New Museums

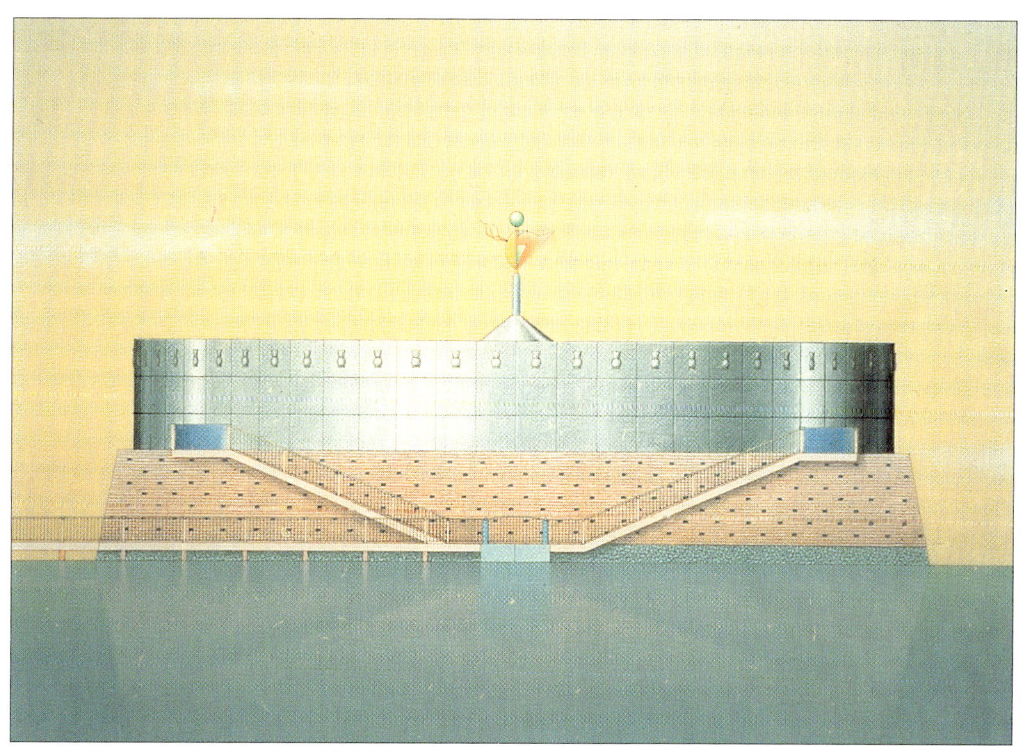

PHILIPPE STARCK, GRONINGER MUSEUM, HOLLAND

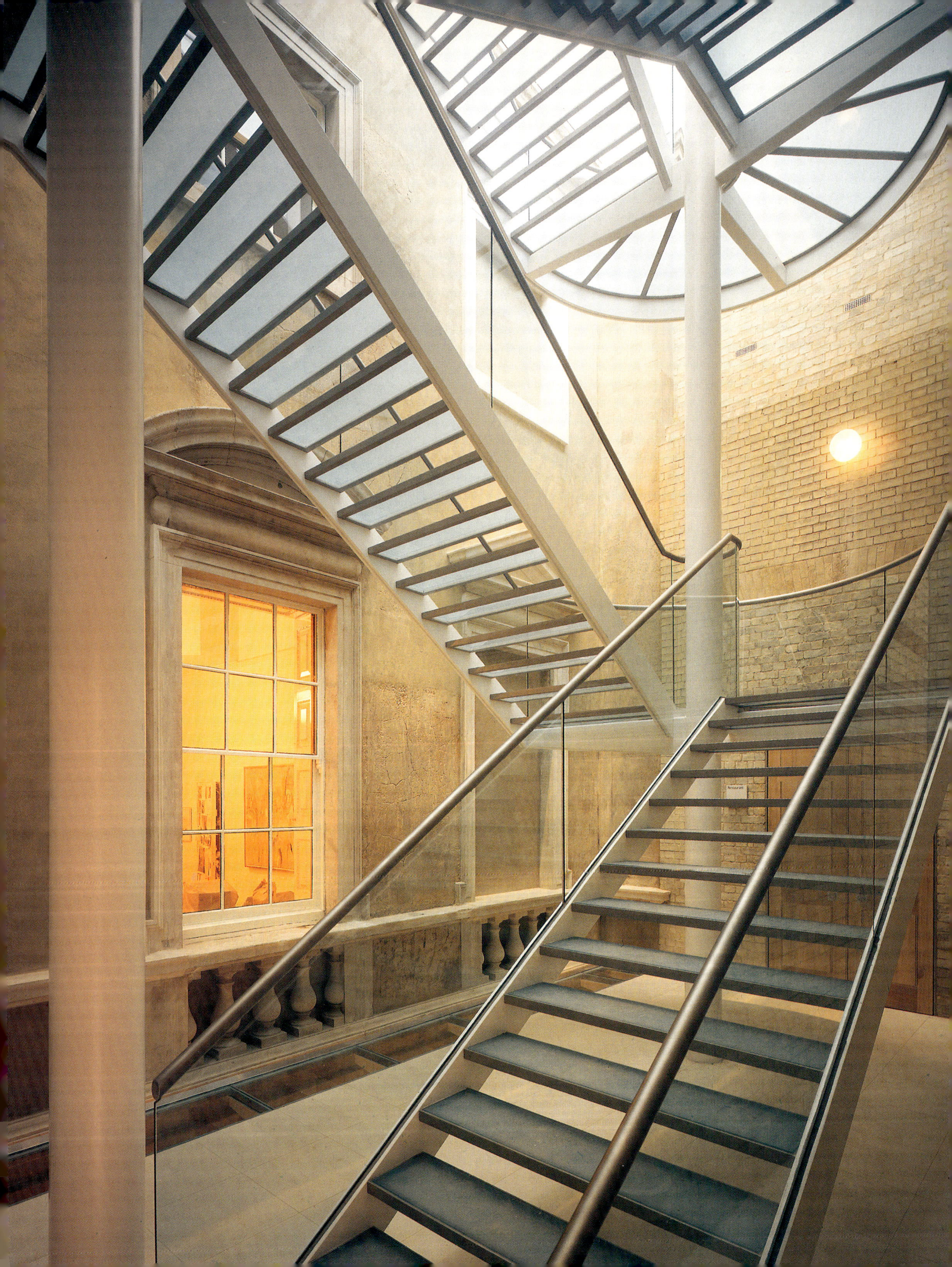

Architectural Design

Edited by Andreas C Papadakis

New Museums

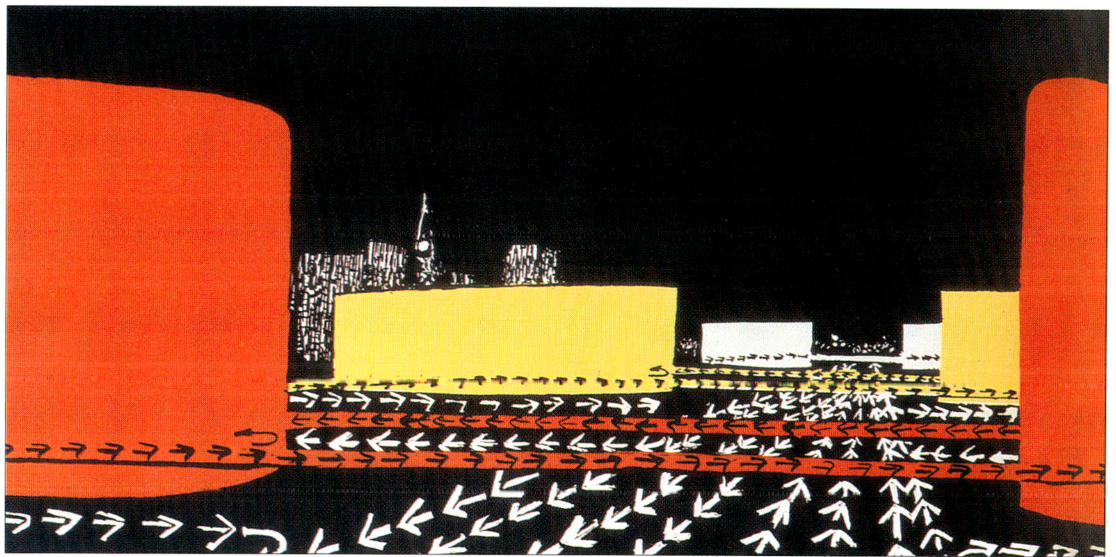

ABOVE: Arata Isozaki has designed the forthcoming exhibition of the work of Louis Kahn which opens at the Philadelphia Museum of Art. The design was inspired by Kahn's plan for the Mikveh Israel Synagogue, a pivotal unbuilt project.
OPPOSITE: Sir Norman Foster, Sackler Galleries, Royal Academy of Arts, view up towards galleries through staircase. Taken from the forthcoming Architectural Monograph *Foster Associates, published by Academy Editions.*

ACADEMY EDITIONS • LONDON

Acknowledgements
This issue takes its theme from the two events organised by the Academy Forum in collaboration with the Royal Academy of Arts. The discussion on
NEW MUSEOLOGY
and the
INAUGURAL ACADEMY ARCHITECTURE LECTURE
which took place at the
ROYAL ACADEMY OF ARTS

The lecture by Kisho Kurokawa took place at the RIBA and the lecture by Robert Venturi and Denise Scott Brown took place at the TUC and was organised by the Architectural Association

We are grateful to President, Sir Roger de Grey and the staff of the Royal Academy of Arts especially MaryAnne Stevens, Librarian and Head of Education, for her collaboration and assistance; Edwina Sassoon for her help with the organisation of both events held at the Royal Academy of Arts; President, Maxwell Hutchinson and the staff of the RIBA; Architectural Association and Charles Jencks for their assistance

We wish to thank the architects for their participation and Sir Norman Foster for agreeing to inaugurate the Academy Architecture Lecture

The interview with Ian Ritchie was conducted by Maggie Toy and the interview with Wolf Prix by Vivian Constantinopoulos

The material for 'What a Wonderful World' pp64-73 was supplied by the Groninger Museum.

We wish to thank the Frankfurt Museum of Modern Art for providing material for the presentation on pp80-87

All material courtesy of the architects unless otherwise stated

Photographic Credits
Front cover, p52 Dieter Leistner; pp2, 36 Dennis Gilbert; pp6, 80, 82-83, 86-87 Rudolf Nagel; p8 Philip Starling; pp28, 41, 84 (right)-85 Andreas Papadakis; pp42-51 Jocelyne Van den Bossche; pp92-96 Rahul Mehrota & Abhay Thamane. Other photographs by *Architectural Design*

EDITOR
Dr Andreas C Papadakis

EDITORIAL OFFICES: 42 LEINSTER GARDENS, LONDON W2 3AN TELEPHONE: 071-402 2141

First published in Great Britain in 1991 by *Architectural Design* an imprint of the Academy Group Ltd

ISBN: 1-85490-117-6 (UK)

Architectural Design Profile 94 is published as part of *Architectural Design* Vol 61 11-12 /1991
Published in the United States of America by
ST MARTIN'S PRESS, 175 FIFTH AVENUE, NEW YORK 10010
ISBN: 0-312-07145-0 (USA)

Printed and bound in Singapore

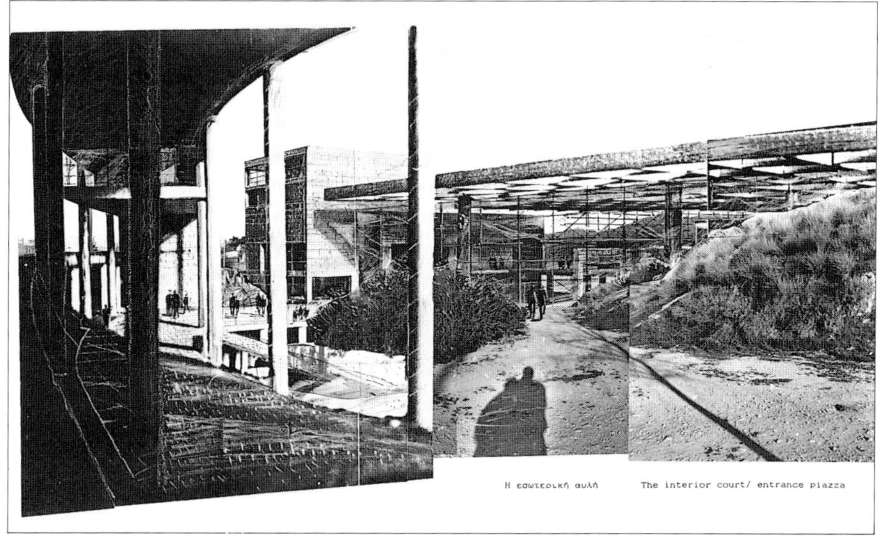

TASOS BIRIS, DIMITRIS BIRIS, PANOS KOKKORIS & ELENI AMERIKANOU, ACROPOLIS COMPETITION ENTRY

Contents

ARCHITECTURAL DESIGN PROFILE No 94

New Museums

 Subscription rates for 1990 (including p&p): Annual Rate: UK only £49.50, Europe £59.50, Overseas US$99.50 or UK sterling equiv. Student rates: UK only £45.00, Europe £55.00, Overseas US$89.50 or UK sterling equiv. Individual issues £8.95/US$19.95. Plus £1.50/US$3.00 per issue ordered for p&p. Printed in Singapore. [ISSN: 0003-8504]

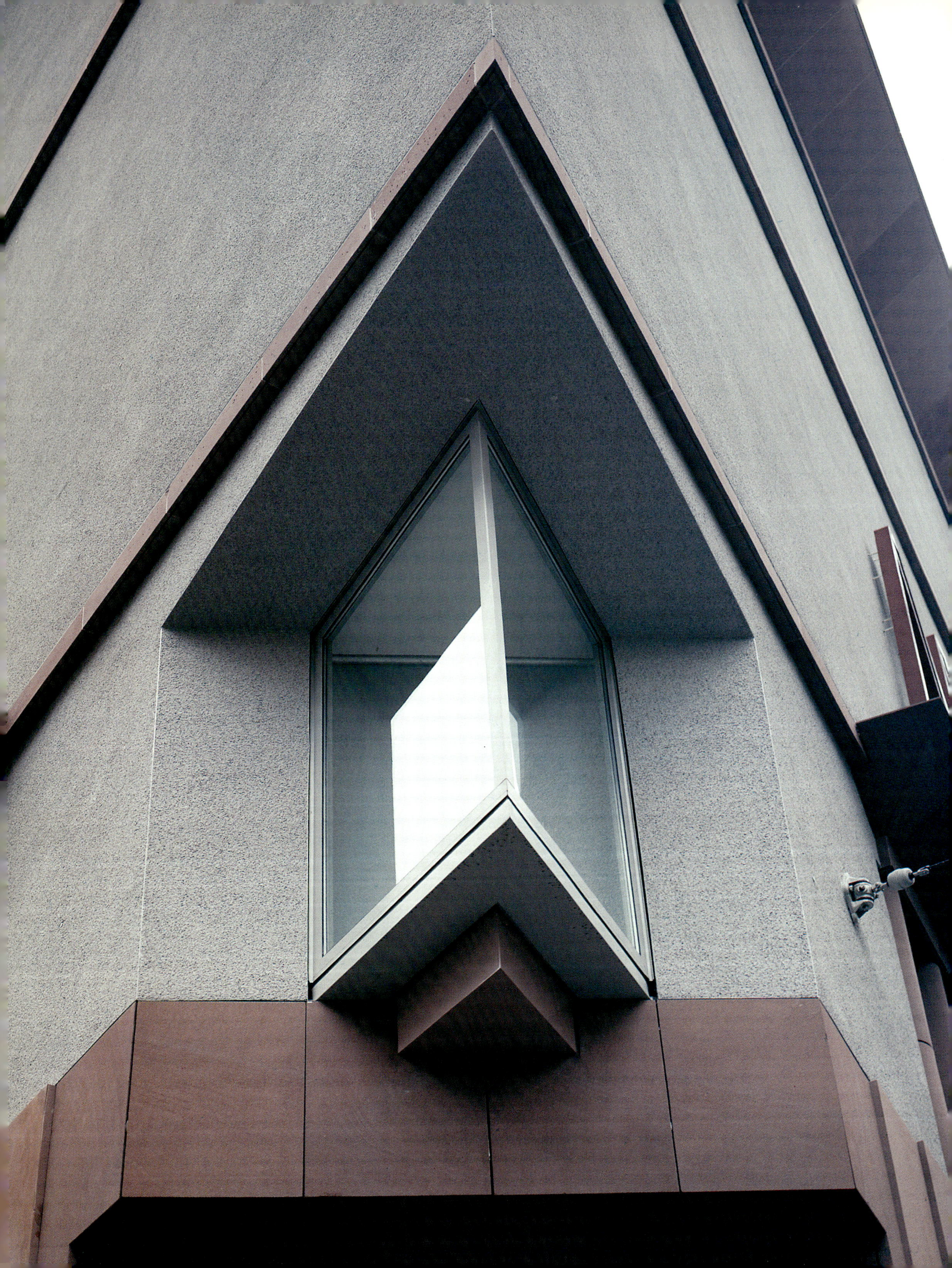

KENNETH POWELL

NEW MUSEOLOGY

Hans Hollein, Frankfurt Museum of Modern Art

A shrine of the arts, a temple of the muses, a repository of timeless values – or a laboratory of change, a flexible container for an ever-evolving programme of multifarious activities? A scholarly sanctuary – or a thronged entertainment centre, where tickets for the principal attractions must be booked well in advance, as for some Broadway or West End show? As museum building has boomed in the last quarter of the 20th century, the role and nature of museums have been brought ever more into question. Museums have simultaneously become the vehicles of architectural ambition, making or breaking reputations. Pei and Stirling, Foster and Venturi, Meier and Isozaki, Gehry and Eisenman – the leaders of world architecture – do battle for commissions. It was not always so.

As opinion in London polarises over the respective merits of Foster's Sackler Gallery and Venturi/Scott Brown's Sainsbury Wing, few can recall who designed the original Tate Gallery or Victoria and Albert or National Portrait Gallery, all second-rate l9th-century products. If the name of William Wilkins, architect of the Regency monument to which Venturi defers, is familiar, it is principally because his National Gallery is almost universally rated one of the worst London buildings of its era. IM Pei's East Wing at the National Gallery in Washington is thrilling – for all its oft-remarked airport terminal ambience – partly because of its proximity to the icy correctness of John Russell Pope. At the Louvre, Pei's architecture draws greater crowds than the Mona Lisa ever did. Rogers and Piano's Pompidou is the longest-running show in Europe, and shows no signs of losing its strange appeal to millions who show only cursory interest in the objects displayed within it. The museum has on occasions itself become the principal artefact.

The diversity of contemporary museum architecture naturally reflects the lack of consensus about the function of a museum once apparently not a matter for dispute. Peter Eisenman's brief for the Wexner Centre stipulated that the building be 'dedicated to experimentation and vanguard artistic activity' (a convenient enough injunction for an architect bent on the demolition of certainty). At London's National Gallery, Venturi and Scott Brown were charged with creating a secure container for a finite collection – the problematic elements of their building are the result of an attempt to introduce contradictions where they do not (or should not) exist. (But they *do*, insist the architects, pointing at the confused, occasionally turbulent, life of the square beyond the gallery walls . . .)

The high tide of modern museum building has coincided with the triumph of the Post-Modernism of which Venturi was a progenitor – Stirling's Staatsgalerie is probably the most celebrated of all recent museums. Wolf Prix has lashed 'the complacency of Po-Mo architecture – don't touch anything as the old city is so beautiful while the new structures are so ugly'. Yet Stirling's Stuttgart is not so much 'complacent' as disturbing, disorientating in its restless dialogue with history. There is a need for a new serenity in museum design, within the pluralistic context of current architecture. It is hardly surprising that the art museum designed by Louis Kahn, notably the Kimbell at Fort Worth and the Mellon Centre at Yale, are relentlessly worked over by architects and critics alike. A museum which outshines its contents is as vulgar and pointless as an over-ornate picture frame, whereas Kahn deals not in detail and elaboration but in space and light.

These are vital ingredients equally of the work of the leading contemporary Japanese practitioners, including Mozuna, Isozaki, Maki, and, most intriguingly perhaps, Kisho Kurokawa, whose work moves beyond any sort of obvious Modern/Post-Modern definition. (Kurokawa's theory of symbiosis, indeed, dismisses the Modern/Post-Modern polarity as a Western fancy.)

The creation of a new museum architecture which is both numinous and reverent, practical and flexible, sharing the characteristics of a workshop and a repository, is a daunting task. Perhaps the architects have run away with the museum and used it for their own ends, while the curators struggle to hold them back. The work of the Japanese school (and Japan has greatly broadened the concept of a museum), of Botta and Foster and of Rafael Moneo, whose Merida Museum of Roman Art has an almost Roman nobility, points in the right direction.

At the same time there is scope for the growth of what Douglas Davis (in a challenging recent study of the museum phenomenon) has called 'the anti-museum'. Frank Gehry's low-budget 'Temporary Contemporary' in Los Angeles (retained by popular demand after the completion of the permanent museum scheduled to supersede it) and Max Gordon's economical fit-out of the Saatchi Gallery in London are especially successful examples of the genre and the new Reina Sophia Museum in Madrid one of the most ambitious. The best museum is not the most costly.

The museum may no longer be a shrine, sealed away from everyday life. Yet it must surely be set apart in the sense of being a special place, where life takes on a different dimension and there is time and space to think and feel, and room for Kahn's beloved silence. As the agenda of modern architecture moves forward from a narrow, technology-obsessed functionality to a concern for the whole human being in the context of society and nature, the auguries are good for a spectacular new generation of museum buildings.

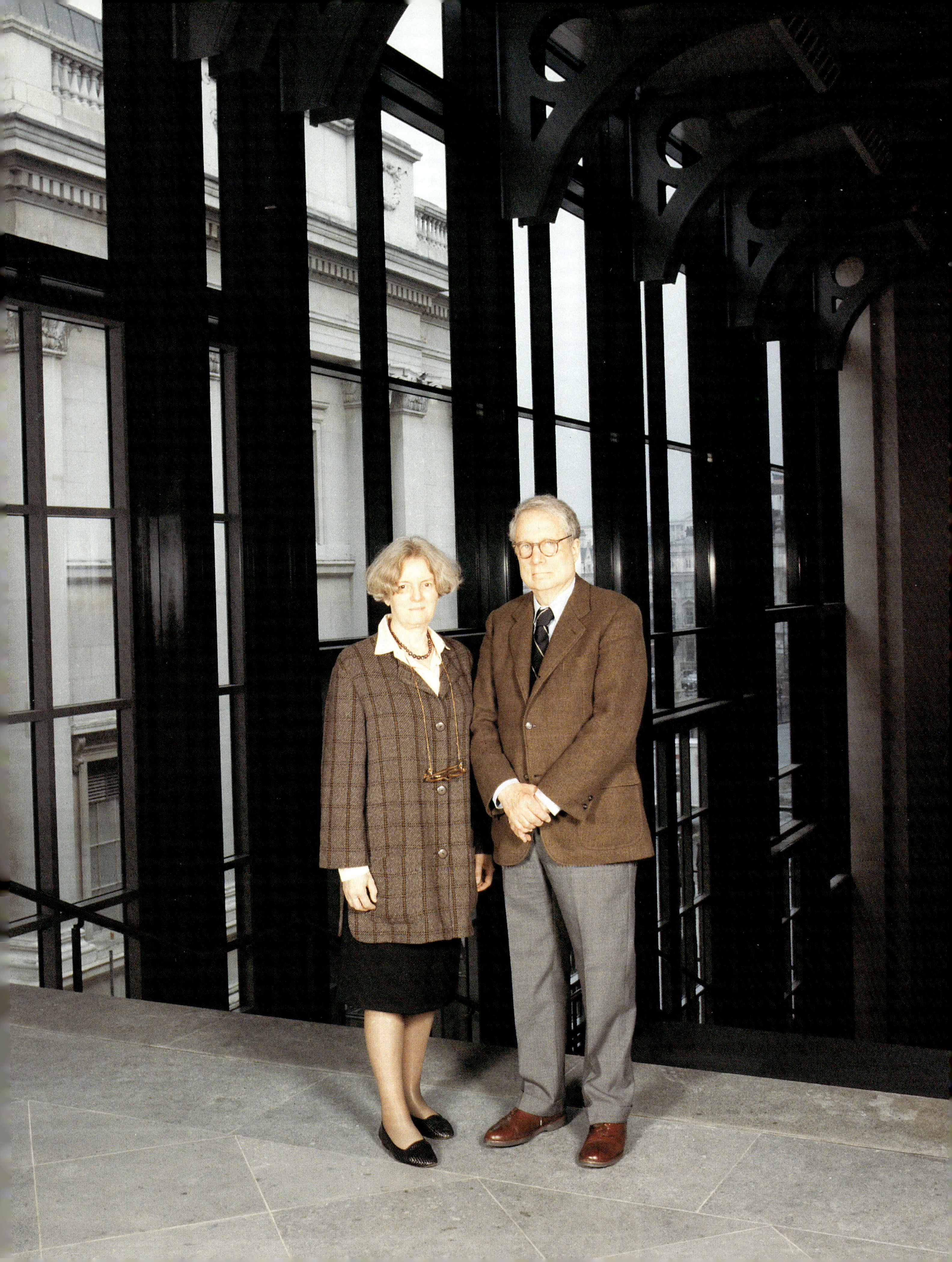

ROBERT VENTURI & DENISE SCOTT BROWN

ARCHITECTURE AS ELEMENTAL SHELTER, THE CITY AS VALID DECON

Robert Venturi and Denise Scott Brown at the top of the main staircase of the Sainsbury Wing, National Gallery, London.

Theory and criticism are disciplines which need a space to breath set off from the pressures of sectarian debate, and the imperatives of a deadline. Robert Venturi and Denise Scott Brown have made a unique contribution to architectural theory, especially in two books: Complexity and Contradiction in Architecture *published in 1966, which helped formulate the Post-Modern paradigm around the notions of complexity, ambiguity and historical memory) and* Learning from Las Vegas, *published in 1972.*

Specifically, they injected into the debate two discussions which had been very strong in the 60s: the lessons of mass culture, and semiotics, the theory of signs, both important for considering the question of 'meaning in architecture'. Today, in most countries (except Britain), the notion of architecture as a language has superseded the previous paradigm – that it is a functional tool. At the very least a building must communicate *its functions before it can function well, and the Venturi Scott Browns have helped establish such points.*

Their recently completed extension to the National Gallery has upset a few Modernists and Traditionalists, not to mention Purists of all sorts. It sends out carefully considered hybrid *messages, calculated oppositions between a high-tech grammar – done where that is appropriate – and a Corinthian curtain wall, clipped on* and *constructed where that is suitable. The great point of this doubly-coded architecture is to come to terms with the fact that we live in a plural culture. To express this honestly is truthful and pleasurable; to deny it with a purist solution is to paper over the cracks.* **Charles Jencks**

We were asked specifically to discuss issues outside architecture: if that means 'don't show slides of your work', we're OK. If it means 'relate architecture to literary criticism, semiotics, philosophical theory, psychology, and strange ideas about perception', we're in trouble because that's what we're not going to talk about, and the significance of that avoidance is the subject of what follows.

Intricacies of the Avant-Garde

When we read today's architectural literature we are often confused by its obscurity, distressed by its pretensions, or bored by its banality. Yet architecture and its perception and meaning should not be difficult to describe by an educated person to a literate reader, because architecture is a discipline that has to satisfy basic functional and structural requirements and meet obvious responsibilities, economic and social.

Architecture, as the most social and prevalent of the arts, must sublimate its esoteric dimension or, at least, not *try* to be esoteric; it is inevitably a part of mass culture and as such must be likeable and readable by lots of people – literate and illiterate – who have to use it and live with it over time. As we lament the current trend toward simplistic, if obscure, ideology we are reminded of a statement by Sir Edwin Lutyens on Sir Herbert Baker: 'God asked Adam to name the animals *after* He created them. Baker names his animals first and then starts to create around a name and words.'

Ideology is an enemy of art. The trouble once was that architect-ideologues would read only one book, then name a movement; now they read too many books and drop too many names.[1]

In what follows, we hope you will understand what we say. We will try to talk about important things in an easy, straightforward way; speaking American, not translated French, German or Italian. We have an old-fashioned belief in being understandable to others and even to ourselves, so don't hold us suspect if you find you understand us.[2]

There is, as well, a second weakness in our position: our criticism of current tendencies in architectural theory may not contain a proper amount of persuasive detail because we cannot understand a lot of what we've read or tried to read. If you can't understand it, you suspect it's not worth understanding. You may question how we can disagree with what we don't understand or have much patience with, but we would argue that this contradiction is the substance of what we are criticising, and that, although we don't understand or agree with much of what we currently read and see, we still claim most of it parallels what was written in *Complexity and Contradiction* 25 years ago, and *Learning from Las Vegas* 20 years ago, but – a significant but – in an extravagant or misunderstood manner: is Decon *Complexity and Contradiction* in Modern dress?

Take the element of contradiction that permeates and often dominates theory and practice in our time (although it is called by other names). As in music, all dissonance leads to no dissonance. If contradiction in architecture is everywhere, it is nowhere, for contradiction must work as an exception to a perceived order or remnant of order, no matter how faint, or to a 'difficult whole' as described in *Complexity and Contradiction.* An architecture of Mannerism must refer to an original order. By facing function and context as realities of experience rather than facets of ideology, you will break open your aesthetic system and this may be aesthetically good. Constant contradiction and consistent inconsistency, in the end, either grate on the sensibilities or bore. Contradiction cannot be forced and, by definition, cannot be total: the exception must prove, not make, the rule.

Although some of the theory we refer to, and the architecture *it* refers to, parallels that of *Complexity and Contradiction*, it ignores the warning in the Gentle Manifesto that introduces that book, the warning against 'the incoherence or arbitrariness of incompetent architecture' and 'the precious intricacies of picturesqueness and expressionism', and the preference for a 'complex and contradictory architecture based on the richness and ambiguity of the modern experience'. It seems that the late Modern articulated expressionism that we reacted against in the early 60s, what we called 'heroic and original' architecture in *Learning from Las Vegas*, and the extremes of Post-Modernism that we disassociated ourselves from in the early 80s in *Plus ça Change*[3] have now been reinvented by the academic avant-garde (another oxymoron) as the architecture of Deconstructionism today: *plus ça change* once more.

Ubiquitous contradiction and gratuitous ambiguity are not deduced from program, structure and meaning, or from the complexities and ambiguities inherent in modern cultural and social experience, but are derived from arbitrary, formalist-aesthetic games and clothed in the, by now, truly historic symbols of the late-lamented industrial revolution, or shrouded in obscure references to esoteric perceptual theory, or girded by extravagant and pretentious intellectual argumentation – these, in the end, bore more than they irritate.

Is what is wrong here the result of the age we live in or the age we are? We have an aversion to older architects criticising younger architects – having suffered from that when we were young – so our criticism, so far as it goes, is anguished as well as confused. On the other hand, we can ask ourselves, are we flogging a dead horse? Has Decon already self-destructed?

Against Mo, PoMo and NeoMo

We have written elsewhere of the need, in our time of cultural and social diversity, for an architecture, or better, for architectures, of richness and ambiguity rather than clarity and purity, of variety rather than universality, and we have made a plea for an eclecticism of symbolic reference that accompanies a complexity and contradiction of form, and for the vernacular and the conventional over the progressive. We have stood against the 'shock of the new' *throughout infinity*, and against Modernism as a universal and perpetual avant-garde.[4] But we have also criticised the irrelevance of historic reference and the arbitrary employment of Neo-Classical and Art Deco symbolism in much Post-Modern architecture. We have written, too, of the validity of ornament, of the trouble caused by the rejection of explicit ornament and pattern by the Modernists and late Modernists, and of the trouble the consequent substitution of functional and structural expressionism gets them into. And today's Neo-Modernists are no different. What extremes the terror of ornament drives them to: they will perform structural and architectural acrobatics, vaudeville acts and extravaganzas to avoid ornament; applying a fragment of a truss here, suspending a tilted column there or creating, via glass roofs, an architectural greenhouse effect – all to catch your eye. But total bravado is no bravado. And how expensive all that trouble is. Even when coloured up, is it worth it, dollar-wise and beauty-wise, when such simple pleasures can be derived from decorative pattern or the sheltering surfaces of a building and its framework, or in the decorative shapes of its details?

Neo-Modern disdain for historical reference does not expand to the Modern style, which is the symbolic basis of the NeoMo architectural vocabulary. Yet this derivation of an industrial vernacular is a historical style by now, no less so than is highfaluting Neo-Classicism, and NeoMo offers little that is relevant to current practice in construction. Everyone else knows the industrial revolution, begun 200 years ago, is dead as a doornail and that naked iron or steel hanging dizzily from a facade, or exposed ducts zigzagging through space are now, like any exposed parts, boring in the end, bedraggled looking, neither thrilling nor practical when left out in the rain.

In their fervour to uphold Modernism – its style, not its principles – against historical reference, Neo-Modernists' vehemence is almost menacing. Granted many works of Post-Modern architecture are bad, and their allusions irrelevant to our era's cultural diversity, but why such emotion? Perhaps it's because the Neo-Modernists rely solely on purist Modern as a source for their Post-Modern pastiche.

Pure pastiche is, of course, a contradiction in terms. Pastiche works only when it is diverse or impure, if not haphazard. And Modernism was based on anti-pastiche in the first place. What an irony! Modernist elements, derived from an International Style, Russian Constructivist vocabulary, are used literally but as decor rather than as rational and 'honest' manifestations of function and structure – and they're coloured up at that. The effect is that of a Puritan lady dancing the can-can. Would Walter Gropius have hated Decon even more than PoMo?

Those of us who respect and love the Modern architecture of 60 years ago and have learned immeasurably from it, are offended by the Neo-Modern parody of it. Yet perhaps we should not be. Decon, whose decorative use of structural elements is the ultimate 'construction of decoration', may be today's equivalent of Art Deco – that poignant and beautiful last attempt by the rearguard to graft the old Beaux Arts onto the new Modern style. Perhaps Art Decon is the Art Deco of PoMo. That ironical last gasp was effective and had its place. Is the Decon we are flailing a dying, but not dead, horse?

Against Arbitrary Ambiguity

So far we have criticised these easy ways out:
- theory and criticism that substitute for architectural art.
- built theory; architecture as frozen theory over frozen music.
- architecture as diagrams and words, used as a means to express complex meta-architecture as building and shelter, dedicated to use and aesthetic meaning.
- ignoring varieties of context, promoting a universal ideology.
- substituting boring-shocking for real avant-garde; promoting a pseudo avant-garde that is truly a central, if not rear, garde.
- demonstrating, rather than revealing, ideas.
- achieving cockeyed picturesqueness through the consistent use of contradictions.
- pretending the Modern style is not a style.
- pretending the Modern style is Modern.
- promoting symbolic shapes as abstract forms while forgetting meaning. Association and reference are inevitable after you're two years old and are OK, but you have to admit to symbolism in order to use it effectively.
- self-righteously denigrating the broad range of our culture and denying the significance of popular and mass culture as artistic sources in the rich mix of our arts.
- advocating a single, dominant, ominously elitist taste culture, oxymoronically avant-garde and universal; what Jim Collins refers to as a 'semiotically impossible *universal* grammar – a sole *official* culture' – within our pluralist ethos.
- substituting expressive articulation for applied decoration; the whole building as an ornament.

Here is the inherent ambiguity of art taken to the

ridiculous extreme, ambiguity for its own sake rather than to enhance richness and depth of meaning. It is based on a lack of recognition of, or accommodation to, the complexity and richness of contemporary experience, which in the end demands in its art truthful disorder, anguished disorder, an expression of chaos derived from reality not affectation, not sensationalism but vigour.

Building as Pavilions, Building as Town

In the works of architects as different as James Stirling, Peter Eisenman, and Frank Gehry there is a shared tendency to disengage parts of what would be conventionally considered a single building into separate units – to create the buildings as pavilions. In buildings by these architects, the separate units are connected so you don't get wet in the rain moving from one space to another, but the units are emphasised and the connections played down; it's as if the building is a town. This approach is for some reason strongly advocated by Leon Krier, whose buildings would all, ideally, consist of series of separate, proximate pavilions, little and mostly low.

In our youth we risked our reputations arguing against the megastructure, when the town tried to be a building, because we felt that this approach ignored the inherent quality of a town as an incremental entity evolving in time and form, depending for its development on complex relationships among finance, technology, infrastructure, bureaucracy, function, taste, and aesthetics, not to mention cars. Now we don't think the current building-as-town has as bad problems as the town-as-building, yet the building-as-village – the village after an earthquake, the frozen image of an explosive gesture – contradicts some basic principles of architecture and common sense: think of roofing all those connected but distinct architectural phenomena, exposed to the elements.

The building-as-town is essentially anti-urban; its fractured, relatively small components contrast with, rather than reinforce, the scale of the existing city, and break the continuity of its building facades. People pass through and between the pavilions of what seems like a small-scale village within a city. But the combination is more like spaced-out rooms than pavilions and resembles Los Angeles sprawl more than it does European urbanism. Its buildings are orthodox-Modern in their separation, articulation, and expression of interior functions but, in that its spaces are enclosed rather than free-flowing, they are anti-Modern. Also, the occasional ornamentation of the pavilions, through pattern or surface articulation, accentuates their anti-Modern (that is, anti-International Style) formal and spatial disjointedness. The final effect is of Swiss Pavilions without the slabs.

OK, so we love Los Angeles (and Las Vegas and Tokyo *and* Rome), but not *too* much; not to the extent of transforming our buildings into it. The house as village represents an extreme in the ranking of scatter over shelter. The spatial and sculptural articulation of virtually all elements of a relatively small building is an extravagant gesture indeed.

Building as Objects, Building as Sculpture

Beyond being a building that is not *a* building (or a building that is buildings) the deconstructed building is also not an architectural expression of shelter. It is an object, or rather a set of objects, left out in the rain. Or it is sculpture all right, in the rain. It has no window, or wished it hadn't: yet aren't windows the soul of a building, the main signifier of its character, the elemental and eloquent contradiction to the wall, and the modulator of interior light? Decon architecture has no eaves, or wished it hadn't, its reluctant roofs are usually of the same materials as its walls, or its walls are made of roof materials; there is aesthetically no difference between wall and roof, side and top. But this defines sculpture. Decon tends towards sculpture not shelter, sculpture in lead-coated copper.

But you don't have to live in real sculpture and you don't have to maintain it or worry if it leaks. Think of maintaining all the flashing that protects the connections that join the roofs that cover the links that connect this architecture's disconnected objects. This use of flashing promotes structural abstraction and spatial articulation but it contradicts architecture's basic, sheltering quality, and the articulations are expensive both to construct (they have more external wall surfaces) and to maintain. So we suspect a flashy architecture based on flashing.

Some Decon buildings are more unitary, their articulations resembling less a town and more the bumps, lumps and carbuncles on a washed-up shipwreck. But buildings are not boats or cities; they are not even good analogies for them. For us, it is too easy to derive tension and drama from extreme forms of articulation and manipulation of volumes and spaces, or to produce picturesque compositions by setting building elements at unusual angles. We prefer to derive tension from the contradiction and ambiguities of complex architectural programs, rather than by promoting exciting effects or accommodating obscure theories. Decon bores you in the way a crazy person does. Be anguished, not crazy.

Against Arbitrary Distortion

Contradiction has had a long history in architecture. A tendency to modify and distort the order of architectural parts is found in the angles and curves of Alvar Aalto, or in mosque complexes turned towards Mecca, or in the layouts of Renaissance palaces, distorted to accommodate to medieval sites, or, more violently, in wall dividers within a Corbusian grid; or in medieval town plans as they accommodate the eastern orientation of a cathedral.

In our early work, starting with the North Penn Visiting Nurse Center, we employed diagonals in plan to accommodate to programmatic, spatial, or contextual circumstances, and have seen this device become a characteristic architectural element of our time; but current distortions are more violent, and they have become a motival element in plan, section, and elevation. Such configurations aren't intrinsically wrong but they generally appear to be used for little or no reason – unless you consider sensational effect and the promoting of avant-garde images acceptable determinants for architecture.

So we are back to the exception that becomes the rule, the contradiction that's baseless, the constant dissonance that smothers dissonance; to picturesque expressionism not based on the richness and ambiguity of experience – *plus ça change, plus c'est le même chose*, yet once again.

Architects should remember they are working for beings who walk upright and resist gravity, whose buildings should not convey only private or esoteric meanings, tailored to the inside critic, writer or reader. In fact, architecture, as the most everyday of the arts must be readable on many levels, including the popular. Architects should become sculptors if they want but, if they remain architects, they should embrace the wonderful limitations of their field, loving the constrictions inherent in their

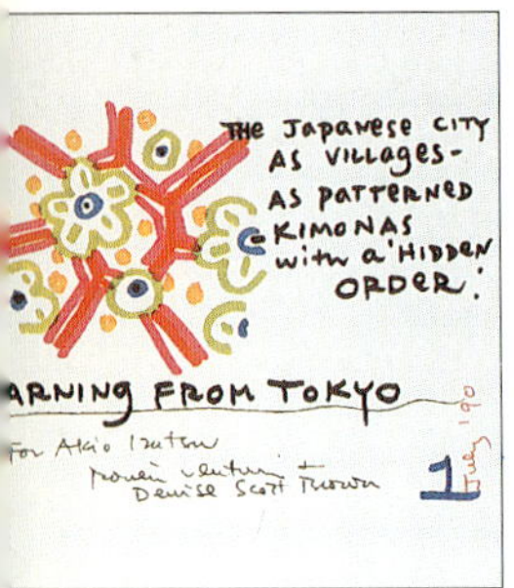

Robert Venturi and Denise Scott Brown, Learning from Tokyo.

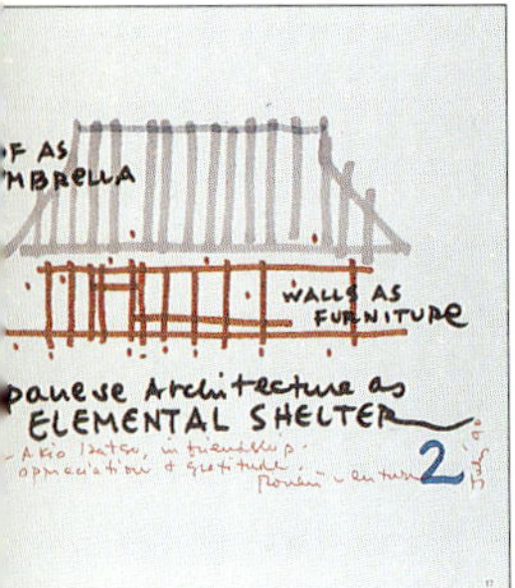

Robert Venturi and Denise Scott Brown, Japanese Architecture as Elemental Shelter.

medium – resisting them, once in a while, for the sake of a valid and artful *tour de force*, but not seeking to surmount all the limits all the time.

Practising architects might have to be lawyers, business-people, psychiatrists, and performers to get and implement a job, but that's another matter, as designers and theorists they should not be literary critics, semiologists, psychologists, philosophers, or calculating obfuscators: they should be artist-craftspeople who love architectural detail. And the convention in their art should not be scorned on one hand or evolved into whimsy on the other; the job of an architect is to lead *and* to follow.

Architecture as Shelter and the Decon City

We have been viewing some recent trends with alarm and thereby illuminating where we aren't in architecture, we hope this exercise can work to illustrate where we are. The positive side of our argument makes the case for multiple architectural vocabularies, rich and varied tastes, historical and geographic contexts, symbolic and ornamental systems that evolve from contexts, and conventional building methods that architects tolerate at the risk of being thought outmoded. The positive argument sees the building as an elemental unit of shelter, and the city of now as a valid deconstruction. Recent trips to Japan and Korea have helped us to formulate this view. Until these trips, our most vivid images of architecture as shelter were the archaic classical temple of 'The Primitive Hut' described by Abbé Laugier. At another extreme might be a child's drawing of a house, with a big roof, a chimney near its centre, walls punctuated by a door and windows that are holes in the wall filled with conventional window panes, and decoration over the door to make the entrance explicit.

Each generation of Western architects has seen in Japan what it has wanted to see. The interpretation our generation inherited from the early Modernists focuses on the minimalist, structuralist, modular purity of the villas and shrines of Kyoto. These images of a particular historical architecture, conveyed through the early Modernists' cameras and the careful cropping of their almost always frontal photographs, made us think of Japanese architecture as pure but dry, as 'goody-goody'. And by editing out the poignant counterpoints of complexity and simplicity, of intricate and plain, of big and minute, our forebears made this architecture seem irrelevant to us.

We felt Kyoto could wait. But our first day there, when it did arrive, contained a revelation. There was the scale of the Sanmon Gate and the foundations of the Nanzenji Temple, not itsy-bitsy 'human scales' but comparable to Italian civic scale in their monumentality – a kind of *terribilité* in wood. Second, there was the juxtaposition of the rich colour, pattern, and variety in the sublime kimono upon the pure and apparently simple architectural convention of the temple. For us, both elements, architecture and robe, must be included and envisioned within the aesthetic equation. Unlike our Modern predecessors, we needed to see the simple building as context for the patterned kimono – as it is depicted in the classic Japanese print – and to see the *connection* between the temple, its gardens and the market beyond.

We loved the juxtaposition of ancient temple and tourist ephemera – the clutters of objects that are truly precious, not tiresomely precious: dolls, dishes, balls, boxes, boxes in boxes, hairpins, statues, chopsticks, chopstick holders, parasols, comic books, and idols; made of, among other things, plaster, porcelain, paper, bamboo, and lacquered wood, all skilfully crafted and coloured. These items – kitsch or otherwise – on sale in the marketplace outside the temple, play against the severity of the architecture and are perhaps substitutes for the patterned kimonos that once moved among the screens, mats, spaces, structural grids, and overhangs of the buildings. The juxtapositions of extremes in scale are comparable only to those in the buildings of Michelangelo or in the art and architecture of the pharaohs. Here, in the joy and vigour of its small objects, was a Japanese version of 'God in the details'.

Then there were the gardens, which stylise nature, representing and symbolising its diversity within universality with the same infinite genius for multiplicity and miniature that we discovered in the markets. Whereas, in the French gardens of Le Nôtre, nature becomes an abstraction, in Kyoto the temple garden, in its variety, unity, and rich combinations, symbolises the natural landscape as a whole. And real nature cooperated that first afternoon by supplying the raindrops that formed jumping patterns on the ponds, to match the patterns in the linkings of Kimonos.

And then the diversity. In Kyoto temples there was a quite consistent convention of building but, within that, there were infinite exceptions. The contradictions were stunningly tense in their aesthetic and perceptual effect, and valid and understandable in most dimensions; when they weren't, who would worry, given the context of care? Care – the loving attention to multitudinous detail in design, from chopstick holders to gilded temple paintings, from foundations to standards of maintenance – created an aura that permeated the whole of the art, the place.

Later, we discovered that, more than it was deceptively simple and artfully complex, the Kyoto temple architecture was elemental. The elemental sheltering quality of traditional Japanese architecture is symbolised by the roof. The hipped roof with large overhangs is perhaps the dominant element of these buildings. Roofs are everywhere. A gate is a roofed shelter as well as an entrance; a garden wall has a little roof on it to act as coping; roofs are sometimes eloquently redundant, as in the vertical stacks of roofs of a pagoda that shelter it as it ascends.

Subsequent visits to Korea and Nikko made the elemental sheltering roof more vivid. There the complex wooden architecture below the roof is painted in vivid colours and decorated with delicate patterns. Colour is kept out of the rain and seen in shadow. The comparatively delicate walls and parapets with fragile finishes, which people live beside and touch, become essentially furniture. This contrast between the sheltering roof and the furniture under it – between the roof that dominates and makes the building a unit, and the elements at human level that are delicate, intricate, accommodating, and 'forgiving' – make a classic architecture of shelter – not Decon's sculpture or Modern's space – but shelter that we can learn from and cannot forget.

As important for us as the lesson of historical Kyoto have been the lessons of Tokyo today. The Japanese love to describe Tokyo as chaotic; the word for chaos in Japanese is adapted from the English. But is this not a convincing chaos, or an order that is not yet understood? Or an ambiguity not forced or pretentious? Tokyo's chaos derives from its variety of scales, forms, rhythms, and symbols, based on a cacophony of cultures. Village dwellings and urban renewal landscapes; 'pencil' buildings and corporate high-rises; slot machine parlours and *haute-couture* boutiques; shrines and temples; temple markets and western department stores; American fast foods, signs, and monumental traffic jams: all occur in cockeyed configurations and unimaginable juxtapositions in an urban infrastructure of straight streets and wide avenues lined with trees or regiments of commercial signs; or of crooked lanes lined with utility poles draped with myriad wires; or of elevated highways snaking through and above the city.

It is said that the city was designed as a maze to confound attacking armies approaching the shogun's castle. If, beneath the chaos, there are rules, these possibly derive from the early technology of the city, for the spanning capacity of construction timbers, and from the breaks and separations mandated for fire and earthquake protection. Upon this city, destroyed in World War II, a new Tokyo grew in one decade. This city, unified by its 1950 Googie architecture, is now being renewed and upscaled by the demands of Japan's global economy. The results will be an overlaid pattern of different scales and types of urban configuration, reminiscent somehow of the combinations of patterns on a kimono or of the juxtaposition and draping of kimonos in a woodcut.

It is ironic that in Japan, a society known for its discipline, formality and rules of courtesy, architects are able to venture artistically as they would not be allowed elsewhere in our world of design regulation and historic commissions. The results, as in some recent pop-Decon constructions, look better here than they would in Europe or America, and form part of the city's vivid and unique combination of the exotic and the familiar – and the almost familiar. In other cities such buildings might seem irresponsible intrusions in a decaying ethos. In Tokyo, in their context, they dance a jig at a lively party. Pride makes the kitsch OK, and spirit makes the vulgar likeable. The combination of sophistication and *naiveté*, spirit and control, or 'discipline and ease' as George Santayana would have put it, distinguishes this city and its art. In our reactions, we found ourselves employing French words – *joie de vivre*, *jeu d'esprit*, *tour de force*, *élan*, *panache*, *arabesque*, *pastiche*, *incroyable* – to describe these eclectic urban juxtapositions of symbols, forms, scales and patterns. Our own phrase 'valid deconstructivism', seemed to define this curious urbanism.

Decon works for cities; it is more natural to cities than to buildings because cities don't have to keep the rain out or the warmth in (or out), and because the city is the 'difficult whole' *par excellence*, built not all at once but incrementally, now that we have individuals and committees, rather than prelates and princes, as builders and regulators.

What you see in contemporary Tokyo and historical (and contemporary) Kyoto is an accommodation to and a celebration of the realities and tensions of our time; to the plurality of cultures promoted via global communication and flourishing side by side; and to the diversity and quantity of overlapping taste cultures (nine symphony orchestras in Tokyo alone) – these complexities and contradictions and the resultant ambiguities lead to a richness of effect and a spirit that are the fate, and should be the glory, of the art of our time. In our art today, it should not matter if you don't like it all, if this detail isn't quite right, isn't quite to your taste. The tensions between what you like and dislike should, in the end, heighten your tolerance *and* your sensibility; they will allow the city to be disciplined in its elements and the maintenance of its infrastructure, 'chaotic' in its formal configuration, and overwhelming in the prominence of its detail; *and*, in the example of Tokyo, to read as a capital of global business organisation.

Architectural Theory for Architects

What we have attempted here is architectural theory of the kind traditionally enunciated by architects as the means of clarifying their work, to themselves and others, and sometimes to justify it. We did *not* promote a theory of architecture that substitutes itself for architecture, replacing architecture with arconcepture and buildings with diagrams and words, or promoting perceptual conceits or critical apparati, belatedly and laboriously transposed from inappropriate disciplines and ending in extravagant yet boring and frequently irrational and irresponsible buildings. Architecture should not be frozen theory, the victim rather than the subject of theory. Buildings should not be accumulations of cheap thrills and emperors' clothing, theoretically rationalised by the journalistic rhetoric of an academic avant-garde. Architectural theory should confront elemental architectural qualities of shelter, use, and meaning, seeing architecture as 'a thoughtful process of making'[6] and as a highfaluting craft, to be used and perceived through the sensibilities of everyday – to be, in the words of Herbert Muschamp, 'meaningful to the innocent eye'.

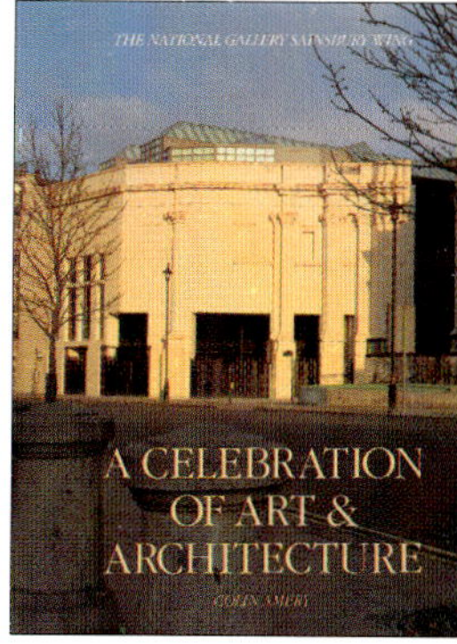

The following titles have all been published by National Gallery Publications to mark the opening of the new Sainsbury Wing: Colin Amery, A Celebration of Art and Architecture; A Guide to the Sainsbury Wing; The National Gallery Report, April 1990-May 1991.

Notes

1 In a recent article of less than 1,500 words by a noted architectural academic, the following names were mentioned: Sigmund Freud, ETA Hoffman, Friedrich Schelling, Legrand du Saule, Georg Simmel, Siegfried Kracauer, Walter Benjamin, Maurice Halbwachs, Eugene Minkowski, Jean-Paul Sartre, Martin Heidegger, Homer(ic), Jean Jacques Rousseau.

2 What we are against is exemplified in the following quotation from the first five pages of an article on architecture by John Shuttleworth called 'The Diffraction of Symbol and Sign: An Essay on Symbolic Thought and Semiological Grammar' in a publication aptly called *Avant-Garde 3* (although 3, rather than 1, is perhaps an oxymoron and, if you call yourself avant-garde, perhaps you're not). The phrases quoted here are strung together by relatively few ordinary words represented by the dots: '... hermeneutics and deconstructive criticism ... logical positivism, mechanistic determinism and pragmatism ... dialectical materialism ... communistic/socialistic or capitalistic/social theories ... auguries of physical, quantitative, inductive scientific thought ... colouration [which] 'reads through' almost all semiologic, structuralist and post-structuralist writings ... schism [existing] since the Ionian tradition of the 6th Century ... emotio-logical thought ... Freud, Jung, Lévi-Strauss ... analytic and synthetic, the motional and rational (etc) [sic] ... cognitive 'feeling' ... literal symbolism, polyvalence of significance ... linear grammars ... The symbolic plays redundancies of meaning to reveal the referent in modal terms. In this way the symbolic rectifies certain of the 'hollowing out' of the implicit meaning which quantifying sciences so arrogantly dessicate in the name of objectivity and illusory democracy ... socio-linguistics ...' and so on for nine more pages.

3 Robert Venturi, 'Diversity, Relevance and Representation in Historicism, or Plus ça Change ...' plus 'A Plea for Pattern all over Architecture with a Postscript on my Mother's house' in *Architectural Record*, June 1982, pp114-19.

4 As described by Jim Collins, *Uncommon Cultures, Popular Culture and Post-Modernism*, Routledge, Chapman and Hall, New York, 1989.

5 *Ibid.*

6 Sylvia Lavin, 'The Uses and Abuses of Theory', *Progressive Architecture*, Aug 1990, p114.

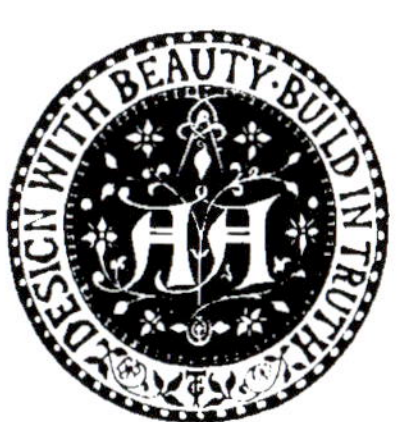

This article is an edited version of the 'Outside Architecture' lecture organised by the Architectural Association and given by Robert Venturi and Denise Scott Brown at Trades Union House on May 2 1991. The lecture was introduced by Charles Jencks and a reply was given by Sylvia Lavin, the text of which follows.

SYLVIA LAVIN
OUTSIDE WITH THE VENTURIS

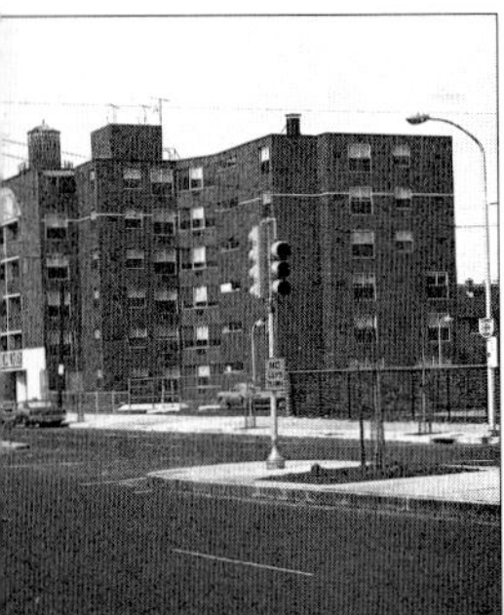
Robert Venturi, Guild House, Philadelphia, Pennsylvania, 1962, general exterior view.

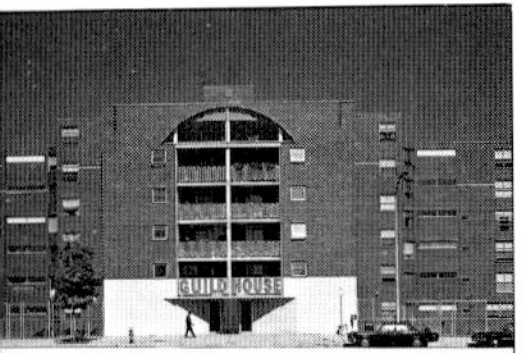
Guild House, exterior view of the main facade.

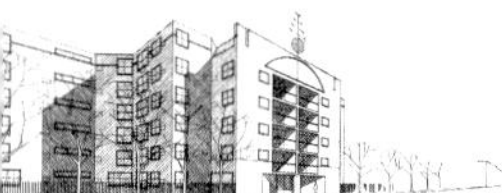
Guild House, pespective.

For someone of my generation, perhaps particularly for an American of my generation, it is rather difficult to step outside architecture in the context of the Venturis. For anyone whose architectural consciousness came into being after the publication of *Complexity and Contradiction* (1966) and *Learning from Las Vegas* (1972) there is no place truly outside the Venturis. Our most basic understanding of architecture was moulded by the ideas presented in those texts. The relevance of history, the importance of context, the intimidatingly puritanical morality of orthodox Modernism, architecture's enrichment through complexity – these ideas and others are today more often points of departure than points of contention.

Paradoxically, the degree to which these ideas developed by the Venturis have infiltrated the foundations of contemporary architectural thought and culture is the degree to which the scope of these ideas has been limited. So successful have they been that their essential nature as ideas has been forgotten – they are often mistaken for architectural truth. This mistake is a serious one with serious consequences because truth, like facts but unlike ideas, demands no critical attention. Truth is believed in and belief simply opens a revolving door leading back to the very puritanical moralising the Venturis were trying to escape. Moreover, the failure to distinguish between idea and truth is an error that has also had at least two profound repercussions for the Venturis' reputation. First, when those who have borrowed the Venturis' ideas have done so uncritically, the critical content of the original ideas has gone unnoticed. In fact, the critical content has often been if not literally repressed, then quite literally domesticated. The result is that the Venturis are placed in a position of responsibility with regard to a radically under-theorised architectural practice that has only the most superficial relationship to its theoretical foundation. This practice is what the Venturis are calling PoMo and although they themselves have never, would never, and could never, simply revisit a historical style, they are held responsible for those that do.

The second consequence of the usurpation of ideas explored by the Venturis and their transfiguration into architectural truth, is similarly repressive but in a reverse form. I am now speaking of their relationship to what is called Deconstructivism, for which they are certainly not held responsible. But in this case, some degree of responsibility – call it giving credit where credit is due – is appropriate. Just a few years ago while on a trip to Philadelphia to see the Venturis and their work, I described the state of quasi-stupor in which I found myself after visiting the Guild House.[1] Robert Venturi was rather pleased with my state of shock because he told me of having just visited the building with a well-known critic whose response to the building had been 'It's hard to tell now what all the fuss was about.' Such a comment wilfully denies the persistently provocative complexity of that extraordinary building. Although some practitioners of Decon may lay claim to ideas about, for example, instability and the indeterminacy of meaning, they do so only by distorting the truth. So, PoMo makes the Venturis' work 'nicer' and more 'polite' than it ever came or comes close to being. Decon takes advantage of this by suggesting that anything as nice or polite as that couldn't possibly have much relevance for something so radical and rude. Thus, despite the recent and somewhat belated recognition of their work – I am thinking of the Pritzker Prize – the fact remains that contemporary architecture in successfully domesticating the Venturis, ironically, has marooned them in a kind of wilderness wherein more success seems increasingly indistinguishable from less.

The Venturis' paper constitutes, in my opinion, an attempt to build for themselves some sort of shelter within this anguishing wilderness. The primary components of this shelter are two sets of interrelated oppositions – elemental architecture versus Decon theorising flash on the one hand, and buildings in their individual integrity versus the city in its multiple complexity on the other. I would like to suggest a few refinements for the Venturis' sense of these oppositions that I offer as a bit of extra mortar for their hopefully temporary campsite in the wilderness. First, with regard to the difference between architecture and 'arconcepture'. It is rhetorically unpersuasive to claim not to understand something while evaluating that same thing all in one breath. As a strategy, it lies too close to what Robert Venturi in *Complexity and Contradiction* called 'carefully maintained ignorance'.[2] Certainly the score of a Mozart concerto is a formidable jumble of dots and lines for someone who has never been taught to read music – just as words such as PoMo, Decon, and Neo-Mod, may not be music to a non-architectural ear. It is therefore safe to say that verbal incomprehensibility should not be in and of itself objectionable. On the other hand, to sense that to exclude is a goal, and that humiliation for the uninitiated is deliberate and wilful, must be anguishing indeed, particularly for those such as the Venturis who have defined their lives' work as making meaning, against all odds, meaningful again. But while this essentially superficial battle wages about how often it is appropriate to ask your audience to look words up in the dictionary, an extremely important battle goes on below the surface. This conflict is between populism and avant-gardism. The question of the viabilities of these attitudes towards culture is sufficiently important to demand direct discussion, however populist or avant-garde the vocabulary necessary for the discussion may be.

Second, there is some irony in defining Decon as nothing more than flashy philosophising verbiage while at the same time describing Decon with great clarity in formal terms – sculpture, object, diagonal, pavilion, etc. This irony is rhetorically persuasive but it still does not get quite to the root of the problem. The irony succeeds in suggesting both that Deconstruction is too philosophical to be useful to architecture and that Deconstruction, once in the hands of architects, becomes poor philosophy which therefore produces even poorer buildings. But fundamentally the real issue is not rhetorical. Rather, and appropriately enough, it is philosophical – not in the sense of whether or not or by how much to philosophise architecture, but which philosophy to turn to as an architect. The Venturis, when they invoke the need for theory to deal directly with architecture and its various specificities, are not being un- or anti-philosophical. They are being pragmatic and phenomenological, both of which are of course important philosophical positions.

The third clarification has to do with the appropriateness of importing ideas from other disciplines. *Complexity and Contradiction* is and was inconceivable without what more simply used to be called literary criticism – Venturi is always one to acknowledge his sources and he names TS Eliot, William Epsom and Cleanth Brooks several times. Once again the issue cannot be with bringing things outside of architecture inside, but is with to what purpose they are put once they are there. The difference in purpose of these borrowings leads me to the second opposition made by the Venturis, namely buildings versus cities. One of the reasons that the Venturis' learning from literature was less problematic than is Decon's dabbling with Derrida was that the act of borrowing was manifestly of a piece with the ideas that were ultimately formulated. Borrowing from all over the place helped weaken the foundations of old hierarchies that had placed literature above the other arts with architecture at the bottom, and building even lower. The Venturis' foray outside architecture, in other words, functioned to reveal what was already inside by dismantling hierarchies across disciplines. Venturi was able to demonstrate unforeseen parallels within the discipline of architecture. This notion of the continuity of culture was explored in *Complexity and Contradiction*, but was exploded to an urban scale in *Learning from Las Vegas*, where a revolutionary description of the continuous nature of the urban experience was movingly depicted. High versus low art, literate versus illiterate, good versus bad, ugly versus beautiful were cataclysmically catapulted into a magical union bonded by semantic parity, all of which together reinvented the space of the modern city.

However integrated a view of the city and its buildings the Venturis may once have held, their paper distinguishes between what is almost okay for cities, at least for some cities, and what is not okay for buildings. 'Decon works for cities,' they write, 'it is more natural to cities than to buildings because cities don't have to keep the rain out or the warmth in.' True, cities don't have weather envelopes – yet – but they certainly have serious and complex jobs to do. If Decon's formalist concerns, in the Venturis' opinion, lead to sculptures in the rain and not to buildings, there is no reason to think that formalism on an urban scale will lead to anything other than really big sculptures left out in a torrential downpour. Moreover, when the Venturis write 'buildings are not cities; they are not even good analogies for cities,' they are not challenging a recent Deconstructivist idea but a very long standing tradition. In his *De Re Aedificatoria* Alberti said 'if the city is like some large house, and the house is in turn like some small city, cannot the various parts of the house be considered miniature buildings?'[3] It is of course not by accident that Alberti said this at the very time that the design of cities became a conceivable activity for the first time in the modern era. This occurred not because a prince had assumed absolute control of the environment, but because the existence of urban order was noticed for the first time – the medieval city was no longer seen as without order but as conveying deliberate disorderliness. The fact is that Alberti did for Medieval Florence what the Venturis did for Modern Las Vegas. However, while the Venturis may have changed their thinking from the days in which they described the urban phenomenon as stretching from the parking lot of the A&P to the ugly duckling a little further down the highway all joining to form a coherent and humanistic system of communication, their comments here suggest otherwise. To describe Tokyo from Kimono to traffic jam is to reinvoke the idea of urbanism as a seamless cultural garment that embraces everything from solid buildings to empty spaces, from tiny details to the city as totality. Indeed, the Venturis' article here indicates that what was learned from Las Vegas was a fundamental methodology for urban analysis that as such embraces and hence transcends the specificity of particular cities as well as the buildings within them. In the end, therefore, it is almost unnecessary to teach us about Tokyo and to distinguish categorically Tokyo as city from Tokyo as architecture. Today, phenomena as apparently diverse as urban geography with its emphasis on material culture to the Deconstructivist impulse to read context as immaterial text, coalesce in the idea that the design of cities is the most fundamental activity of social making. This view distributes the burden of the quality of the urban experience amongst all members of society and amongst all facets of the landscape, good and bad. This view is the hope of our cities' futures and is in large measure the result of the Venturis' insight.

All of my comments are unthinkable without the precedent of the Venturis' thoughts. Thus, rather than constitute a provocative manifesto, I hope they have been a gentle reminder to the Venturis of the breadth of their own ideas. These ideas are of such breadth that they can easily afford to lend a bit of themselves to others. I cannot assuage the Venturis' anguish by claiming that their ideas have been unilaterally borrowed with the same elegance, acknowledgement and sense of purpose with which the Venturis borrow things. But, and however cold, I hope it is comforting to them to know that they have enriched architecture and urbanism almost beyond our capacity for recognition, much less for description. Finally, now that we can look at history without apology, thanks again to the Venturis, I hope also to remind them that history often surprises us by allowing substance to survive style, however appealing its flashiness may be for the moment.

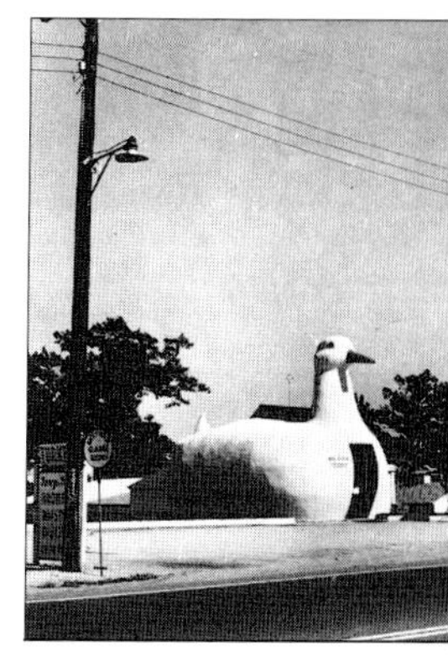

'Long Island Duckling' from Learning From Las Vegas *by Robert Venturi and Denise Scott Brown.*

Notes

1 I would like to mention that of the many revelations that induced my stupor, one was the presence of a Baroque chain-link fence. The architectural 'discovery' of this material, and its subsequent domestication, is always connected to Frank Gehry. Of course Gehry and the Venturis' use the material in very different ways. However, if its use is to be admired, then the architectural profession has in this case discriminated against the Venturis.

2 Robert Venturi, *Complexity and Contradiction in Architecture*, New York, second edition, 1977, p13.

3 Leon Battista Alberti, *On the Art of Building in Ten Books*, J Rykwert, N Leach, R Tavenor, trans, Cambridge, MA and London, 1988, book 1, ch 9, p 23.

Sylvia Lavin is Assistant Professor of History and Theory at the Graduate School of Architecture and Urban Planning, University of California, Los Angeles.

GEOFFREY BAKER

THE SAINSBURY WING AT THE NATIONAL GALLERY BY VENTURI, SCOTT BROWN AND ASSOCIATES

The fact that the Venturi, Scott Brown Sainsbury Wing has attracted rhetoric ranging from 'pretentious architectural rubbish' or 'picturesque mediocre slime' to 'quiet compliment to London', points up both the feelings stirred by such an emotive monument and its location and the problems facing the architects.

The same kind of response and strength of feeling has also surfaced about Paternoster Square, and in each case the protagonists (in the blue corner the Prince of Wales, the general public, Terry Farrel *et al*, and in the grey metallic corner the architectural media representing the avant-garde) have their case argued by strident critics who each manage to avoid a really close look at the architects' intentions. With this in mind and in the belief that the creative act can be an enormously challenging struggle, I think it's worth trying to discover some of the intuitive thought mechanisms that seem to have guided the Venturi Scott Brown design.

We must begin by recognising that Robert Venturi has a distinguished academic pedigree. *Learning from Las Vegas* and *Complexity and Contradiction in Architecture* can properly be regarded as seminal works that played a major role in changing the direction of 20th-century architecture. And as with Corbus' Ronchamp or Stirling's Staatsgalerie the extension to the National Gallery gave Robert Venturi a fine opportunity to draw together a lifetime of observation and analysis and in so doing to confirm his theory with one definitive affirmation. It was Venturi's background that enabled him to bring to the problem an unusually perceptive recognition of the idiosyncratic nature of England and London and to pick up subtle site resonances. As he has explained:

> The vitality of Classical architecture in this country lies in it being Mannerist, impure, idiosyncratic, and that involves very much Inigo Jones from the beginning, Hawkesmoor and very much Soane, Greek Thompson and Wren in the churches. It involves Archer to learn from, Vanbrugh, Lutyens. I find it the most thrilling country, along with Italy and Japan.[1]

Such observations colour the architects' approach to the problem and on close examination the building makes many references to earlier writings.

The design of the Sainsbury Wing may be discussed in two ways: firstly there are some basic premises regarding the site and role of the extension in relation to the National Gallery that seem to determine the formal organisation; and secondly the design approach can be considered in relation to Venturi's own analytical investigations as outlined in *Complexity and Contradiction in Architecture*.

The National Gallery is in essence a horizontal slab which stretches

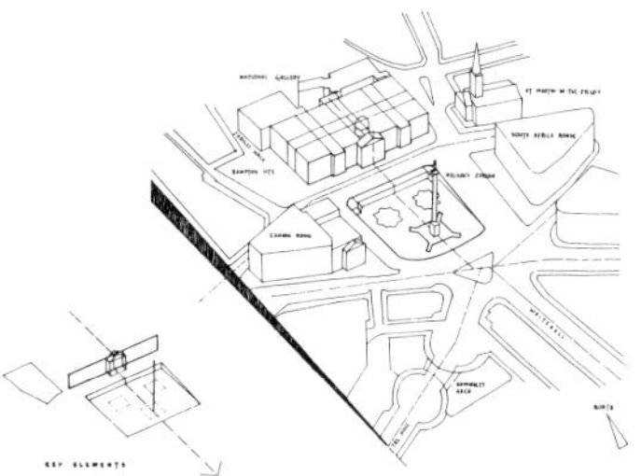

Trafalgar Square.

along the northern edge of the site, forming a low-key backcloth to Trafalgar square. At the north-eastern corner, James Gibbs' St Martin in the Fields acts as a stop to the Gallery, whilst at the opposite end the hole left by the destruction of the Hampton Furniture Building during the Second World War forms the site for the extension. To the left and right are Smirke's Canada House and Baker's South Africa House. The sense of enclosure dissipates to the south, as the square becomes a large traffic roundabout. It is held together by the symmetry of the Gallery facade and this symmetry is retained in the Square by the positioning of the fountains and Nelson's Column. At the western edge of the National Gallery, Jubilee Walk links Trafalgar Square to Leicester Square.

The programme called for a new, permanent home for the Early Renaissance Collection, including such masterpieces as Ucello's *Battle of San Romano,* Piero della Francesca's *Baptism* and Jan Van Eyck's *Arnolfini Marriage*.

Rather than relating the design to the rectilinear geometry of Wilkins' National Gallery, the architects here take the site configuration as a starting point and exploit the divergent axis where Whitcomb Street meets Pall Mall East.

The wedge shaped angle of the

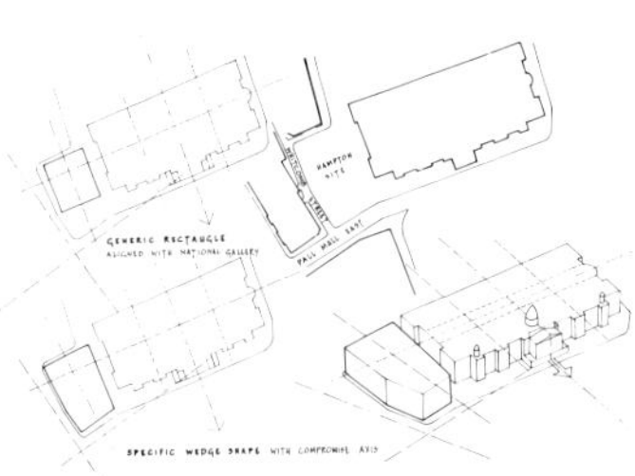

Venturi's configuration responds to the angle of Whitcomb Street and Pall Mall East with 'compromise' axis.

site to the south-west (Whitcomb Street and Pall Mall East) results in a 'compromise' longitudinal axis at an oblique angle within the configuration. This offset axis, at an angle to the orthogonal grid of the National Gallery, sets in motion a range of important possibilities, later to be exploited.

At the corner where contact is made with Trafalgar Square, a radial entry zone has been created which erodes this corner of the mass.

This entry zone radiates from the main longitudinal axis. At the upper level the main galleries are placed to the west of the main longitudinal axis.

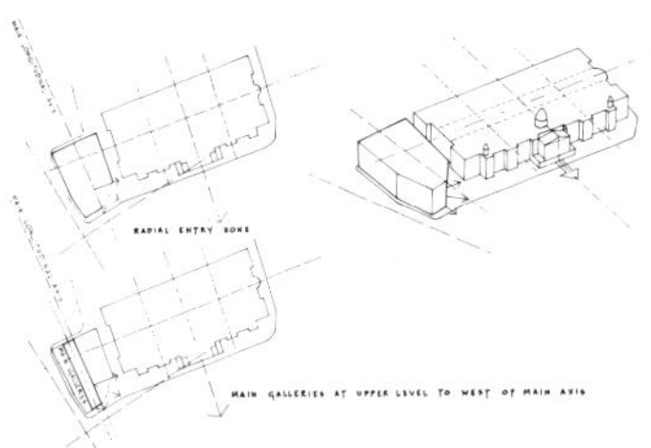

Entry zone radiates from main longitudinal (compromise) axis. Galleries are at upper level to the west of main axis.

At the ground level of the entry zone the radial theme is taken up by a double skin shaped like a boomerang and closed at the western corner by escape stairs which lock into the right angle where Whitcomb Street meets Pall Mall East.

The outer skin is masonry pierced by large openings which invite entry, while the inner skin is glazed and affords a view of the entry

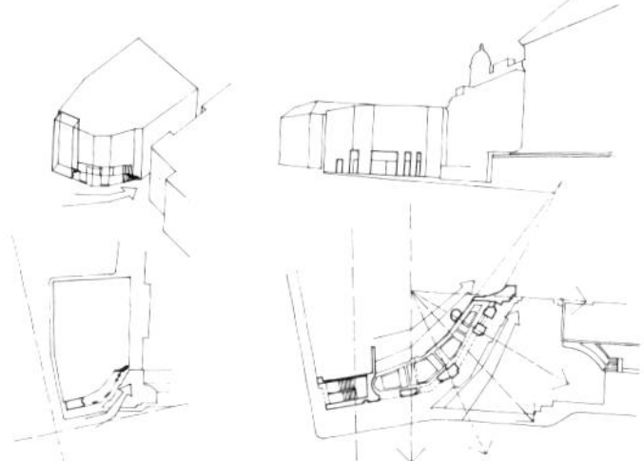

Entry zone double skin – boomerang creates anti-clockwise movement vector terminated by a sculpted pier.

foyer. The combined effect of the boomerang shape and radial formation – stopped by the escape stairs into which are fashioned a niche – creates an anti-clockwise movement vector towards the National Gallery, stopped by a substantial and carefully sculpted pier.

The contrast between the outer, pierced, solid skin and the inner transparent skin is furthered by the staccato punctuation of the outer layer, as the series of columns and pilasters visibly move towards a stuttering conclusion in the corner. Their plan profiles are distorted by radial and movement pressures and also by the continuous bonding of each layer. In the original design, the floor pattern between outer and inner skins expressed the dynamism and richness of this interaction, conveying something of the energy generated by the tension between inner and outer layers. And in its original form the sweeping boomerang curve produced ripples in the forecourt between it and the National Gallery, echoed in the form of curved steps at the corner of the front terrace to the National Gallery. (This has been replaced by a simple curve.)

The idea of entry on the corner resembles that of Peruzzi's Palazzo

Massimi, particularly in the way columns have been used to define the outer skin and allow a subtle

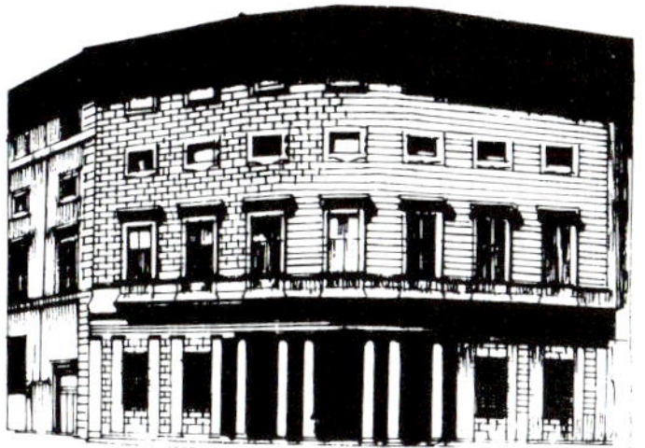

Baldessare Peruzzi, Palazzo Pietro Massimi, Rome.

form of penetration into the mass. In *Complexity and Contradiction* Venturi explains how on the Palazzo Massimi, 'a curving rather than an angular distortion accommodated the facade to the street, which also curved before it was changed in the 19th century'.[2]

However, in the Sainsbury Wing, a giant order is used which is detached from the general facade pattern. In *Complexity and Contra-*

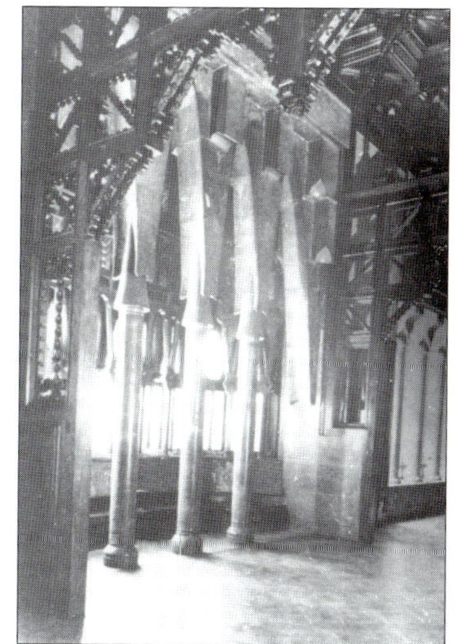

Gaudi, Casa Güell, Barcelona.

diction Venturi refers to the way the columns on Gaudi's Casa Güell are disengaged and superimposed on contrasting window patterns.[3] He cites numerous examples of this which he terms superadjacency, and explains that this play of layers of openings is sometimes discordant in rhythm and scale. His description of the layered facade to the extension shows how this resembles the layering of Wilkins' facade.

Entry into the building is towards the western edge of the boomerang, so that the route to the galleries from Trafalgar Square enters at the widest point of the portico and then takes a right turn towards the stair.

The stairs act as counterpoint to the entry boomerang, reversing the enclosing membranes so that the

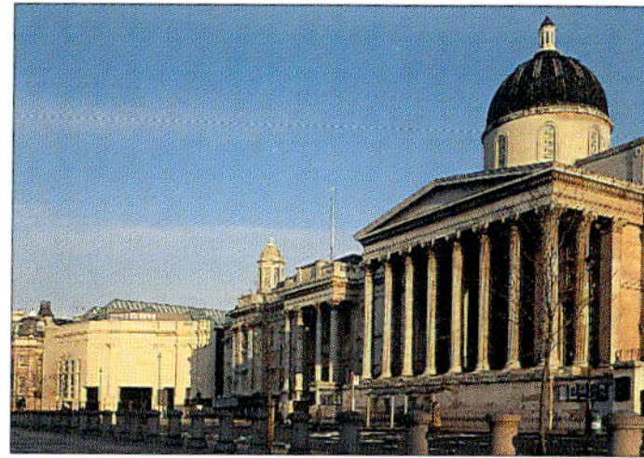

Venturi & Scott Brown's layered facade to the extension resembles that of the National Gallery.

outer skin is of glass and the inner of masonry. The sculpted column acts as the intermediary between these circulation zones.

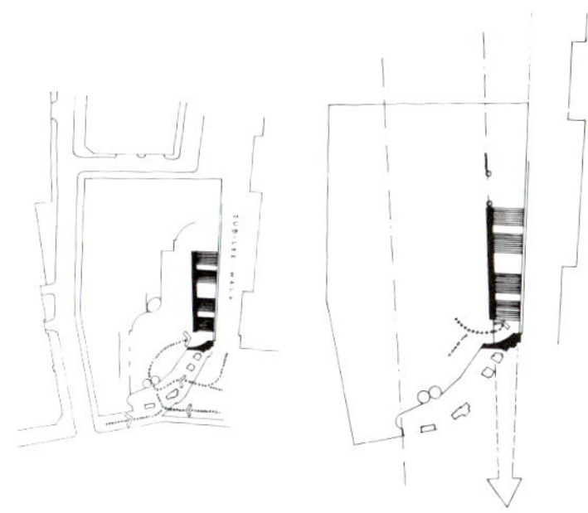

Entry at ground level. Stair reverses boomerang in having outer glazed and inner masonry skins.
Stair resolves two axes (extension and National Gallery). Sculpted pier resists tendency to thrust outward and is shaped to accommodate movement.

The inner masonry wall of the staircase is aligned with the internal axis of the main gallery, whilst the outer glazed skin is parallel to the National Gallery. This angle gives the stairs a momentum which threatens to thrust outwards, piercing the sculpted column; this is resisted by the strength of the main pier which is shaped so as to turn movement from foyer to staircase.

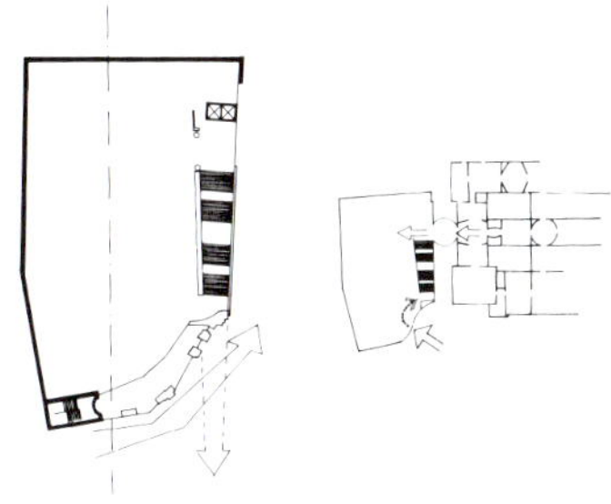

Stair 'held' by twin elevators. Static rear and west sides hold swirling south-east corner.
Entry routes from National Gallery and extension meet at the top of the stair.

At the opposite end the stairs are held by twin elevators. Looking at the plan as a whole, it is evident that the surging energy of the eastern edge is contained by the static rear and west sides of the mass. The outer swirl of the boomerang is countered in part by the implicit thrust of the stairs, and in the southwest corner is stabilised by the escape stairs.

Unquestionably the staircase is the central idea of the scheme; it fulfils several roles. On a geometric level its angled sides reconcile the two axes of extension and National

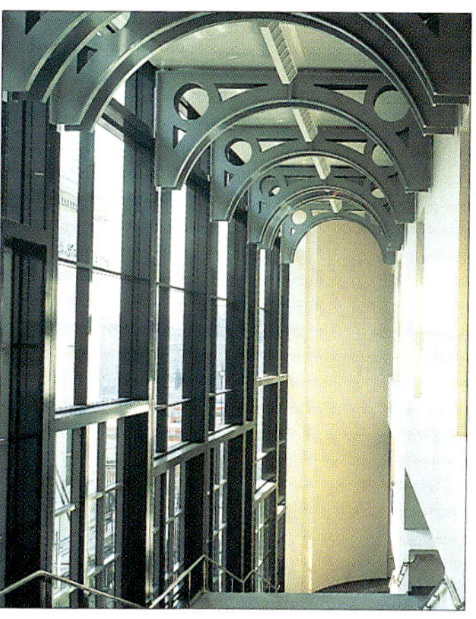

View down Main Stair.

Gallery. The reversed layering of enclosing membranes reminds us of Chapter 9 in *Complexity and Contradiction,* 'The Inside and the Outside', in which Venturi refers to complex layering in Baroque architecture. Psychologically, the monumentality of the staircase, with its broadening perspective, is enhanced by its multiple readings. Moving up the staircase, the presence of the National Gallery is confirmed by the sight of its outer wall surface to the right, with an implied reflection of this wall to the immediate left. So we are simultaneously made aware that we are in a 20th-century building by the message of the glass wall, and we know we are part of a 19th-century ensemble by virtue of the masonry wall and view towards the National Gallery. The carved Roman lettering on the inner wall of the staircase is an appropriate gesture to its senior neighbour, whilst the curved steel trusses above speak of a British engineering past. Moving down the stair we are provided with a glimpse of Nelson's Column in Trafalgar Square.

The juxtaposition of entry and stair solves the circulation problem of the extension at a stroke. Externally entry is at the obvious point, where the site ends and invites access; inside, those moving into the extension from the National Gallery and those entering from the extension arrive at the same gathering point before moving into the galleries.

The entry foyer responds to the twin zones of boomerang and stair, echeloning alongside in deference to them.

To the immediate left of entry is the gallery shop, entered through a third double skin; it has its own entry zone, fashioned by columns of a different size and shape, placed on

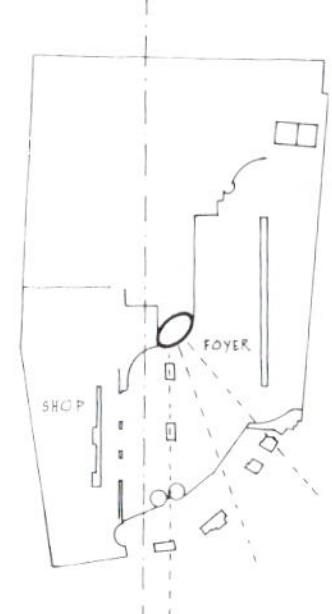

Entry foyer echelons. Oval information desk forms visual and radial focus. Double skin entry to shop.

the same axis as the permanent picture galleries above. The inner skin of this foyer curves around as the space changes shape. At the central point of curvature, a sculpted oval information desk forms a visual focus which implies a radial source for the membranes of the boomerang.

The entry foyer ceiling is organised in rectangles on an orthogonal grid in stark contradiction to the radial plan. In contrast (adding to the complexity) the floor plan consists of diagonals whose intersections form angled squares. Larger angled squares are connected by small squares on the orthogonal grid. As the stair descends from foyer level to the basement, Venturi introduces an overscaled 'Mannerist' cornice broken into angled segments that do not coincide with the stair landings.

The treatment of enclosing membranes has distinctly Baroque overtones in its dynamic pulling and pushing of surfaces and space. Chapter 10 of *Complexity and Contradiction*, entitled 'The Obligation Towards the Difficult Whole', refers to 'almost equal combinations of contrasting directions and rhythms in columns, piers, walls and doors in the Church of the Holy Sepulchre in Jerusalem', which is similar to the composition of the Berlin Philharmonie by Scharoun.[4] As exemplifying the inclusive whole in an architecture of opposites: 'The unity of the interior of the Imatra Church or the complex at Wolfsburg' is seen as being 'achieved not through suppression or exclusion but through the dramatic inclusion of contradictory or circumstantial parts. Aalto's architecture acknowl-

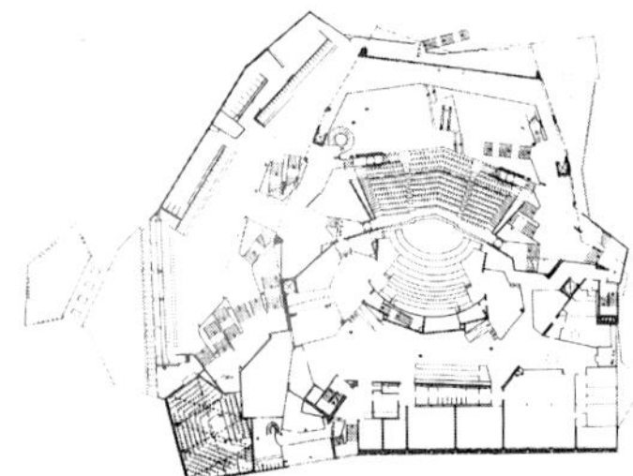

Scharoun, Berlin Philharmonie, plan.

edges the difficult and subtle conditions of the programme, while 'serene' architecture on the other hand works simplifications'.[5] Continuing this argument Venturi illustrates Gaudi's Dressing Table in the Casa Güell, Barcelona, 'representing an orgy of contrasting qualities of form' . . . with 'complex and simple curves, rectangles and diagonals, contrasting materials, symmetry and asymmetry, in order to accommodate a multiplicity of functions in one whole'.[6]

These messages show preference for a resolution of functional requirements acceding to the 'difficult and subtle conditions of the programme'. Forms are used which create spaces enlivened by con-

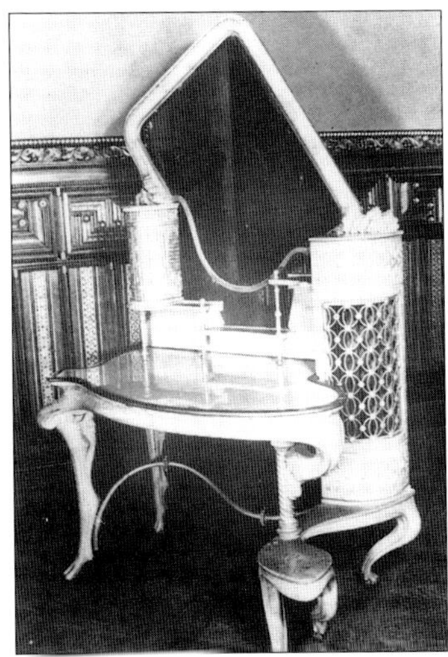

Gaudi Dressing Table, Casa Guell, Barcelona.

trasting demands – in the case of the Sainsbury Wing revelling in the contrasting demands made by entry, stairs and foyer.

The extension is linked to the present building by a circular volume. This configuration divides the two buildings and establishes a pause between them. It is part of a piercing thrust along the main longitudinal axis of the National Gallery which is emphasised by a narrowing down as it penetrates the Sainsbury Wing. This is experienced as a series of receding arches, suggesting a Renaissance false perspective.

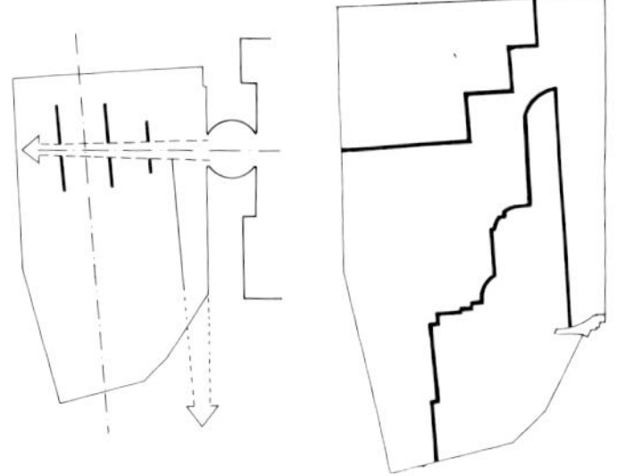

Circular volume separates extension from National Gallery and starts to thrust into extension.
Echelons interact.

At Mezzanine level two echelons interact, the one, rectilinear at the rear, the other, with curved corners, picking up the boomerang/staircase movement. Between these two systems the Information Room acts as a mediator, with a pronounced curve that relates to an undulating wall opposite, which is part curved and part echeloned. The resultant space forms the head of a 'scythe', into the corner of which nestles the kitchen, and beyond which radiates the cafe. At its northern edge the cafe becomes a snack bar, almost rectilinear, as its enclosing walls are formed on the internal axis of the extension; but at its outer, southern edge, the cafe belongs partly to the outer skin and partly to the inner as it extends the idea of the double skin at entry. To the right of the snack bar a landing forms the circulation route as it overlooks the stairs, reinforcing not only the eastern edge, but also the general S-shaped movement along this edge.

Michelangelo's Sforza Chapel of St Maria Maggiore, Rome, is described as having layers implied 'in the violent penetrations of rectangular space and curved space in plan and of barrel vaults, domes

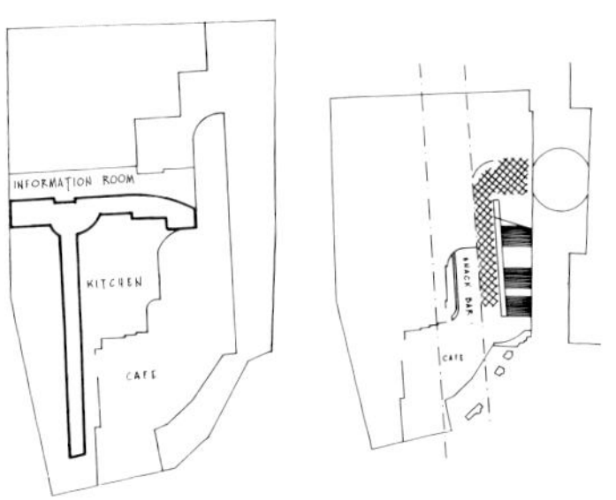

'Scythe' encloses kitchen from which cafe radiates outward.
Snack bar on axes. Cafe extends double skin idea at entry. Stair landing supports S-shaped movement and strengthens movement energy along this line.

and niche-vaulting in section'.[7] These volumetric sculptings, in which spaces respond to their immediate surroundings, remind us again of Aalto,[8] and also of the quotation from Sinnott's The Problem of Organic Form which begins Chapter 9 of *Complexity and Contradiction*:

> The external configuration is usually rather simple, but there is packed into the interior of an organism an amazing complexity of structures which have long been the delight of anatomists.

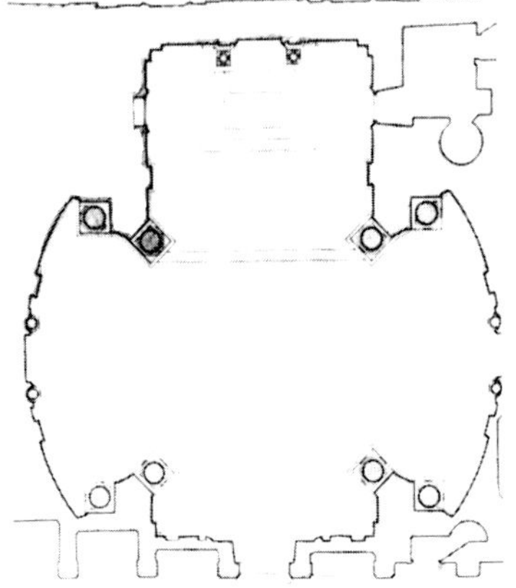

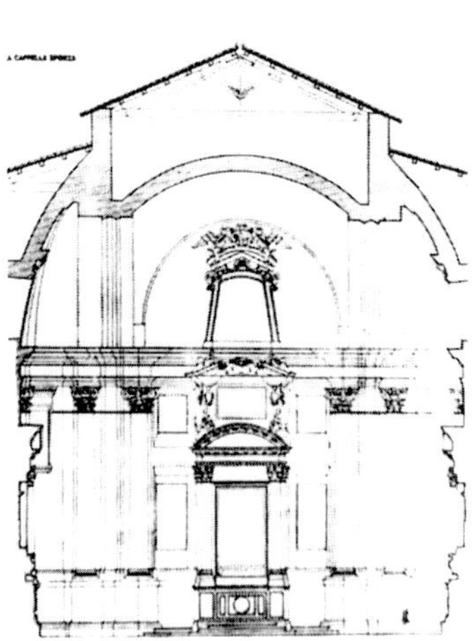

Michelangelo, Sforza Chapel, St Maria Maggiore, in plan and section.

> The specific form of a plant or animal is determined not only by the genes in the organism and the cytoplasmic activities that these direct but by the interaction between genetic constitution and environment. A given gene does not control a specific trait, but a specific reaction to a specific environment.[9]

This kind of specificity becomes a major technique throughout the extension. At the basement level the auditorium reinforces the main axis, whilst to the east movement shifts round a curved cloaks pod to emerge at a circular node placed directly adjacent to the bottom of the lower flight of the main staircase. This turn of the stairs forms an axis which passes through the circle into the Temporary Exhibition Gallery.

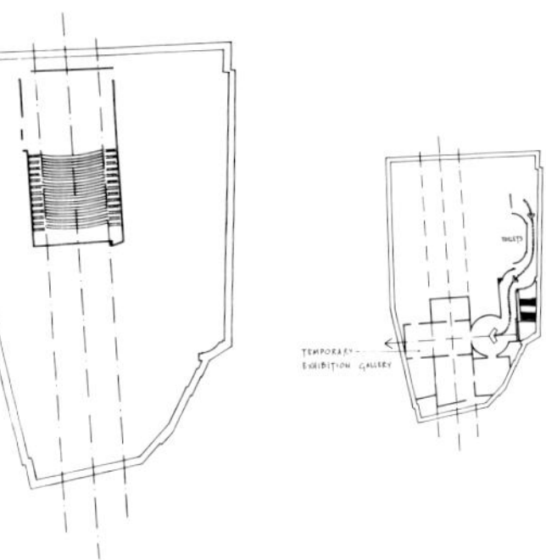

Auditorium reinforces main axis. Movement bends round cloaks to reach circular node on axis from stair towards Temporary Exhibition Gallery.

Again, there is a response both to the main longitudinal axis (in the auditorium, which centrally reinforces this axis), and to the south-eastern edge (with a swirling route and a circular node which respond to the radial boomerang above). The circular node picks up a device used in the National Gallery to express points where circulation axes meet.

The window wall, where the cafe overlooks Pall Mall East, extends the general theme of layering, furthering extensive discussion in *Complexity and Contradiction* of the possibilities afforded when inside and outside are juxtaposed. At Mezzanine level the cafe has four windows which look directly into the street.

On the facade this punctuation of the wall plane looks ordinary. It takes the form of a Regency window whose scale and shape relate to Pall Mall East. Inside, however, in

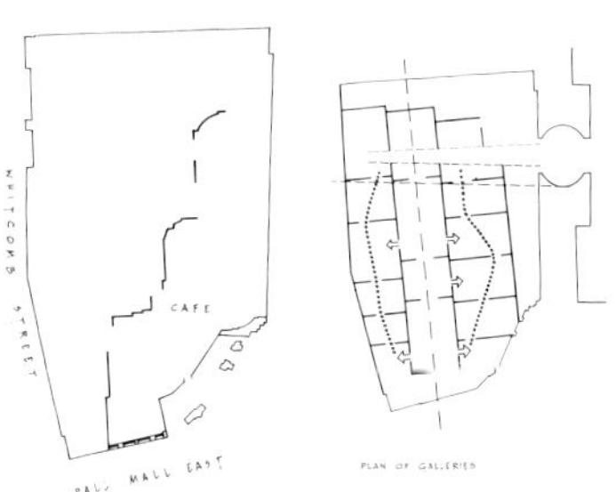

Four windows from the cafe overlook Pall Mall East.
Circulation thrust from National Gallery sets in motion an echeloned plan which shifts the gallery positions on either side of main central galleries.

the original design a double height space is created next to the outer wall so that a double wall exists above at gallery level, with three windows looking over the void, which is itself top lit by rooflights. The reason for this becomes apparent when we study the plan of the main galleries.

This ensures the primacy of the main axis and is terminated at each end by a right-angle. On the southern side this right-angle abuts the void, whose outer skin is angled with Pall Mall East. By this means, the void and creation of a double skin mediates between an inner and an outer condition. The outer windows, facing Pall Mall East, observe the outer condition, the inner windows to the gallery observe the inner condition (the inner windows to the gallery in the original design have been removed at the client's insistence to give more wall hanging space). This intended 'tension' between inner and outer is discussed by Venturi in Chapter 9 'The Inside and the Outside' in

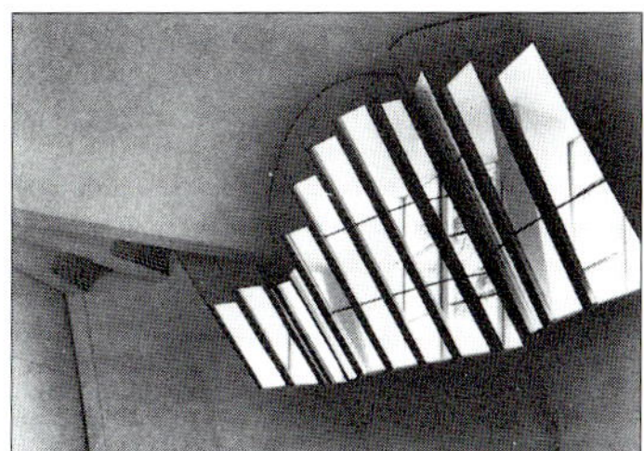

Aalto Church, Vuoksenniska, near Imatra, Finland.

which he refers to 'the detachment of the inner and outer window openings in Aalto's Imatra Church'. In Aalto's Church and the extension, the skin layering responds to inner and outer conditions, the interest being created by the difference in these conditions. This dynamism may be compared to the comparatively static double skin of Sir Norman Foster's Sainsbury Centre,

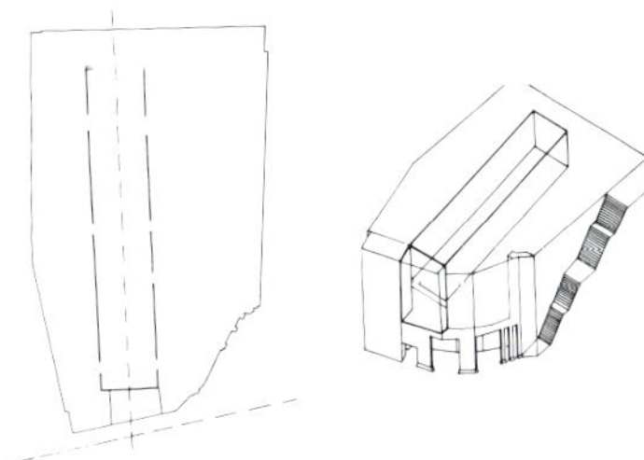

Gallery plan showing inner and outer conditions.
Double height top-lit space with windows looking into this space from the galleries and with outer windows looking onto Pall Mall East. Windows and wall angles observe inner and outer conditions.

which represents the opposite minimal modernist position.

To the rear of the galleries an echeloned plan formation also mediates between the galleries east and west of the central 'nave', in a stepping down which is set in motion by the angle of the circulation thrust from the National Gallery. Circulation within these side galleries is further angled to set up a counterpoint with the regular rhythm of rectilinear compartments, and, as the architect points out, to give views of paintings opposite door openings.

The main galleries define the north-south axis with large arches separating the rooms. Openings at the sides allow glimpses of the side galleries. Gallery illumination depends on daylight and electricity. Daylight is admitted through banks of clerestories at the upper perimeter of galleries. Prismatic glass in the clerestories filters the light distribution to the wall surfaces below. The gallery windows overlooking the staircase give a pleasing effect with their views towards the National Gallery.

This analysis of the architects' main design strategy has sought to

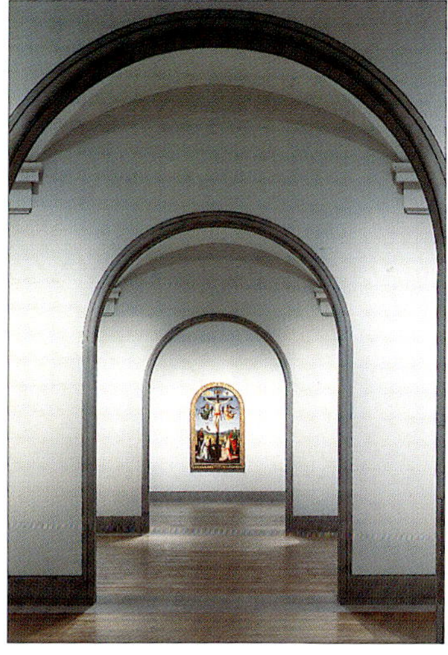

View of Galleries.

show how the Sainsbury Wing has been designed according to a set of principles drawn from both historical and modern architecture. Addressing such issues as inside and outside, the obligation towards the difficult whole, ambiguity, reversal, and other topics treated at length in *Complexity and Contradiction,* the project offers an approach intended to be appropriate for a major cultural work in a historic context in the late 20th century. The analysis has gained by having Robert Venturi's theory already in place. This philosophy results in a building far simpler in its articulation than current trends by architects such as Meier, Morphosis or the Deconstructionists. These recent modern trends towards complex articulation are replaced in the Sainsbury Wing by simpler elemental statements. The facade becomes important again in its surface modulation. Instead of a series of ramps we have a grand staircase. The complexity is there, but it is of a different order to that of much contemporary work. This difference lies, to a large extent, in the area of meaning. This draws on a symbolism derived from close study of precedent intended to engage a wide audience. This approach (with its incised Roman lettering along-

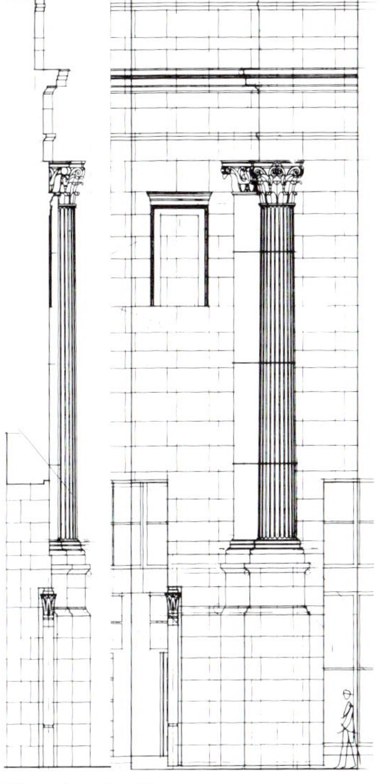

Elevation detail.

side the stairs, 'pictra serena' stone door casings and Mannerist columns) is more profound than the decorative superficialities of Post-Modernism. Its integrity and authority reside in its origins. Mannerist, Baroque and Rococo architecture manage to be both complex, contradictory and accessible in terms of inherent meanings. In Zimmermann's Wieskirche, an example quoted by Venturi, the colonnade does indeed 'make changing rhythmic juxtapositions against the pilasters and window openings of the walls'.[10]

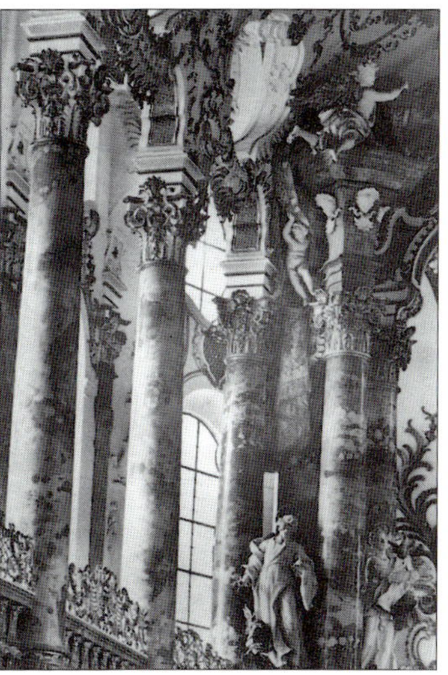

Zimmermann Wieskirche, Steingaden, Bavaria.

Because of the nature of the elements and their intention, these juxtapositions seem relevant and appropriate. To transfer such 'super-adjacencies' into a modern language is the task Venturi and Denise Scott Brown have set themselves.

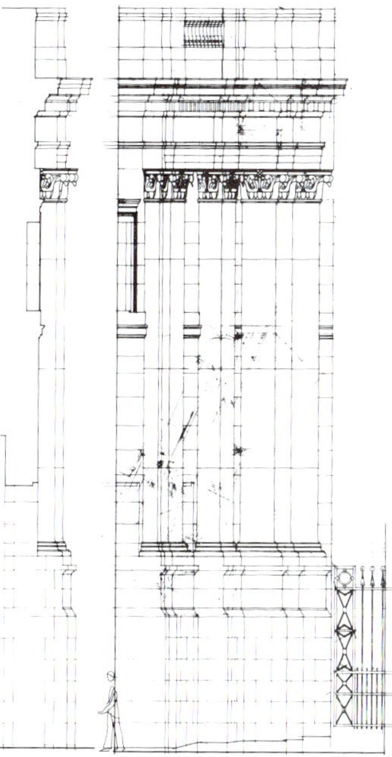

Elevation detail.

Notes

I would like to thank Lance Hiatt and Jonathan Siegel for help with the diagrammatic drawings of the extension to the National Gallery, Donald Gatzke for his comments and Gregory Ensslen for help compiling the illustrations.

This article is taken from a paper given to the Association of Collegiate Schools of Architecture, Chicago and published in the conference proceedings. It is reproduced with the permission of the ACSA.

1 Interview with Charles Jencks, AD Profile No 91, p57.
2 R Venturi, *Complexity and Contradict-ion in Architecture*, The MoMA, New York, 1966, pp45-46.
3 *ibid*, p64.
4 *ibid*, p102.
5 *ibid*, p102.
6 *ibid*, p102.
7 *ibid*, p78.
8 See GH Baker, 'Analysis of the Town Hall at Säynätsalo', *Design Strategies in Architecture: An Approach to the Analysis of Form*, Chapman and Hall, London, 1989, pp159,185.
9 Edmund W Sinnott, the Problem of Organic Form, Yale University Press, New Haven, 1963.
10 Venturi, *op cit*, pp70-87.
11 *ibid*, p66.

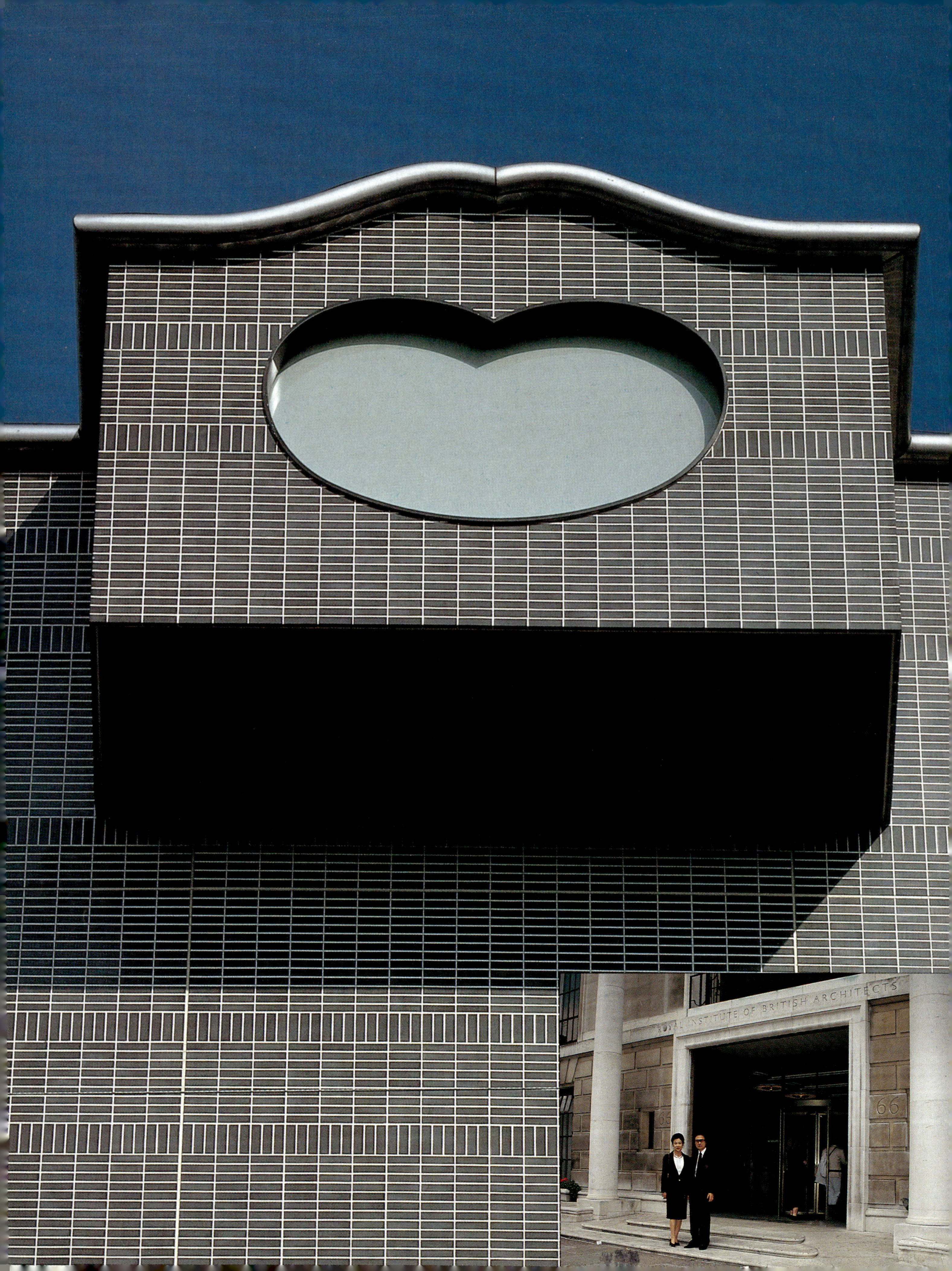
ROYAL INSTITUTE OF BRITISH ARCHITECTS
66

KISHO KUROKAWA
FROM METABOLISM TO SYMBIOSIS

Kisho Kurokawa has had a close relationship with the RIBA since he was awarded an honorary fellowship in 1986. As a prolific designer, writer and teacher he continues to grow in stature throughout the world yet remains one of Japan's most important and controversial architectural figures.

As we in this country have had our battles of the styles, Tokyo has had an enduring architectural battle over the new city hall in Sinjuko, designed by Kenzo Tange, Kisho Kurokawa's professor. Kurokawa has become the new hall's sternest critic and adversary. In so doing he has articulated much of his architectural philosophy and approach:

> *the art of architecture is an expression of the spirit of an era . . . buildings which we architects design today should be part of the cultural heritage of future generations. In this sense the Tokyo city hall is nothing but reminiscent of the Medieval age.*

Maxwell Hutchinson

Kisho Kurokawa is a man of wide-ranging interests. He not only designs buildings and redesigns cities but also takes part in political debates, appears regularly on television and is something of a philosopher. What is the philosophy of Symbiosis? For Kurokawa, it is a way of life and aesthetic based on mixing opposites, ambiguity and hybridisation. His buildings interweave dualities: East versus West, abstraction versus representation, organic versus rational, past versus present and future. It is no accident that he is a friend of Prime Ministers and masters of the tea ceremony, high-tech and traditional architects. Nor that he was known as the capsule architect for about 15 years and then spent another 17 years designing a tea ceremony hut in his own house. He refuses to confirm those polarisations which set Prince Charles against the now Sir Richard Rogers. But nor is he for unifying their differences in some Hegelian synthesis. Kurokawa's position is the third way: both the inclusion of opposites and the ambiguous sliding between them.

Charles Jencks

Kurokawa does two things that rarely come together. He challenges our own categorisations of the correct territory for architecture and also questions the correct territory for the Japanese themselves. Japan is an extraordinary combination of a careful, procedural culture and a Toy Town culture, the most 20th-century country of all. But where most Japanese try to brush this ambiguity aside, Kurokawa has chosen to move in on it and to attempt a symbiosis. What cannot come through in pictures is the precision and elegance with which he does this.

Kurokawa holds weekly meetings at his practice where he pummels away at the reasoning behind the work. His philosophy is not just for the international circuit and for the big book, it also comes into the office; it works.

Peter Cook

The Metabolism movement began in 1958. The first book to come out of the movement was published in 1960. It all began, then, 33 years ago.

It is hard to draw clear-cut lines, but my focus of interest seems to change about once every decade. In the 1960s I was concerned with Metabolism, and an architecture of open structure. In the 1970s I talked about in-between space, ambiguity, and an architecture of greys. In the 1980s I spoke of Symbiosis and Intercultural Architecture. In the 1990s I believe I will further pursue and develop the concept of Symbiosis.

Architecture is an expression of the spirit of the age. I think it is fair to say that my interests have changed with the changing times. In the 1960s Japan's economy entered its period of high growth. The ideas of open systems, open structures, a dynamic architecture and urban planning matched the strategies of Japan at that time – its government, economy and culture. That is why a large section of the populace supported my ideas at that time. They accepted and backed our attempts to bring change and growth to art and architecture, to take Modern architecture apart and reassemble it in a contemporary way.

The 60s was a decade in which the curtain rose on Japan as a leader in technology. It was also Japan's last decade as an industrial nation, I believe. For that reason, the architecture of Metabolism not only had an open structure but also tried to express metaphorically the future potential of technology.

The International Exposition in Osaka in 1970 may have been the culmination of those tendencies. The 1970s was a decade when the contradiction between city and nature, between people and technology, sharpened in intensity.

From another viewpoint, the 1970s was a turbulent transitional period when we began to move from an industrial society to an information society. Our value system was shaken, and a change of generations began to take place in government, economics, and the arts. High economic growth faltered, as did the excessive faith we had in technology. In the 1970s I published many writings on my theories of intermediary space, ambiguity,

The National Bunraku Theatre, Osaka, Japan. INSET: Mr & Mrs Kisho Kurokawa.

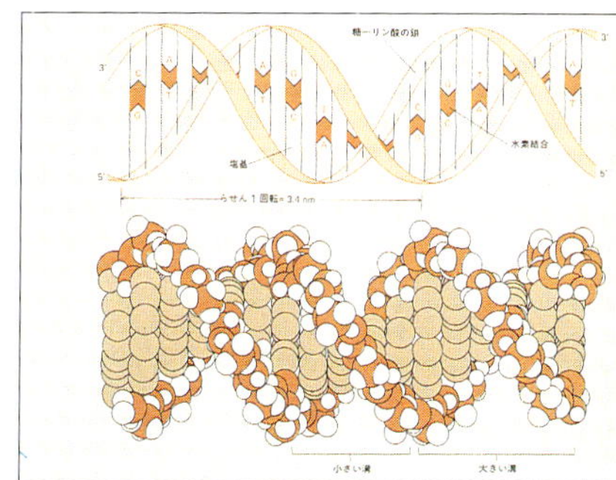

The double helix of the DNA molecule served as a prétexte *for the concept of the helix city, which was offered as part of the declaration of the founding of Metabolism.*

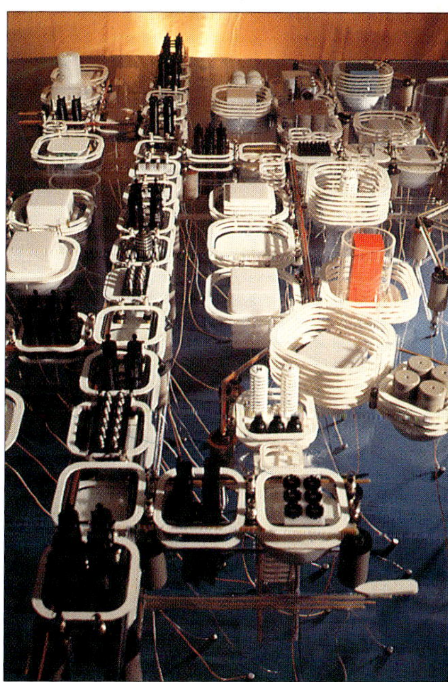

My city concept was one of a city with growth and change. I conceived of cities built on lakes and oceans.

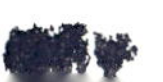

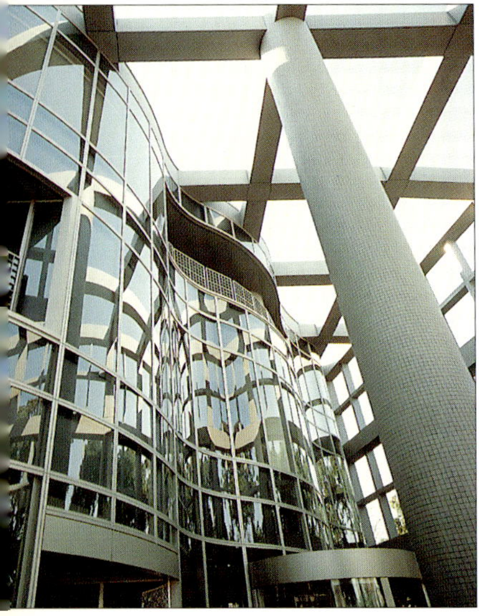

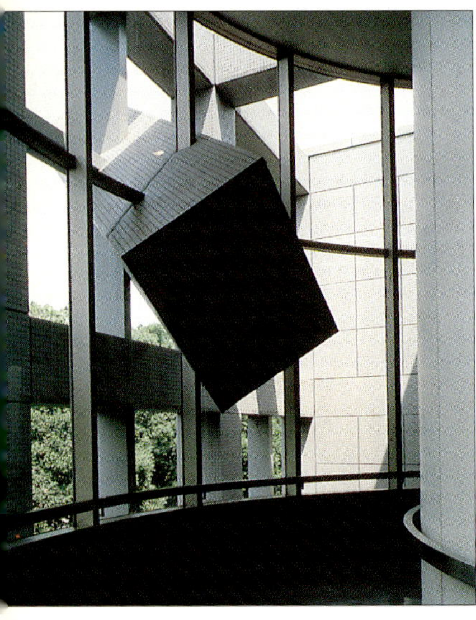

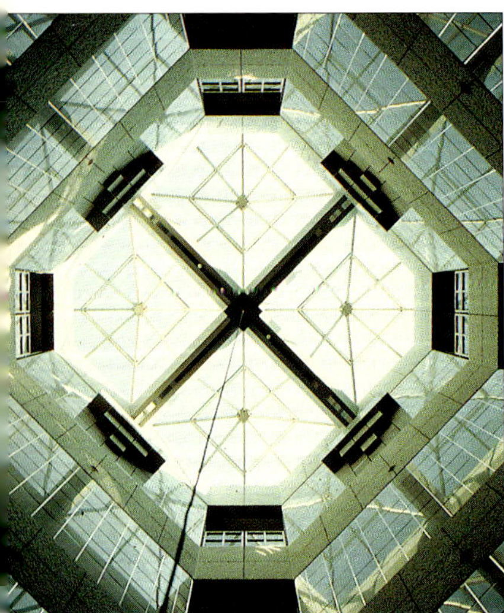

The Saitama Prefectural Museum of Modern Art stands in the midst of a park. To create a symbiosis of the interior and exterior, architecture and nature, I created an intermediary space of three-dimensional lattice work. As an ambiguous, intermediary zone, the facade also acts as a device to challenge artists. The object pierced by the lattice is a sculpture by Yonekichi Tanaka. It was created after the building was completed.

and ambivalence. It was during this period that I was using phrases like 'an architecture of greys' and 'a culture of greys'. I focused on intermediary spaces between private and public, the part and the whole, the individual and society, architecture and the natural environment, and interior and exterior as a method to reunify a dissected and disassembled architecture.

In the world of government, middle-of-the-road parties such as the New Liberty Club were born in Japan from the fierce opposition of conservative and liberal forces. I think that my theory of intermediary space was successful in restoring the rich artistry, ambiguous and ambivalent, that Western dualism and binomial opposition had destroyed. Intermediary space acts as a shared or common element between binomial oppositions, differing individuals, and differing cultures, allowing them to exist in symbiosis.

In the 1980s it became increasingly apparent that Japan was being transformed into an information society. Some 70 per cent of Japan's GNP was now a product of non-industrial sectors of the economy such as finance, research, design, education, communication, commerce, trade and the service sector.

The cutting-edge technology such as computer communications, communications media; biotechnologies such as life science and genetic manipulations; and micro machines and fuzzy sensors – all are invisible technologies. In the industrial society, which began with the invention of the steam engine and the Model-T Ford, we were creating a world of visible technologies and machines. Modern architecture existed as an analogy to these visible machines.

We have not yet sufficiently answered the new question of how architecture would express the invisible technologies of the information age. Architecture freed from representing the machine, from representing apparati, will probably become an architecture expressive for its own sake, an architecture that values the creation of meaning, no longer tied directly to mere function or reason. Why? Because the new invisible technologies – especially communications technology – allow form to exist independent of technology.

The independence of the architectural facade, the creation of meaning, the importance of symbolism – all of these are intimately linked to the emergence of information society. In addition, an information age is an age not of substance or material itself but relation. In this age, architecture will become an Intercultural Architecture.

It is not that architecture will be a self-enclosed, independent entity that produces meaning. The relationship between architecture and its environment will produce meaning. The relationship between the distinct spaces within the work of architecture and the relationships between placements of the quoted signs and symbols in the work will create new meaning.

The method of first dissecting a work of architecture into its elements and then freely relocating them and reassembling them is the method of architectural expression in the information age. As a result, symmetry is avoided whenever possible. Placing non-functional open space or *ma* between space and space, form and form, symbol and symbol, produces a dynamic, flowing, Intercultural Architecture.

An age of interrelation means the abolishment of pyramid-like hierarchies. It is fundamentally different in structure from industrial-age society. In industrial society, relations are fixed in vertical hierarchies. The vertical relations of individuals, families, communities, cities, and nations form a fixed pyramid hierarchy.

But in information society, more free and dynamic modes of relation will emerge, I believe. In the coming age, international relations between individuals and cities of different countries, relations that are not funnelled through government channels, will be profoundly important. It will be a time when movements to create a new order will take place at the same time. I think that the concept of Symbiosis will become a key word of this new age of interrelationships. I have explained how the architecture that I created in each period of my career reflects the spirit of the times. But there are two points that are consistent in all my work, from Metabolism to Symbiosis.

The first is, I have always attempted for these 33 years to express the spirit of the age in terms of biology, organic life and living systems, in contrast to Modern architecture which has taken the machine as its symbol or analogy. I intentionally took the terms 'metabolism' and 'symbiosis' from the life sciences.

The connection of part to part in a machine allows for no ambiguity. Play, waste, and areas without significance are eliminated. But in a living organism, biology or life systems, the parts are connected to each other through information which includes ambiguity and play or leeway.

The theme of my architecture – metabolism, change, growth, intermediate space, and a symbiosis that transcends the binomial opposition of dualism – all are expressions of the most important features of living organisms and system or biology. And today, the key concept of Symbiosis is becoming the newest theme in many fields, including life science, physics, biological chemistry, electronics, medicines, and philosophy.

Mandelbrot's fractal geometry, for example, explains natural phenomena as possessing an order which encompasses chaos; and Arthur Koestler sought a philosophy of symbiosis of part and whole in his theory of the holon.

Physicist David Bohm's theory of implicate order says that the order of the whole is inherent in each part. There is a symbolic medicine that is researching methods for us to live to 100 by living in symbiosis with other organisms, including viruses.

There are fuzzy computers and fuzzy robots with ambiguity programmed into them. We see an increasing value placed on ecology in the context of our environmental problems. There is the new French philosophy of Deleuze and Guattari, Derrida, and Kristeva, which seeks to transcend binomial opposition.

If there is one common theme to be found in all

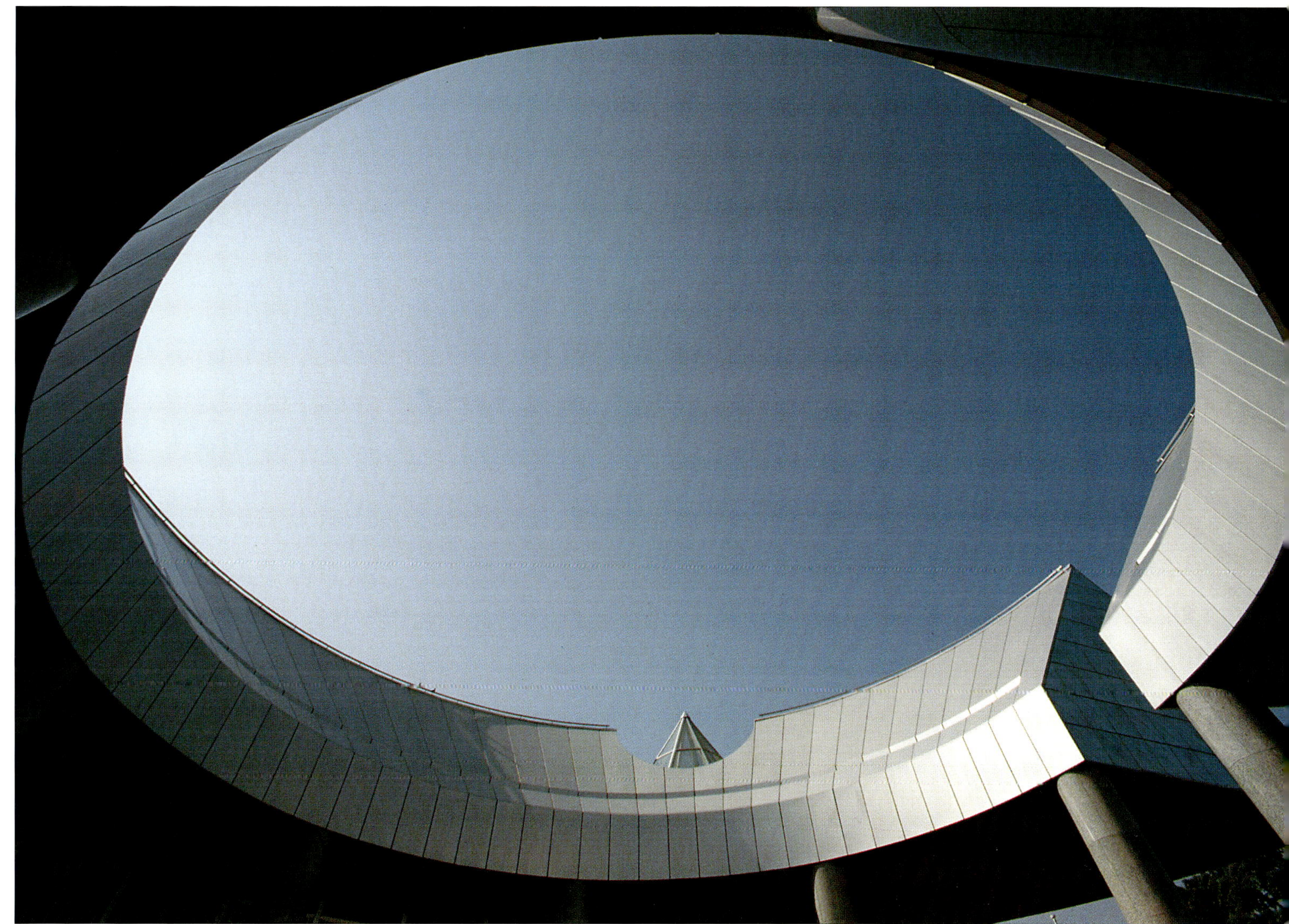

The central rotunda of the Hiroshima City Museum intentionally expresses the absence of the centre. It resembles the atomic bomb cloud, and at the same time a UFO. The round part of the rotunda is chopped off in the direction in which the bomb fell. And on the pillar base, stones discoloured by the explosion have been used.

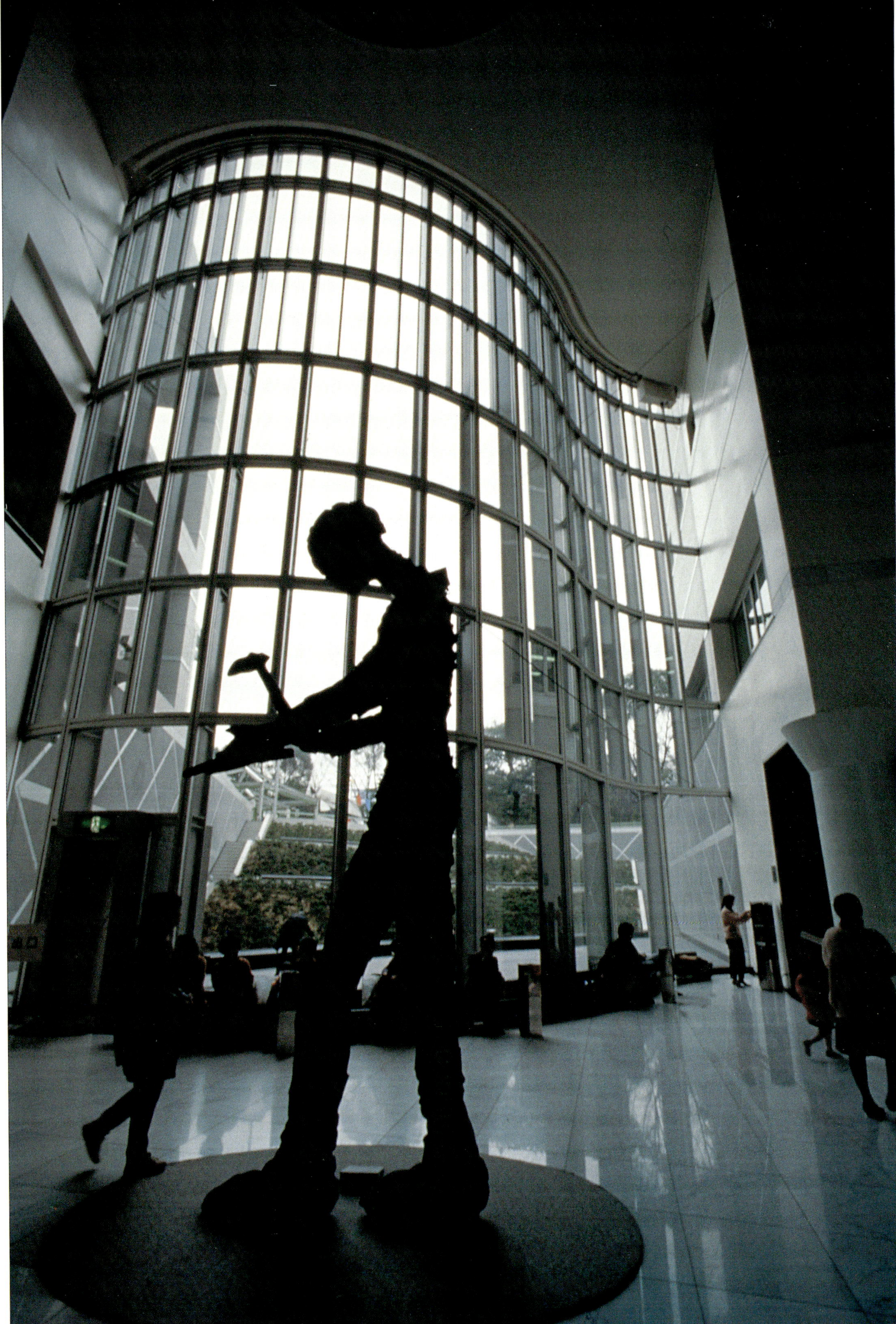

these new directions, it is a 'life system,' a theme that moves beyond the theme of Modernism, the machine.

The second common thread that can be found in all my work of the past 30 years, from Metabolism to Symbiosis, is Buddhist philosophy, which is at the root of Japanese culture. Traditional Japanese architectural models such as Ise Shrine, Izumo Shrine, and Katsura Detached Palace were the *prétexte* of the Metabolism Movement.

Ise Shrine has two distinct sites adjacent to each other. It is a unique structure that has been built anew, in exactly the same way every 20 years for the past 1,300 years, 20 years being the life of the wood used. It is also a suitable interval for transmitting the techniques of rebuilding the shrine from generation to generation. The Izumo Shrine is not rebuilt at such regular intervals, but in its 1,000-year history it has been rebuilt several times. Katsura Detached Palace was added to twice in 150 years.

This is a reflection of the Buddhist concept of impermanence. Architecture and cities are always changing, always going out of existence. Their structures should be open, and the relationship between architecture and nature valued. We should not be preoccupied with matter, with substance.

This special characteristic of Japanese culture penetrates every aspect of Japanese society. Japan has a view of life and death that doesn't make life the absolute – life and death are viewed as related. The Japanese aesthetic cherishes the scattering cherry blossoms. Its human relations are free and open, not restricted to any one community, class, or religious sect. Even the Japanese industrial structure reflects these ideas. Japanese industries are always rebuilding their factories to incorporate the latest technology, easily accepting the newest technological revolutions.

One of the reasons Japan has become an economic superpower is that Japan has faithfully studied the Modernism and rationalism of the West. But it is impossible to explain Japan's success by that alone. The special character of Japanese culture, growth and change that I have mentioned is deeply involved in Japan's scientific, technological and economic success today.

Intermediate space is another expression of the special character of Japanese culture. *Ma* is the interval of space that exists between opposing elements or spaces. In the traditional Japanese residential architectural styles – the *Shoin* style and the *Sukiya* style – there is a veranda called an *engawa* that is an intermediary space between the garden and the house. The veranda links the garden and the house in symbiosis. By placing third space, an intermediary space between two opposing spaces, the ambiguity and ambivalence that are excluded by the dualism and binomial opposition of the West are introduced. A rich and suggestive architecture is created. A semi-public, semi-private intermediary space between public and private space enriches the urban environment. The streets as an extension of living space (in 1962 I called this 'Architecture of the Street'), atria and pocket parks are examples of semi-public space.

Zeami, who systematised the aesthetics of Japan's traditional *Noh* drama, used the term *senuhima*, meaning 'interval when nothing happens,' to describe the silence between words. He valued this silence greatly. The white space between the lines of Japanese calligraphy is also a very important intermediary space.

The concept of Symbiosis is also intimately linked with Buddhist thought. In fact, the idea of Symbiosis is at the very root of Buddhist philosophy. The fundamental difference between Christianity and Buddhism is that a Buddhist (aside from monks) is bound by nothing. He is free to be a follower of Christianity or Islam and still remain a Buddhist if he chooses. Buddhism in not so much a religion as a philosophy or a way of living. This is why Symbiosis, which is at the core of Buddhist thought, was able to transcend the bounds of religion and become the basis of Japanese culture as a whole.

We can explain the uniquely Japanese elements not only in architecture and urban planning but also in *Noh* and other traditional arts and literature with the concept of Symbiosis. Once, 1, 600 years ago, the only way for the tiny country of Japan to survive next to its giant neighbour China was for Japan to take positive steps to absorb Chinese culture, and that of other foreign nations. Japan had to find a way to make its culture live in symbiosis with other cultures, yet preserve its identity.

Today Japan still has a remarkable curiosity regarding other cultures. Symbiosis is the best word by far for explaining the nature of Japanese culture, for in Japanese culture we see the symbiosis of nature and architecture, the symbiosis of tradition and the latest technology, the symbiosis of subtlety and boldness, the symbiosis of different cultures that are opposing entities.

I think you can now see that over the 30 years during which my architecture has evolved from Metabolism to Symbiosis, the two concepts of 'life systems' and 'Japanese culture' have been the consistent themes.

And today I am beginning to believe that Symbiosis is a philosophy that encompasses and distils all my work over those three decades, including Metabolism and intermediary spaces.

I am also beginning to think that we will be able to explain the coming 21st century through the concept of Symbiosis. I don't think anyone would argue that we don't need to rethink Modernism and Modern architecture. But I cannot accept a Post-Modernism that is conceived in the narrow terms of historicism. I think the binomial opposition between Modernism and Post-Modernism is an extremely Western dualism, and I don't think it is a meaningful argument. Nothing could be more meaningless than to totally reject Modernism. What, of Modernism, then, can we keep, and what do we need to revise? I think the two most important revisions of Modernism and Modern architecture are the following: first, we must revise our Euro-centrism; second, we must revise our belief in logocentrism, or universalism.

Up to now, European culture has been regarded as the epitome of human civilisation. It was only right, it was assumed, that the whole world should

Here at the Nagoya City Art Museum a three-dimensional lattice structure and a sunken garden play an important role in creating symbiosis between interior and exterior, architecture and nature.

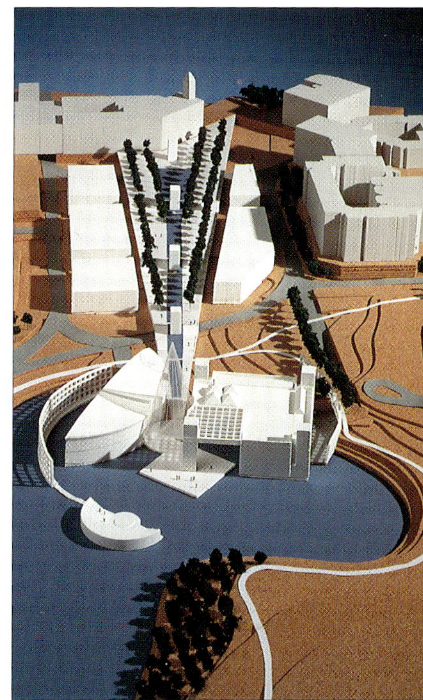

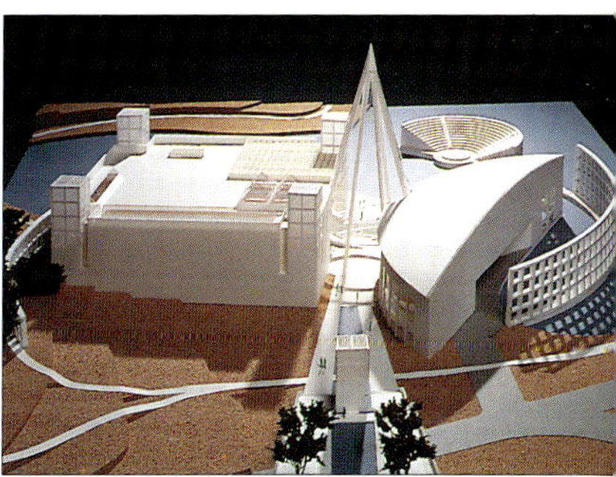

The Art Museum of Louvain-la-Neuve, Belgium is an example of Intercultural Architecture. The functions of the art museum are divided into an exhibition hall, an auditorium, and atrium that serves as an entrance hall, and an outdoor theatre. Each of these areas is made independent while, at the same time, joined in relationships as a single architectural entity.

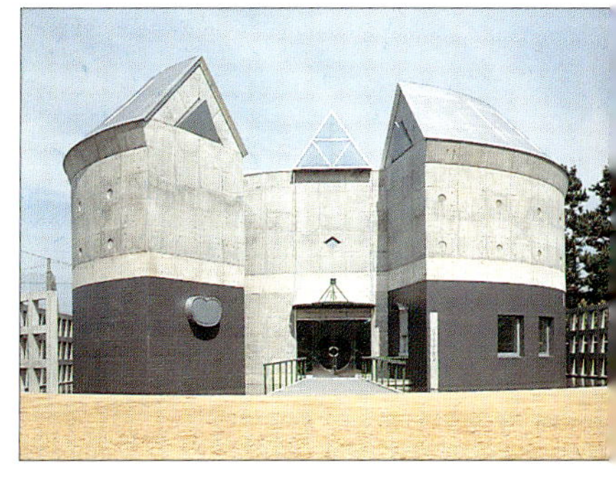

The Honjin Memorial Museum of Art is a subtle transformation of a circle. One part is pulled away, just as if a piece of fruit were cut and a slice removed. In the interior, the missing wedge becomes a skylight, emphasising the symbiosis of diverse elements in the work.

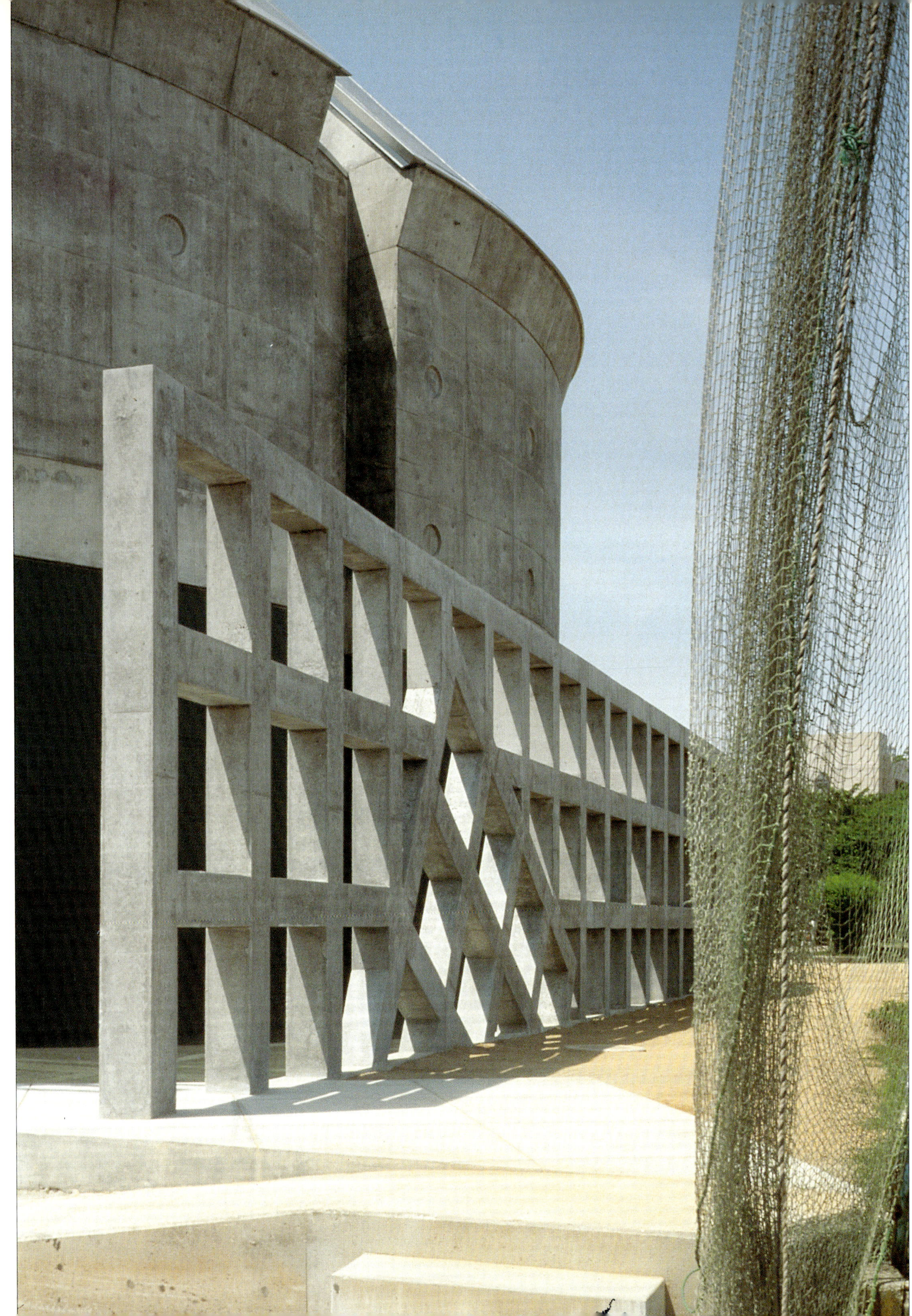

aspire to be like it, that it should spread universally. Progress has meant to become like Western culture. Heidegger called Euro-centrism a visible culture. The world consisted only of what could be seen by the distinctively tinted glasses worn by Western eyes.

In contrast, Symbiosis regards a world in which more cultures live in symbiosis as a richer world. Lévi-Strauss's Structuralism relativised Euro-centrism by looking at Western society from the standpoint of the 'uncivilised' world. The philosophy of Symbiosis carries this even further. It aims for a culture that values what can be heard. The ears hear more things that they want to hear. Activity and passivity are sought simultaneously.

I don't think that Japanese culture is superior to any other culture. And I am strongly opposed to an exclusivist tribalism, nationalism or racism. I believe the goal of architecture for the new age is a symbiosis of universal order and regional culture, a symbiosis of different cultures.

The age of Symbiosis moves forward simultaneously with the information age. It is the age of invisible technology, the age when the significance of architectural surface gains autonomy from architectural function. The formal architectural modes of expression, sign and symbol, will produce multivalent, ambivalent meanings. The age of information society will be an age when the identities of individuals and regions will be re-evaluated. Multiple ways of reading and interpreting architectural expression or form will be sought.

An important creation of Modern art and Modern architecture has been abstraction. Abstraction is common to Modern architecture, modern art, and modern philosophy. The abstract geometrical forms of Modern architecture were used as weapons to destroy the ornamental traditions that had existed before.

In Symbiosis and Intercultural Architecture, abstraction in form will be a method to create multivalent meanings. I think that the abstraction of Modernism or Modern architecture will continue to be effective in creating multiple interpretations of experience.

In ancient times, abstract geometrical forms such as pyramids, cones, squares, and circles symbolised a vision of the universe that transcended regional cultures. Abstract geometry has a double significance. It not only possesses a common recognitive universality that different cultures can share in, but also has a special historical significance.

Symbolism also plays an important role in the Philosophy of Intercultural Architecture. In contrast to the historicism that directly quotes classic style or the architectural forms of certain eras, new meanings can be created from indirect quotation of historical symbols or signs of the future. This is done by dissecting and transforming them. It is also possible to quote historical symbols or signs of the future not as similes but as connotations.

I believe that we can preserve the identity of regional culture, the unique nature of place, and the symbolic nature or sanctity of individuality, in symbiosis with a universal order.

One of the faults of modern society is that the existence of the secret zone or the un-understandable zone is considered to be unscientific. I believe that the symbiosis of different cultures will be made possible by respecting the secret zone in each of our different cultures.

OPPOSITE: The Honjin Memorial Museum of Art is a symbiosis of the universal form of the circle and Japan's tradition of asymmetry.
BELOW LEFT: The Nagoya City Art Museum.

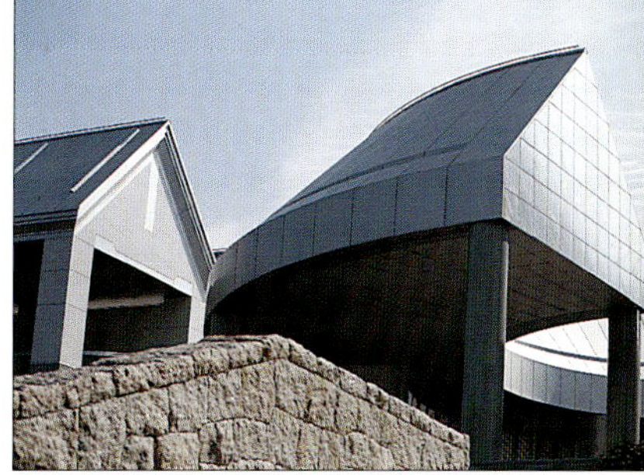

The Hiroshima City Museum of Contemporary Art stands on a hill in the middle of Hiroshima City. The masterplan for this park of the arts was drawn up more than a decade ago. Eventually a museum and a local historical museum are to be built here as well.

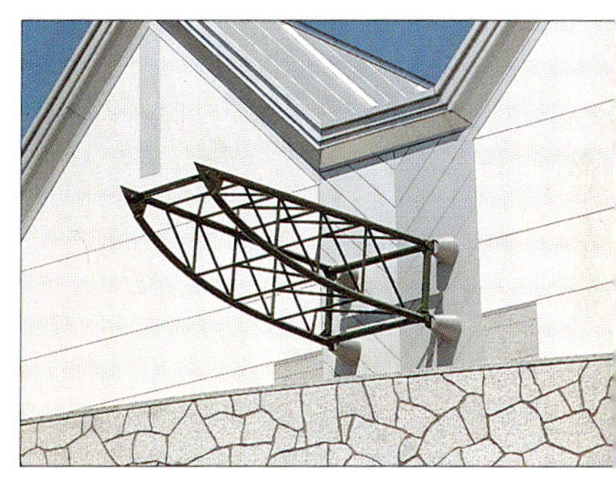

Gable roofs are used repeatedly in the Hiroshima City Museum of Contemporary Art. The image was a village. It represents a symbiosis of the accumulation of parts and the whole.

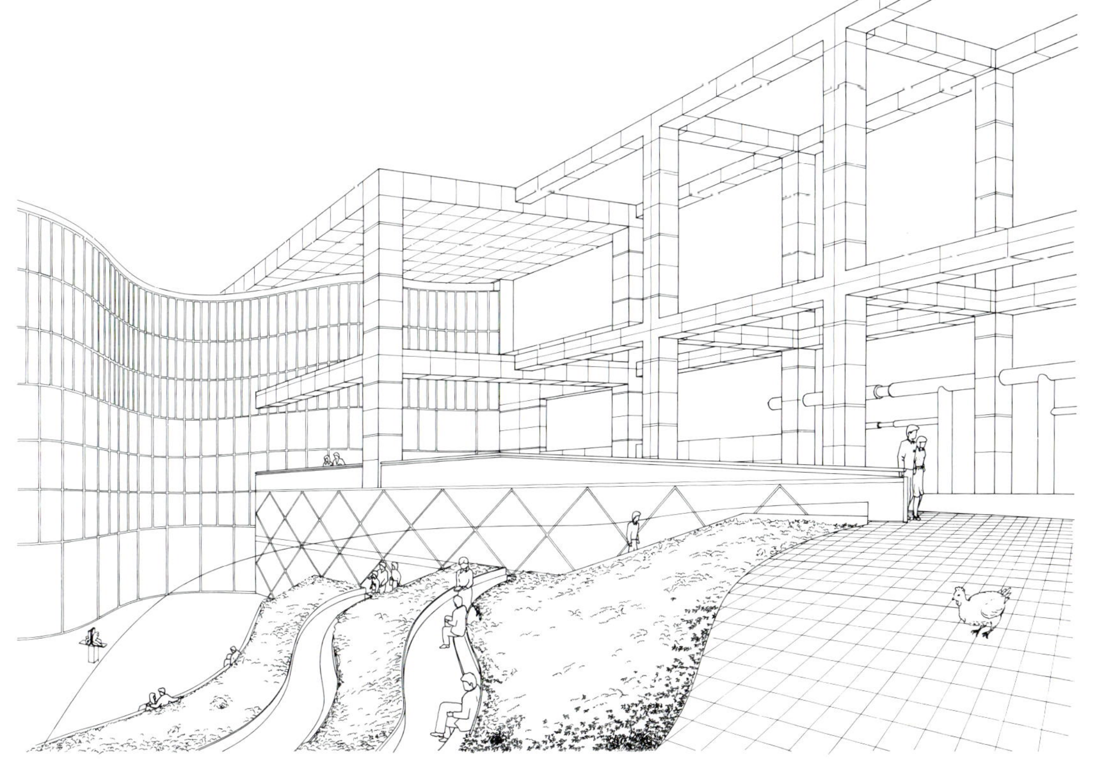

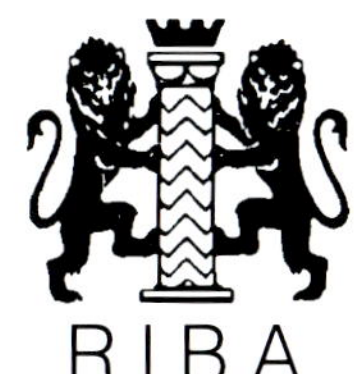

This article is an edited version of a lecture given on June 20 1991 at the RIBA to mark the publication of Kisho Kurokawa's book Intercultural Architecture – The Philosophy of Symbiosis *(Academy Editions). Introductions were given by Maxwell Hutchinson and Charles Jencks, with a summing up by Peter Cook. This is one of a series of events presented by the Academy Group in celebration of their 25th year in publishing.*

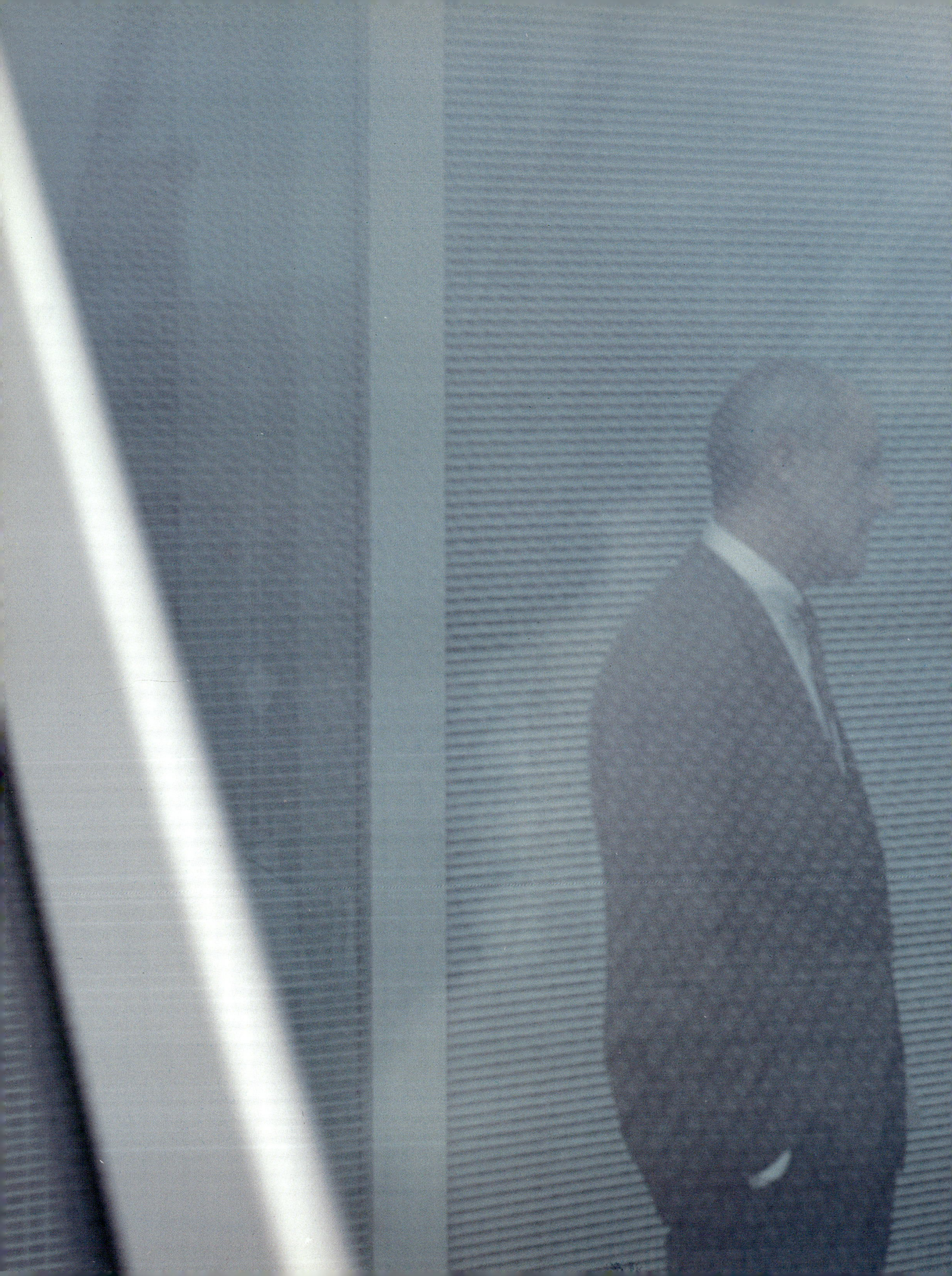

SIR NORMAN FOSTER

INAUGURAL ACADEMY ARCHITECTURE LECTURE

About 150 years ago the dying Turner is supposed to have said: 'the sun is God, my dear', and the exploration of the limitations and horizonless possibilities of light – light as solidity, light as a factor in the density and mass of a building – is what I think Norman is about, and why few of us have any doubts that he is one of the century's most important architects.

Norman makes a nonsense of the dichotomy between technology or engineering, and nature. It has always been a nonsense but it is a nonsense which is deeply embedded in some sensibilities. Technology has indeed always been there but sociology and economics sometimes interfere with it. Historians tell me that the Romans had all the knowledge and raw materials necessary to produce steam technology and therefore a railway civilisation. But they didn't because labour was very cheap; a sociological phenomenon got in the way.

There is an exciting democracy about architecture. We not only have the guiding spirit of the eye and the idea but also the teamwork between the engineers and all those on the planning and administrative side. The problem with architecture is that it is the most collective of all human endeavours and it is therefore all the more inspiring and exciting when collective endeavours come off. I believe that in spite of the habit in this country of castigating itself by comparison with countries overseas we are on the mend visually, and Norman Foster is one of the people who is bringing this about. **Lord Gowrie**

I gave a talk recently, whilst in Japan for the opening of our Century Tower project there, and in the course of that talk I showed a pair of slides that raised the issue of how you bring together the old and the new: how they relate, what the cultural implications are, the technological and spiritual implications symbolised by the computer chip and the Zen garden. Throughout the work that we've done and continue to do, there is a particular attitude towards the bringing together of the old and the new. There is another analogy that you could draw about function. If function is about keeping the rain at bay and the energy flowing around all these systems then it surely is also about the spirit; if you like, the Zen of the project.

Nothing is perhaps so appropriate to the analogy of function than light. You can measure it, you can quantify it and you can say what is right for a given task. But in the end light and the quality of light in a building or an external space is something that is far more subjective – you can't measure it. One of the themes that weaves itself between our projects over the years, is the handling of natural light: how it might inform, diffuse and add another dimension to an interior, whether that's an airport, a building you work in, or a gallery where you look at works of art. With an awareness of the discussion that took place in the International Symposium on New Museology, it seemed relevant to the theme of light to discuss the background to what we've been doing over the last few years in the Sackler Galleries.

It is appropriate to look back to the origins of the Royal Academy. Over time various changes have taken place: from the Burlington additions to the facade of the original house, into the next century and Samuel Wear's elevation of 1815, then in turn to the 'Victorianisation' of the Royal Academy with its elevation by Sidney Smirke, the museum at the rear and the buildings for the learned societies around the courtyard, and in 1875, Norman Shaw's additions which include the staircase to the south rooms that has by and large been sitting redundant, handsome though it is. Each particular point in time is of its time and inseparable from that particular historical context.

I would like to address some of the issues which were raised by the assignment to produce these Sackler Galleries in the 19th-century shell on top of Burlington House. Where do you go? How do you expand? And how do you come to grips with some of the wider issues raised by the insertion of new galleries at this particular point in time? In addition, we've had the challenge of keeping a major public institution working whilst also doing the remodelling and the new works.

One of the first things that became evident was that it was extremely difficult to access these new galleries. The clue was in the seam line: the area between the original Burlington House and the 19th-century Smirke addition. We had the intention of creating the major new complex of galleries at the upper level, while at the same time attempting to solve the problems of circulation that over a long period of time had beset the Academy. You couldn't really move in any sequential way through the spaces in this building and you couldn't move works of art easily from the vaults below. The original Diploma galleries were linked by a staircase and a rather ramshackle lift which Gerald Kelly, the President of the Academy in the 40s, managed to buy from a used car dealer.

If we examine the gap between the buildings we can see just how many little DIY lean-to's had accreted over time. In a way these spaces were 'out of sight, out of mind'; there was no real survey or exact information that charted them. You could get a glimpse of them if you opened one of the frosted-glass lavatory windows and managed to peer through. Our aim was to take all that confusion away; bringing those elements which were intact, cleaning them up and restoring them, at all times trying to make visually clear which was old and which was a new reconstruction. The original diploma galleries, which I know were very dear to some people (I don't personally think they were that distinguished), occupied the upper part of Burlington House. Obviously the cornice line in any reworking within that shell would have to be respected and that in turn limited any upward growth. We discovered that there was a void that could be used for servicing, so the air-conditioning, de-humidification and dust control – all of very high order for these new

Sir Norman Foster pictured in the Crescent Wing extension to the Sainsbury Centre, University of East Anglia.

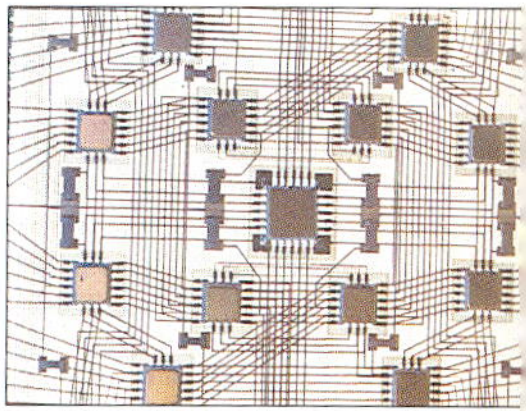

The microchip as symbol of 'new' Japanese technology.

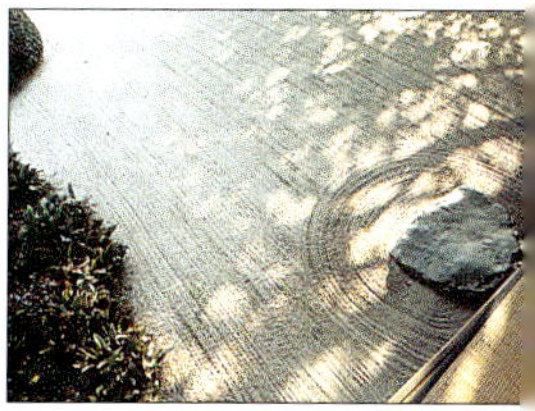

Gravel Garden at the Ryoanji Temple; symbol of the spiritual, 'old' Japan.

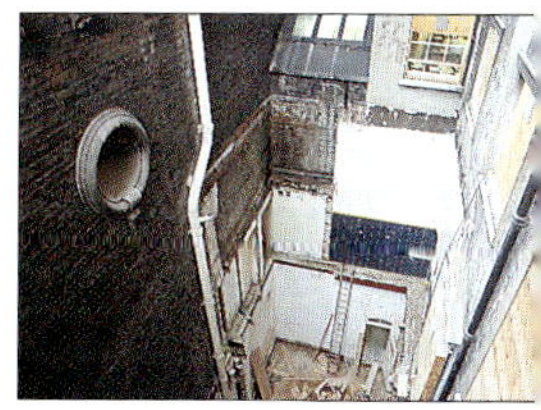

The Royal Academy, London. Seam line between the original Burlington House and the 19th-century Smirke addition, prior to renovation.

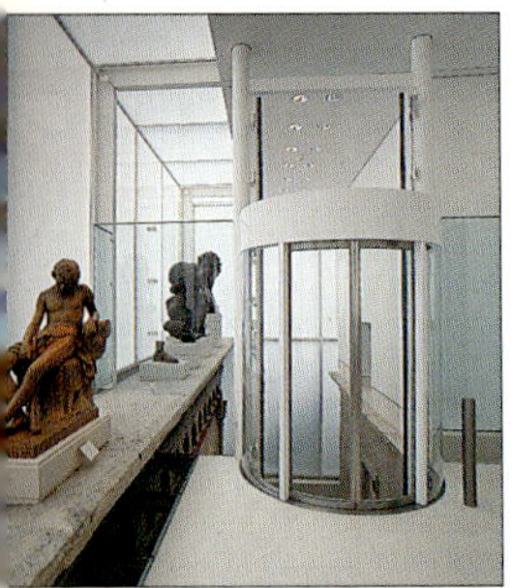

Sackler Galleries, view of the Sculptpure Gallery showing lift inserted into the old seam line.

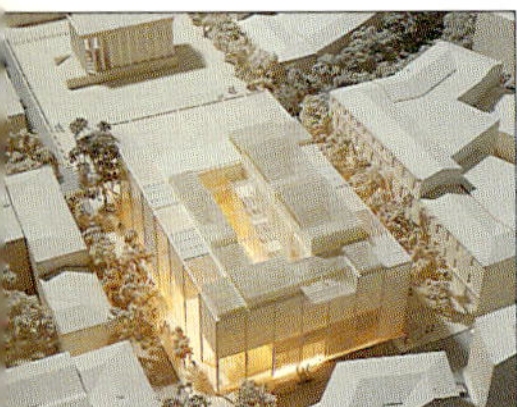

Carré d'Arts, Nîmes, model view.

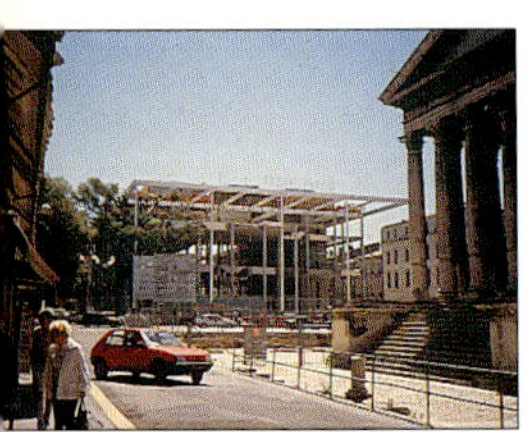

Carré d'Arts under construction.

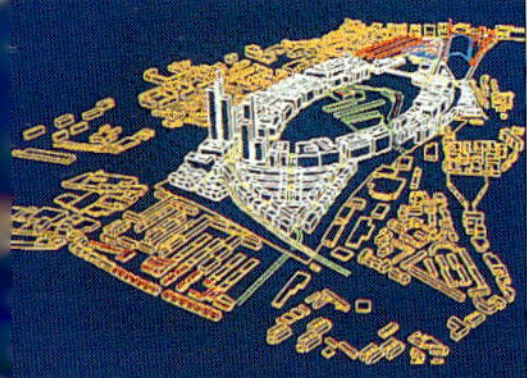

King's Cross Masterplan, computer simulation from the North.

galleries – were quietly, discretely integrated, taking advantage of the nooks and crannies within the existing fabric.

We wanted the new galleries to have that timeless, coved form which is highly appropriate to natural top-lighting, thereby avoiding the problems of shadow. The decision to create a complex of smaller individual rooms was a fairly considered one. We had explored the idea of creating one large space, but it seemed appropriate to create a more intimate grouping of smaller spaces that would more naturally complement the larger ones within the rest of the Academy.

In some of our early model studies of the galleries and the gap between the buildings, the idea developed that a lift could be inserted on one side and that a lot of the very interesting and quite precious rooms could actually be opened up. Before this work was undertaken the Reynold's rooms, for example, had permanent shutters: had no connection with the outside. The possibility of getting top-light down the crack between the original Burlington House, of peeling back time to the end of the last century, was very appealing. It would reveal the Samuel Ware elevation and the 19th-century elevation to the main building which had never seen the light of day.

The knitting together of spaces outside the gallery – the circulation staircase, the lift and the Michelangelo 'Tondo', all came out of an extraordinary chemistry that developed with Arthur and Jill Sackler. Both displayed a wonderful drive, impatience is perhaps too strong a word, but a marvellous sense of endeavour and vision to take a broader view of the total. It was a very creative involvement. I'm sure that there are individuals and institutions that make purely financial contributions to the arts, but the important thing here was that the Sacklers also had a tremendous creative input.

The idea of using glass in staircases and in floors is really quite an old one. Pavement lights are an integral part of historic London, so in using glass and sand-blasting it we were really exploiting those qualities. It is the tradition of exploiting elements special to a given point in time that gives the city its vibrancy, its diversity. I think that many of the qualities of the spaces here come from the fact that this institution has been washed over at various points in time. So it seemed entirely appropriate that we stretch the limits of what we were able to do without any compromise. The glass which provides the side-lighting in the sculpture gallery required extraordinary endeavours to achieve that degree of whiteness. Its translucence is reminiscent of the Shoji screens of earlier Japanese architecture. The interlayer enables natural light to pour in, giving it that luminosity and also allowing the possibility of the wall glowing at night by back-lighting it from the other side. It was only in Czechoslovakia that we were able to find a glass of such purity that it was totally white, without any 'greenness'.

Each age produces its own vocabulary, has its own integrity and makes its own mark. I am quite sensitive to the fact that this is currently an unfashionable view of how you bring the old and the new together, but it is an approach which has been quite fundamental to our thinking.

The proposals for the new Carré d'Arts are inspired by the Roman grid of Nîmes. It seemed to us that that was a powerful generator in its spirit. Rather than trying to ape the trappings of a Roman era, it seemed logical to take the typical Roman grid block and to fill it to the edges, and respect the square in front of it. As it turned out, our traditional response was totally different from the other entries in the competition, which all chose to ignore the fabric both on plan and in height. It seemed important to us to respect the height-lines of the adjoining buildings and to work within them, to continue the grain of the city.

The decision to create a courtyard at the heart of that building was in its own way reminiscent of a lot of Nîmes' historic architecture in which quite deep buildings in the blocks are penetrated by individual courtyards. We were also aware of that tradition of stepped routes through the hill-towns in the region. It was out of that background that the scheme evolved as essentially a low building. It was also rather like a ship in that those areas concerned with 'driving', servicing and storage would be well below ground and those areas that would need natural top light would, quite logically, find their way to the upper reaches.

It was a building that would bring together two cultures: that concerned with the visual arts and also that with information, the mediatéque building acting as a short cut from the main route through the building, on the diagonal, to a minor entrance at the rear. This was a well travelled route that connects the principal monuments in Nîmes: from the Roman amphitheatre through to this square, the Maison Carré and then beyond to the water gardens of Le Notre.

The building was conceived as having a very large portico that would be weather protecting for an upper-level café overlooking the square. Then by 'biting' into the corner we would create a primary entrance. This is a modest building with very simple exposed concrete structures at six metre centres. You really can't do anything more economically or directly in that particular part of France.

There is a transition in the development of the building. Over the later phases we decided it would be more appropriate to break the scale down on the edge, to create an inner grain in front of the main concrete structure. The basement wall adopts a curve on plan to protect the very ancient tree on the corner which is really quite an important ingredient. The steel column on the corner was almost literally threaded through the tree to eventually relate the two together.

As with the Sackler Galleries, the Carré d'Arts brings together the old and the new in a direct and sympathetic way, but without bowing and scraping to the past. It takes the very simple ingredients of a concrete structure, stretching and refining them, and using the steel elements in a conscious dialogue between the square and the historic building which sits within it, but totally removed in time.

The same interplay between past and present took place at King's Cross where our master plan aimed to unify the currently separate stations of King's Cross and St Pancras. The central features of this would be a 25-acre park and at the southern end a new railway terminal related to the channel tunnel. London has its own characteristics which are quite different from grid cities such as Paris, New York, Barcelona, Amsterdam or Washington. London, by contrast, is really a collection of green spaces. Some are large and some small; they roll off the tongue – a London bus or any map will identify Shepherd's Bush, Islington Green, Hampstead Heath; the list is endless. These special places, each with its own character, seemed to us the essence of London.

Our proposed new park is penetrated by Regent's Canal and very much in the spirit of London it learns from the past and attempts in a contemporary way to be informed by it, to take the spirit of it to create another park – the first major park since the last century. And then to bring back from the past the waterway which had been in many cases concreted over by later transportation systems; to excavate those waterbasins; to reinstate the canal; to effect a relationship between the existing historic buildings, preserving the best of them. We aim to develop a dialogue between the hard-edged urban water of a canal, a rediscovered excavated waterbasin, and the soft water that you might associate with a lake or nature reserve or a park. Trying not to be seduced into designing buildings, we wanted to suggest what might be appropriate to the site in terms of massing and enclosures.

We drew comparisons in terms of prime and existing streets that are known in London, comparing our proposals for a major north-south boulevard with Regent Street, hoping to incorporate arcades. Having suggested this framework, we wanted to burst through the insularity, prejudice and petty mindedness that exists in this country. We intended to have architects from Europe, Japan and America doing individual buildings. To do something that so far has not yet happened in this country – our insularity is really a disgrace – especially when you consider the opportunities that Europe and Japan have opened up to architects from Britain. Although the scheme is being negotiated with the planners there is the potential to bring together a very committed and interesting group of people.

At the southern edge of the site we wanted to show how a major new terminal can be integrated and could respect and respond to the two historic stations of King's Cross and St Pancras. It is a project generated by the very powerful geometry on the site of those two buildings. Our building demonstrates how a structure can respond to the site, create a coherent route and also flood the interior with natural light, in a very controlled way.

I believe the original layers of history in a building are made far more real when they are seen alongside the new. The same thing also happens in the reverse. You are in no doubt of what is of this age. This is something we have become blind to, we take it for granted that the richness of so many of our cities is really because each age has had the confidence to make its own stamp in an optimistic and forward looking manner.

This is really the preamble to our work at Stansted airport. As we thought about airports, we realised they have none of the sense of occasion and drama that we associate with the great train stations. It seems that an earlier age had a confidence, vision and a romance with their form of transportation. We felt that we should strive to bring some of that sense of occasion to air travel and to somehow raise the spirits in an airport, that it does not have to be what we have come to regard as a very dreary experience. You could even say that your typical airport is a serious threat to health; the risk of cardiac arrest in an airport is statistically quite high. Another issue at Stansted was the environ-mental one, the impact of putting a large scale terminal on a green-field site – not exactly a green-field site seeing as the centre of attraction was a World War II airstrip for heavy bombers. Nonetheless, a major design implication was how you respected the tree line in this very rural setting.

We felt it would be interesting to go back and to look at the roots of air travel. In the earliest airfields you were in no doubt where you were. You walked towards the aircraft and when you returned you walked towards the road (or more likely a dirt track). There was a clear airside and landside. It had great clarity, you didn't need complex signing systems. Even though the realities of security and immigration could not give you that absolute directness of experience, we wanted to avoid the confusion and muddle that happens as large international airports grow over time, on restricted sites.

By shedding those inhibitions of the past we hoped to see what opportunities might exist and to question how a building like this might be serviced, whether it really made sense to build structures that would not only hold the roof up but also support brick built structures around air-conditioning that negated any possibility of natural light.

The result of that questioning was summed up in our earliest models which took advantage of a fall in the site by digging in a two-storey building, creating the illusion on the landside of a single storey building in which people could move at one level without any changes of direction. Essentially, the idea was to create a large room whose structure would be primarily concerned with holding up a roof that could let in natural light in an energy efficient way. Such a structure could also modulate, order and give a sense of scale to the space. At the same time we had to try to meet some of the more down to earth aspects of the brief: obviously security, through-put, baggage handling times and cost. A major factor in the brief was to significantly reduce the cost of the terminal. Stansted was more than 10 percent cheaper than comparable terminals at Gatwick and Heathrow depending on how you examine the figures.

In our early plans the submerged undercroft contained all those heavy elements that normally sit on the roof, as well as the baggage-handling facilities while the people would be above because you enter an aircraft at the upper level. The idea was to create something that might have the flexibility for change in an industry which is extraordinarily volatile.

In our more developed models, the roof becomes a series of vaults which are very much concerned with natural and artificial lighting as well as removing rainwater. It related to a more developed structural form and to an undercroft that had got bigger. The undercroft now has a full-scale railway station that came in during the early stages of the construction. That flexibility to literally embed a main line station within the fabric of the building was a tremendous bonus; it also allowed for a road through the building so that you can move the shorter-life servicing equipment.

The very large roof will grow in a linear way: its first phase catering for eight million people a year and the final form for 15 million. It is very much about the qualities of natural light. Endless calculations were made that would ensure a shaft of sunlight would go through to produce the high light of a bright patch on the floor. The daylight reflectors suspended below the rooflights would avoid the experience at night of looking up at a black hole. You would actually look up at a white perforated panel, but this would also admit light in a diffused way and cut down the heat gain, while acting as a kind of sculptural element within the shape itself. The roof is really about light and water, and all the heavy equipment is at the bottom. Banished in this approach are those ugly exposed ducts and diffusers, and fluorescent lights and ceiling tiles.

If the structure is a conscious element to give order – to offer a view of aircraft to which you are beckoned notwithstanding the proliferation of security and baggage screens – it is also a means to communicate information on flight times and so on. The poetry of the lighting is for me matched by a different kind of poetry, and that is the hydraulic engineering which allows you to drain water from a space roughly the size of six football pitches and pull it to the edges, maintaining the hierarchy between the structure

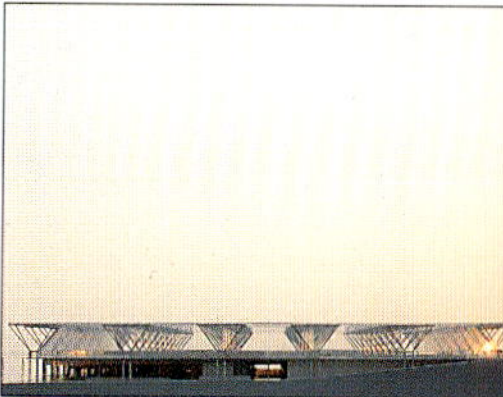

Stansted Airport, model view.

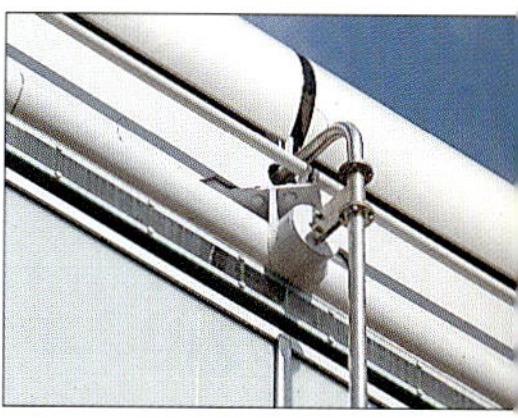

Stansted Airport, detail of roof drainage system.

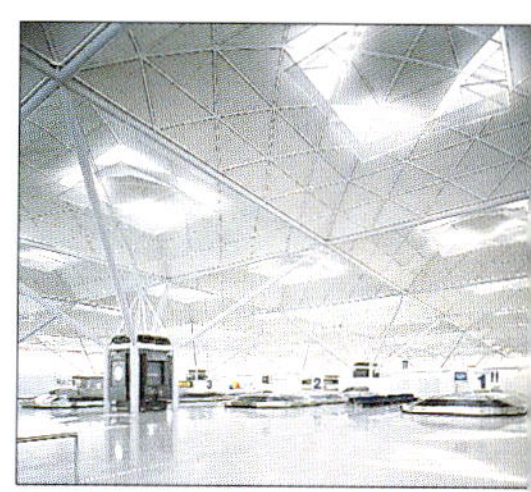

Stansted Airport, view of baggage reclaim hall showing daylight reflectors suspended below the rooflights.

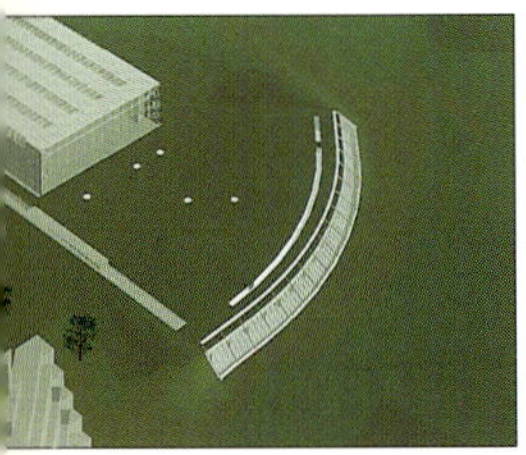

Computer simulation of the Sainsbury Centre and Crescent Wing, University of East Anglia.

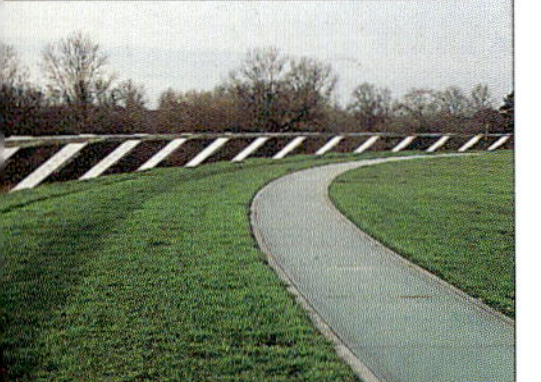

Sainsbury Crescent Wing, view of glass roof.

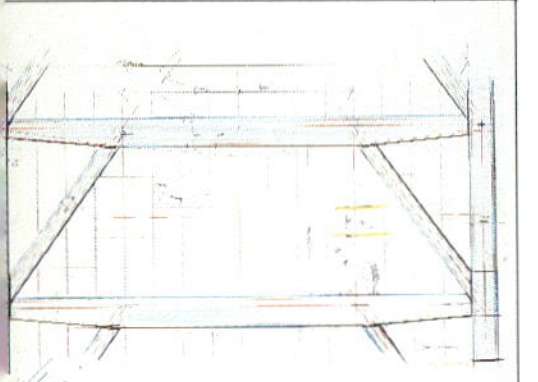

Century Tower, Tokyo, sketch by Norman Foster.

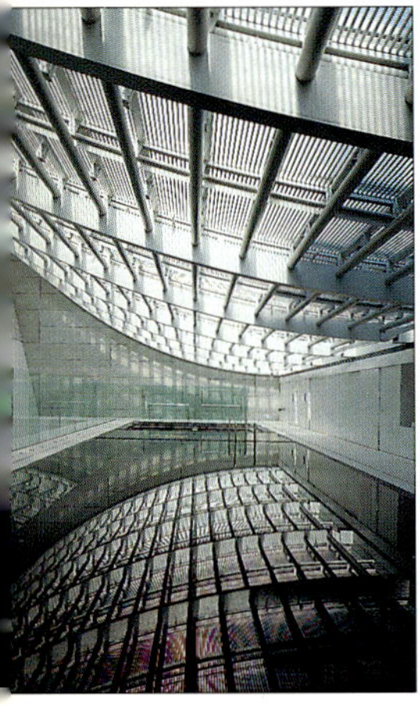

Century Tower, interior view showing swimming-pool.

which is holding up the building and the structure which is holding up those membranes on the outer edge, some of which are translucent on the sides. The use of conventional roof drainage would have had massive implications. I find a certain elegance in the way we have used stainless steel pipes which run absolutely flat in the roof, there are no falls. Using a traditional system we would have something like two metres between the upper reaches of the roof and the lower reaches around the gutters. Our system which starts from the idea that you don't create columns of air with only a thin layer of water around the outer edge but that you create a smaller tube, which when it really does rain is chopped full of water. And that system has proved really quite remarkable in its use. On the edge of the roof are the equivalent of the spoilers on a large jet which break down the air flow, avoiding the problems of uplift in high winds. During construction it certainly did withstand an extraordinary battering in freak gales.

If we compare photomontages prepared for the public inquiry with photographs of the real building, it is interesting to see how discreet in the landscape the realised project actually is. If anything our proposition for the inquiry is more prominent than the reality.

The questions of natural lighting so crucial at Stansted were also quite fundamental to the Sainsbury Centre. In the original building of 1978 the key ingredient was a flexible top-lit space that would integrate a wide variety of activities: those to do with viewing art and studying art history, as well as public spaces: restaurant, faculty club and so on. I am sure if I say this someone will jump up and contradict me, but I don't actually remember saying that this building was constructed to be open-ended for future growth. It did have that capability and we have certainly explored from time to time this way of growing the building, but we have never felt inhibited by that.

It is in the spirit of the cave and the tent that the Crescent Wing expands the original building very discreetly in the landscape and enables its through views to be sacred and unchanged. What is difficult to comprehend is that this new extension is something like two-thirds the footprint of the original building.

The two projects are complementary but also quite different. The Crescent Wing is very much about blockwork and concrete. It is a low cost, almost thatched building. With its very large roof and its earth cover it is very much in the spirit of earlier roofs such as Willis-Faber, and going back even further, the Creek-Vean house in the 60s.

The glass-covered ramp which gives public access to these facilities goes down to a triangular gallery space which is well equipped for conferences, with very good audio-visual facilities. It also descends to a storage area which, as far as I am aware, the only other example is in the Metropolitan. Here you can access, as a member of the public or a scholar, all the works of art contained in the building. So it is the reverse of the typical museum or gallery where the storage area is a vast private domain. Here the density is high, the lighting is of a good order and there are places where you can sit, work and, if appropriate, handle an object.

The triangular gallery also has a system of flexible lighting, so that for the first time it will be possible to teach lighting as a subject, experimenting with it and changing it. So it is doubling up as an element in an academic course as well as the flexible system to light these areas. Even though it is an underground building we have incorporated natural top lights as well as a dramatic sweep of glass inset into the landscaped slope; it is from this that the Crescent Wing derives its name. The top-lighting takes the form of a curved strip which marks the ramp down to the main hall and discs over parabolic reflectors to the laboratories below. These are literally set flush with the grass to leave the main view from the original centre unchanged.

I would like to continue this theme of natural lighting with the Hong Kong and Shanghai Bank. In the Banking Hall one can see sunlight on the cross bracing and on the glass underbelly that visually connects the main public space with the public route below it. That public route is enhanced by sunlight which is pulled in by a system of mirrored reflectors or 'sunscoop' as it is known. Even on overcast days there is a quality of light here which is different from a totally internal space. The building was an opportunity to explore an alternative to the anonymity and the repetition of the typical office building. It was nonetheless a building for a bank and was in that sense a single use and single occupier building. From our own experience it is relatively difficult to demonstrate the potential of new thinking in an owner-occupier building and much more difficult in a building for rental, where the occupants are not known.

Conditions in Tokyo are similar to those in Hong Kong in that the city suffers hurricane wind forces, but unlike Hong Kong, Tokyo also has to cope with the earthquake factor which has very real implications for structural design. One of the many early study sketches for our Century Tower project explored an idea with an orthogonal structural grid on the sides and a raked geometry creating double height spaces and offering a rich mix of spaces for the market. We were working with a client, who was enthusiastic about breaking down some of the barriers between public and private by creating an art gallery, a residential area, a swimming-pool, a club, a restaurant, a tea-house and a public meeting point; and examining whether some or all of those could come together in a building with very different codes and a restricted site.

It was a building that anticipated a degree of growth, and showed an awareness that legislation was changing which might allow more relaxed light angles. This was expected to take place after the completion of the building so mindful of that, the building was conceived as two towers with a light shaft between them. The idea was that they could grow quite independently, as and when the legislation changed. What actually happened was that at a very late stage in the design, the legislation did change and so the building did expand during the design phase. One of the towers has grown, though not as high as the front tower. It is a development of our thinking on the bank, though there are in reality few resemblances, other than that both are see-through from back to front so it is double aspect. The services, lifts and staircases are pulled to the sides so that working spaces are very much about sun and view, and those prime views look right out to the city beyond. There is an interesting linkage here between the above and below ground experience of space. The offices which relate to a vertical shaft of light are now fully let and the combination of single and double heights offers quite a rich mix. The above ground building is linked with the experience below ground by continuing the space, making the staircase that takes you to the galleries below the major element and also linking you across to the glass pavilion which is at the rear of the site, enclosed by a wall. An important ingredient in that is water, with reflecting pools at the base of the wall and water cascading as a flowing film over the granite. So it is really pulling the water, the light, and then effecting the contrast between that structure and the concrete of the base. If there is a striving for a diversity and a greater richness of experiences, then the pool and its catenary structure of glass and louvres further extends the vocabulary of space.

The building works in a special way at night; giving a very distinctive expression of the structure, which many Japanese commentators have expressed opinions about, how it evokes certain characteristics of traditional Japanese architecture. In many ways it is totally removed, but there is certainly a feeling in Japan of an intangible linkage.

In Barcelona there was a different kind of assignment, the outcome of an international competition for an Olympic communications tower on a prominent site on top of the mountains that overlook the city. This is a project about many important things, it is a symbol for the city, but it is also about pollution – visual pollution. The mayor, in an extraordinary civic initiative, said that it was completely out of the question that Telephonica, Spain's equivalent of British Telecom, Spanish and Catalan television should each build their own tall tower. But the idea that these rivals would form one company which would realise and operate the tower seemed quite inconceivable. The Ayuntemiento, the City Hall, were also saying that they should have a minority interest in the company, and just to rub salt into the wounds, demanded that the tower should have a viewing platform to allow the public another perspective of their city, despite the extreme problems of security this would entail.

The removal of a mass of illegal masts, antennae and dishes and their grouping on one new mast was very much an environmental issue. Our proposition was to create the slimmest needle which would make the minimum impact on the site. The site is a national park which certainly compounded the problem, so our aim was to make slenderest possible interventions, taking a totally new look at the nature of a communication mast.

Traditionally these masts are concrete structures. In scribbles done just before the meeting with the competition jury, we showed that a traditional mast on this site would have to be massive: about 25m wide at its base, the equivalent, if you like, of a brick chimney, an image of a past culture. We wanted to get that minimum, most slender element and then to guy it with cables. The technology is really very straightforward, the kind of thing you would associate with suspension bridges.

The related communications building was buried and turfed over and the mountain eventually put back around it. The tower will be almost 300m in its final form. The 13-storey structure of platforms, which is the equivalent of 25-storeys of a domestic building, and weighs something like 30,000 tonnes, was hoisted up the concrete core. That core also is the most basic way that you can move services vertically. It is the thinnest possible pipe, it couldn't really be any smaller. It works rather like a car aerial; there are two further structures at the top which will slide out telescopically, an outer one and an inner one. The final top section, a bit like the droop-snoot on a Concorde, is a crane that can angle and then traverse so that it can move the dishes which will change constantly during its life. The construction started in February 1990 and will be completed by the summer of 1991.

It would be very difficult to talk about buildings and structures without talking about how they are made, how they are put together. I think the label – hi-tech – is in all kinds of ways questionable, I never really understood it. It's almost as if this age has technology and no age in the past had it. If you go 5,000 years back over time, there are earth mounds like Silbury Hill: an extraordinarily sophisticated structure which is 130 feet high, surviving today and undoubtedly at the cutting age of that technology, just like the pyramids, the Alexandria lighthouse of 30 BC, the great cathedrals of the middle-ages, and the explosion of industrial construction at the beginning of the 19th century. Technology is something that has been there throughout time and those structures which have endured or which command attention are always on the cutting edge, stretching the boundaries of technology, and taking to the ultimate the art of making things.

I would like to conclude by remembering two men who are symbolic for all these projects. One is the individual who headed the Swiss team responsible for physically raising the 30,000 kN platform in Barcelona. He symbolises those craftsmen who make the buildings. Even though the buildings site has more and more become the assembly point for prefabricated elements, it still does not mean that craftsmanship and pride have been replaced by robots – the tools might be different but quality is still determined by the attitude and motivations of people. Finally, the other individual is the mayor of Barcelona. He symbolises the patron – the prime mover – in many respects he is the true architect of the tower because without his initiative, continued commitment and support it would never have happened. Of course I should also mention Jill and Arthur Sackler, Sir Robert and Lady Sainsbury, Sir Norman Payne . . . it is a long list. But then the story of architecture is the story of patronage.

Conceptual sketches of the Barcelona Communication Tower by Sir Norman Foster.

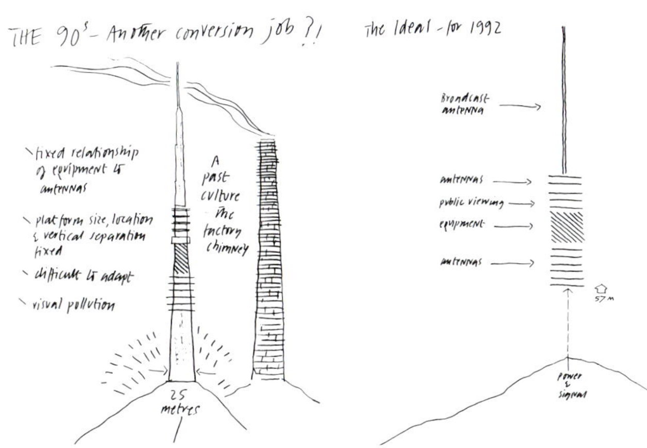

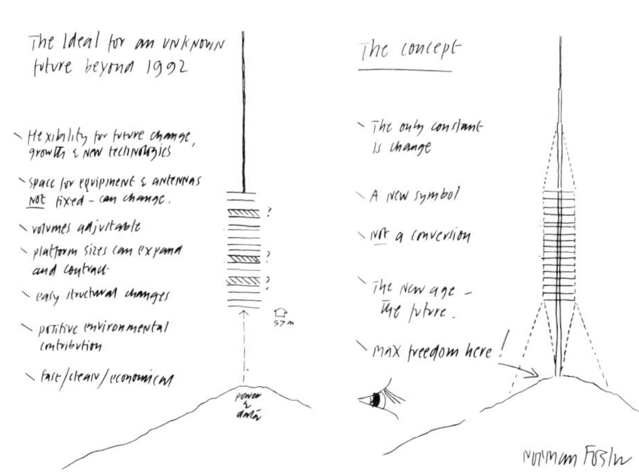

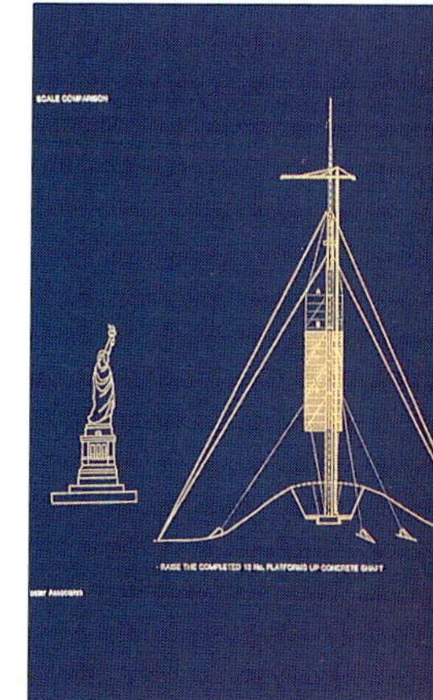

Bercelona Communications Tower, computer simulation showing height relative to the Statue of Liberty.

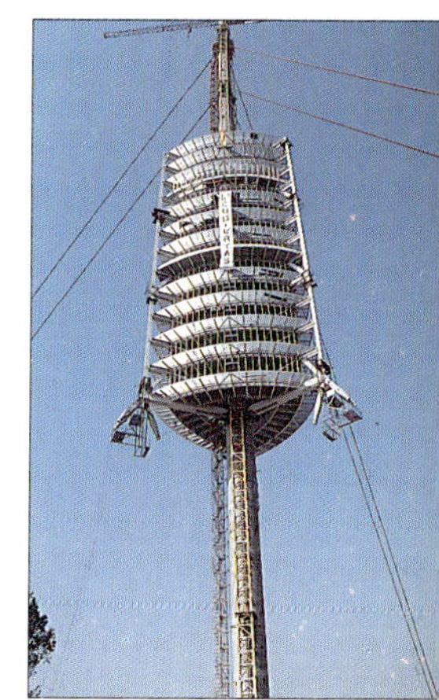

Barcelona Tower, view showing 13-storey platform structure attached to concrete core.

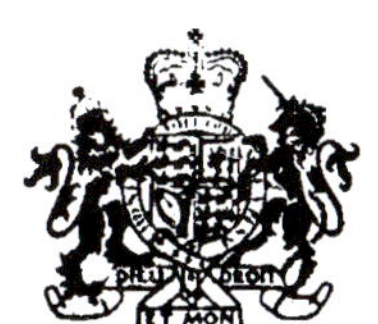

ROYAL ACADEMY OF ARTS.

Sir Norman Foster delivered the inaugural Academy Architecture lecture on June 15 1991 at the Royal Academy where his design for the Sackler Galleries has just been completed. We here present an edited version of the evening's proceedings.

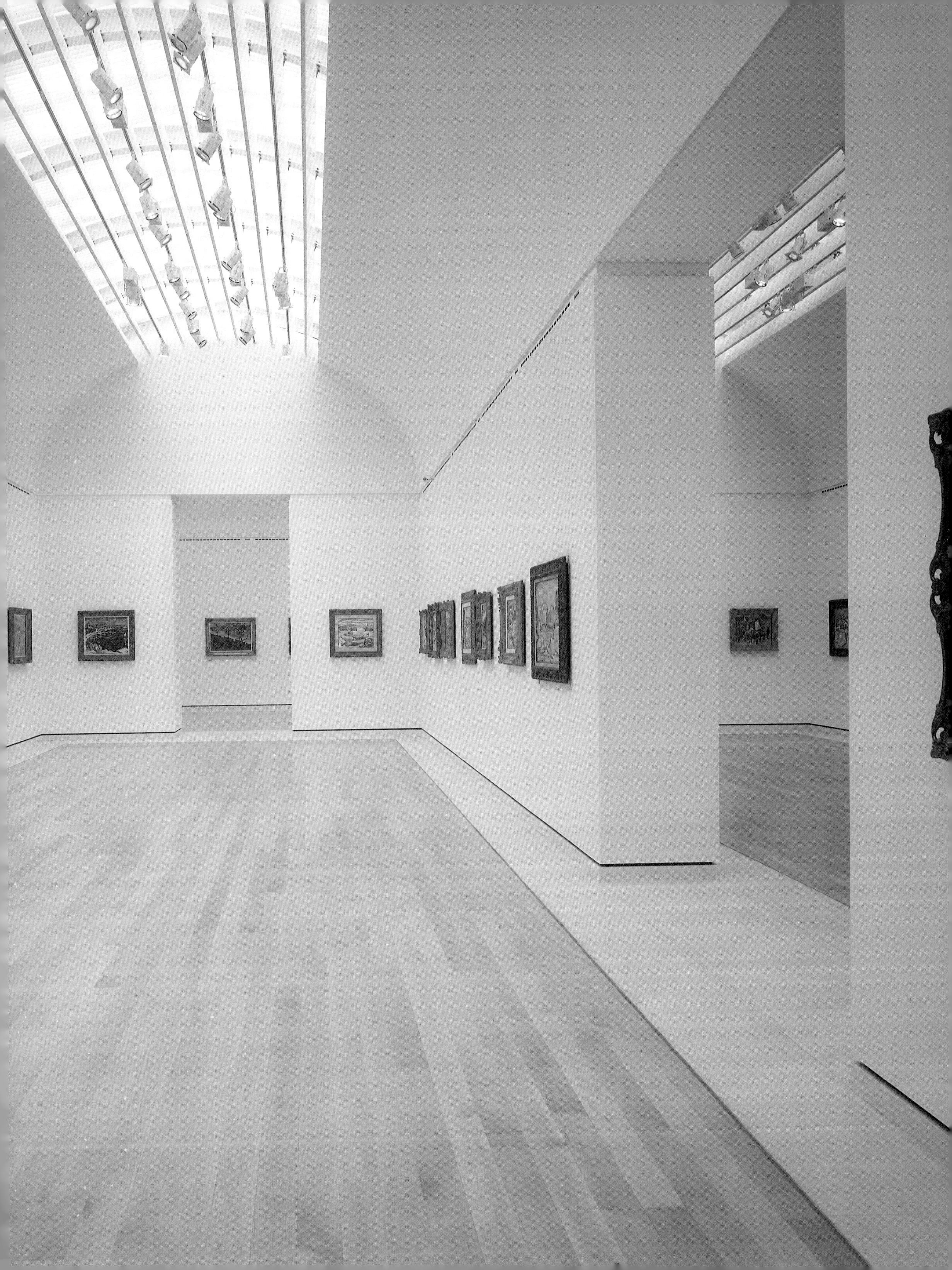

THE SACKLER GALLERIES

The Sackler Galleries represent a radical remodelling of the Victorian Diploma Galleries, which were relatively little used because of their inadequate servicing and poor access. The new galleries, created in the shell of the old, naturally lit from above, with a sophisticated system of louvres to monitor light levels, are fully air conditioned and thus suitable for the display of prestigious loan exhibitions.

The problem of access has been solved by inserting both a new staircase and a glass-walled lift in the lightwell between the original Burlington House and the Victorian galleries behind. In the process, the facade of Burlington House has been revealed after more than a century hidden from view. The new lift and staircase provide easy communication between all floors of the Academy, while remaining completely invisible from the entrance hall and main staircase. The lift, in addition, transports works of art from basement storage areas to all gallery levels. The scheme provides a new system of circulation around the complex building enabling the Royal Academy staff to cope with the ever increasing number of visitors to its main exhibitions. In addition, access for disabled and infirm visitors is now vastly improved.

A striking feature of the scheme is the new reception area sitting over the original light wells and incorporating the parapet of the main galleries as a plinth for sculpture. Glazed edges allow daylight to freely penetrate the space below. This also includes a permanent, secure location for the Academy's most precious possession, the Michelangelo Tondo.

The project demonstrates the approach of the practice to all of its schemes – a careful evaluation of the potential of what exists and a strategy for beneficial change. In the case of Burlington House, long-neglected areas of the building will form the new axis for visitors, and the rich and complex history of the building has been revealed in the process.

OPPOSITE: Interior of Sackler Galleries
BELOW: Cutaway sketch by Norman Foster
OVERLEAF: LEFT: Lift shaft within 'the gap'; RIGHT, ABOVE: Reception area; Longitudinal section; CENTRE: View up towards galleries through new staircase; Plan; BELOW: Detail of existing cornice; Cross section

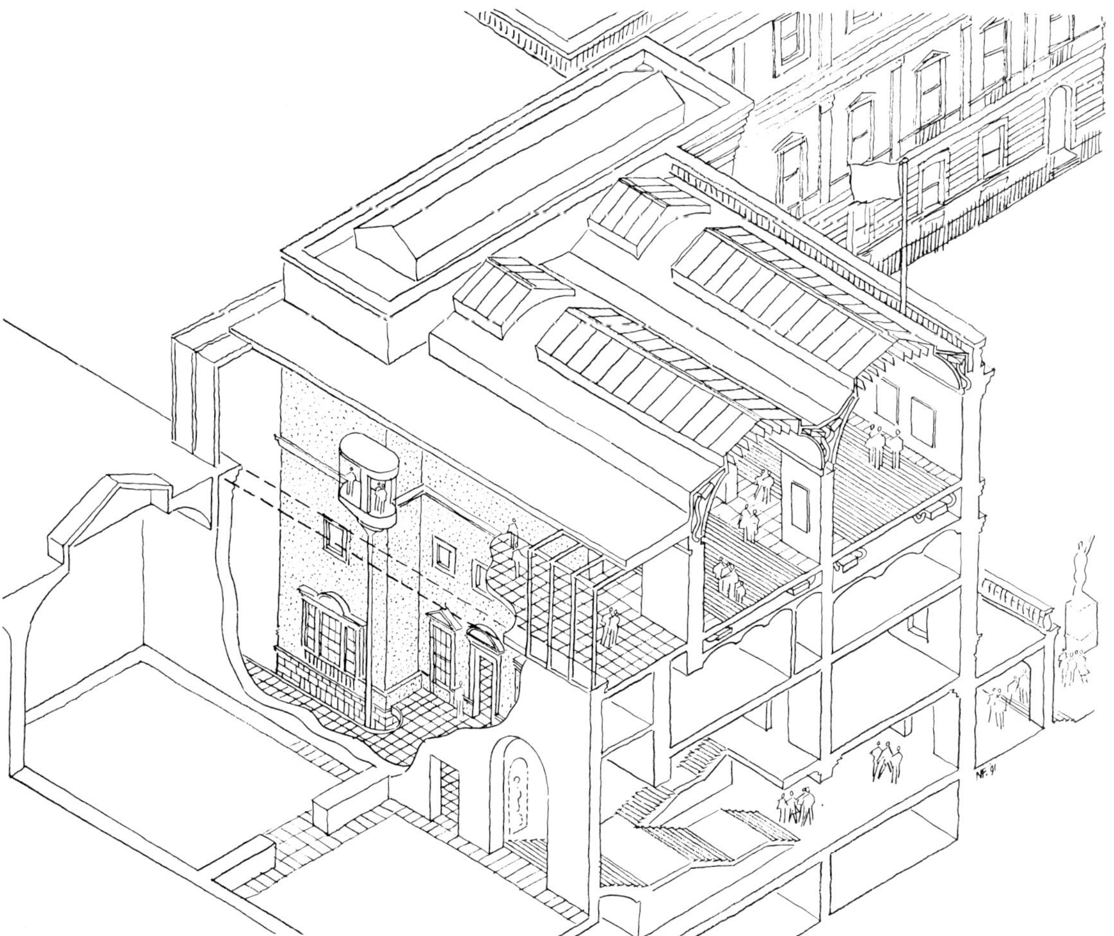

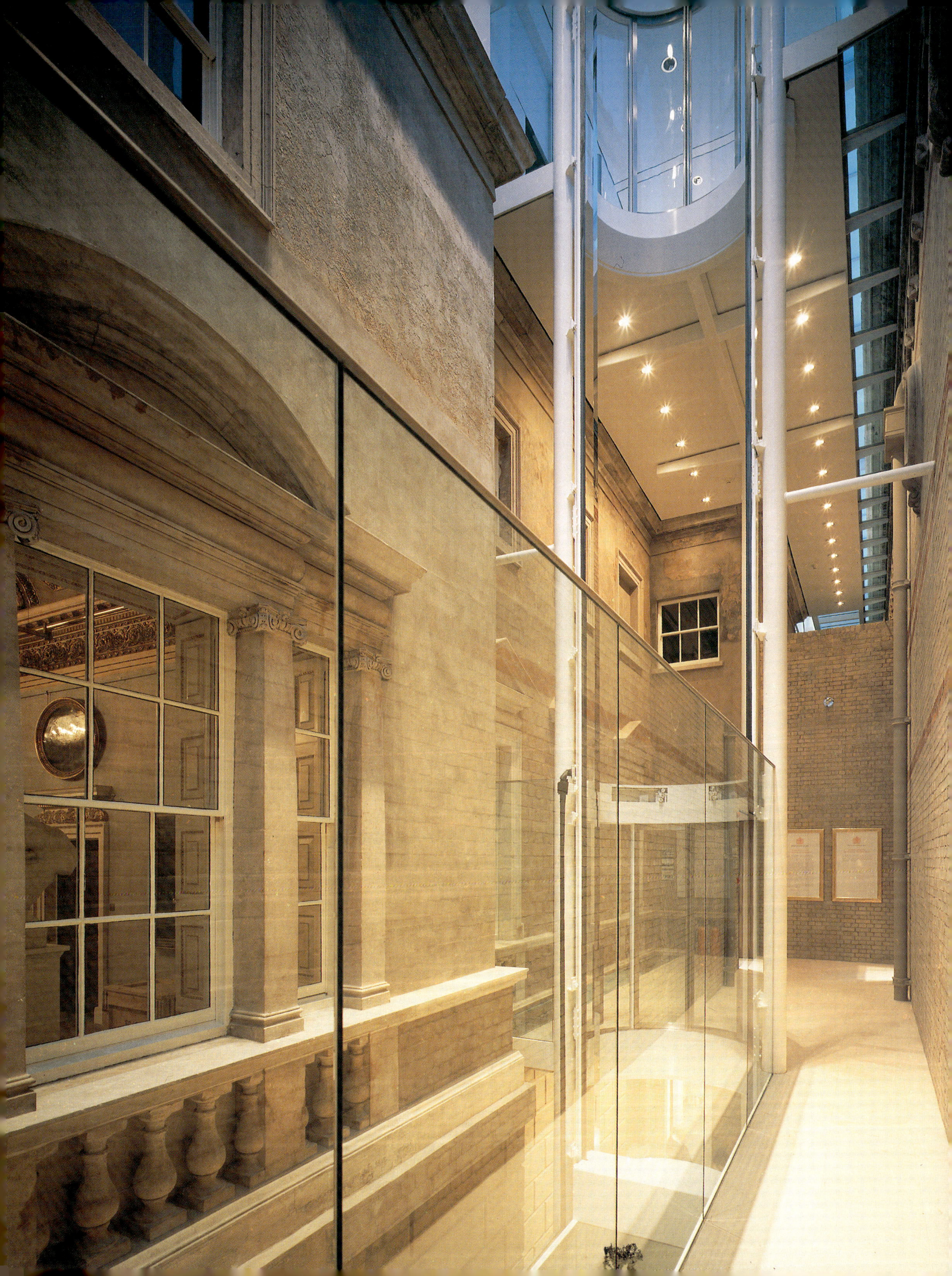

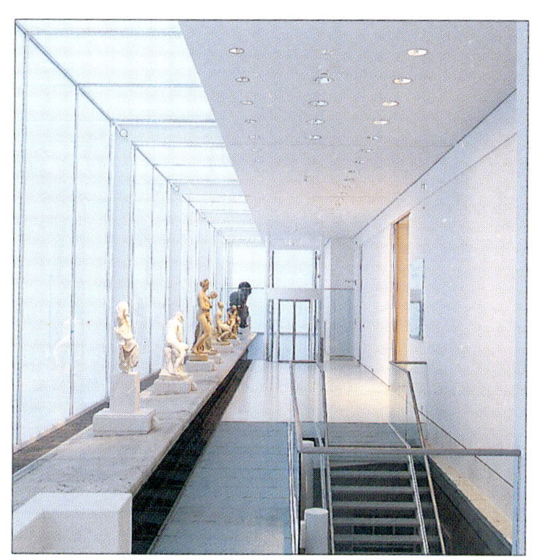

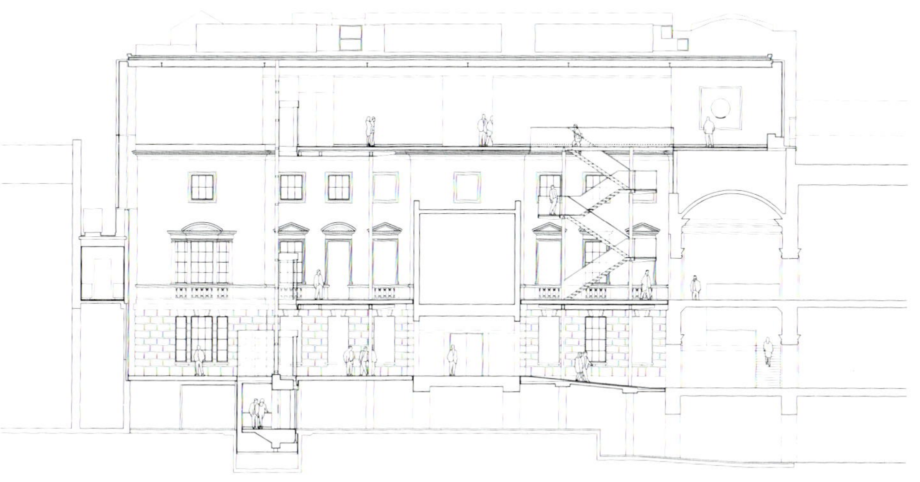

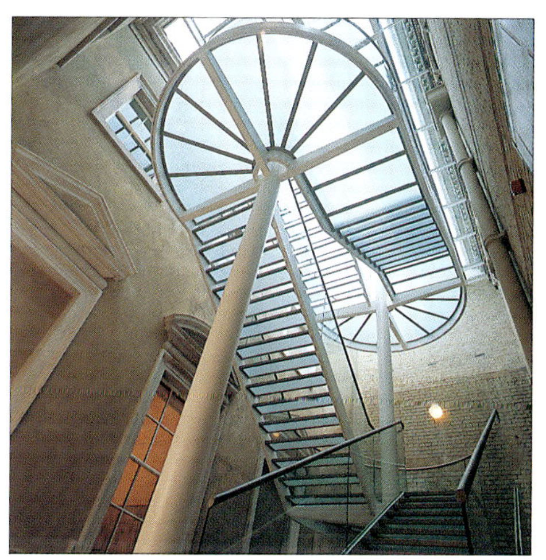

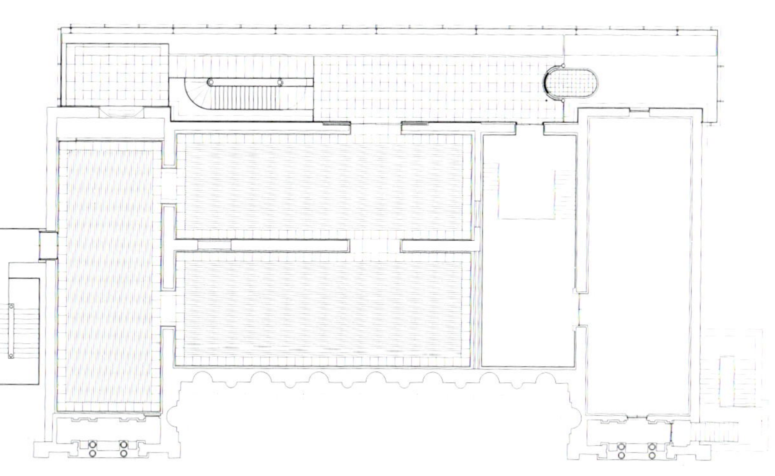

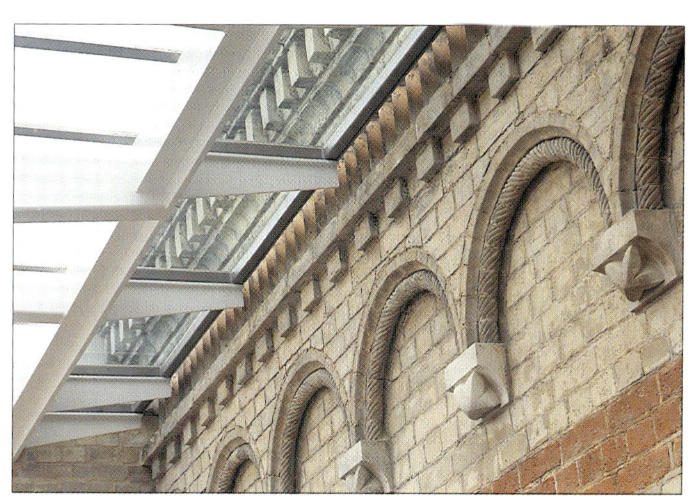

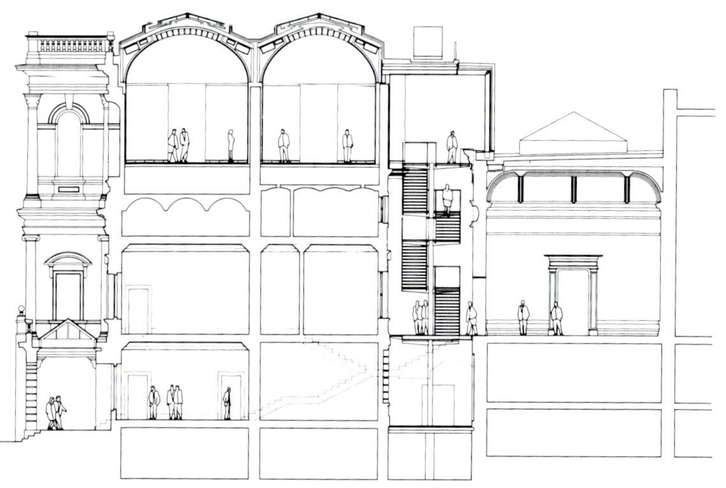

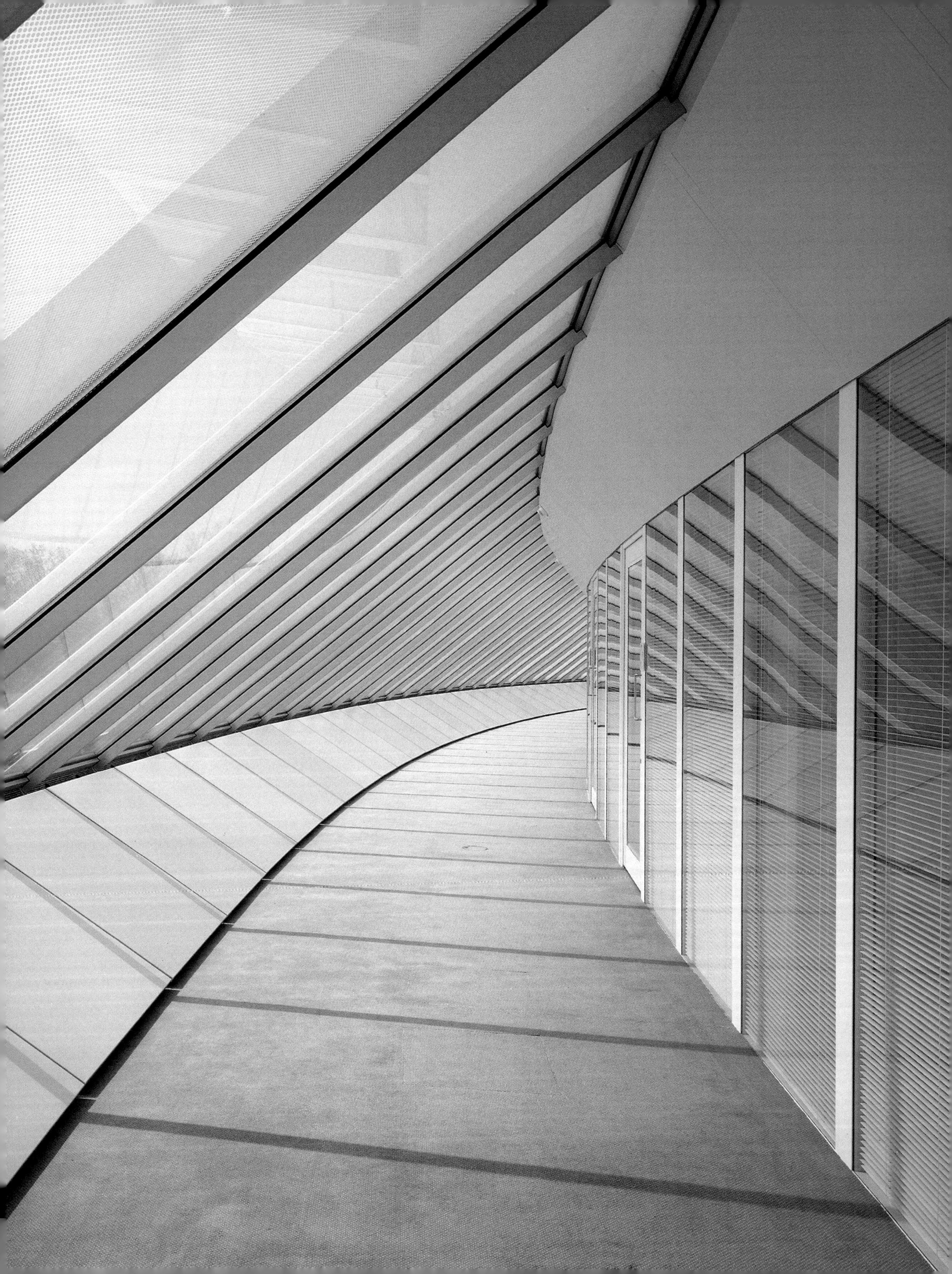

THE SAINSBURY CENTRE FOR VISUAL ARTS

The Sainsbury Centre for Visual Arts was built in 1977. As well as housing the Sir Robert and Lady Sainsbury collection it also provided a wide range of facilities for public and academic use under a single large-span roof. The new Crescent Wing adds a major new public exhibition space as well as providing a range of specialised study and working areas. The new Lower Gallery, which has state-of-the-art audio visual equipment, is entered by a gently descending ramp. The conservation facilities and workshops will rank as the best in the world for three-dimensional objects. A Study Centre, of which the only other example is in the Metropolitan Museum in New York, houses storage in glass display cases for the student and scholar to access. There is also a special area in which to experiment and to teach gallery lighting, the first faculty of its kind.

The New Wing extends out underneath the grassed forecourt at the west end of the Sainsbury Centre. By digging into the natural slope of the site a vast crescent of glass, angled to be flush with the landscape, creates a major internal route and offers a magnificent prospect to the lake beyond. This, the glazed ramp for public access and the occasional roof light set into the glass, are the only visible traces of the new building.

The new facilities, which utilise the most up-to-date architectural, lighting and museum technology, will satisfy the Centre's requirements for many years to come. The way in which this energy-conscious design has been discreetly integrated as an element in the landscape belies the fact that an area almost two-thirds the footprint of the existing building has been added to the site. Both the original Centre and its New Wing have been generously funded by Sir Robert, Lady Sainsbury and their son David Sainsbury.

OPPOSITE: Interior view of corridor
BELOW: Site plan
OVERLEAF: LEFT: Overall view from southeast; RIGHT, ABOVE: Detail of southeastern wall showing balustrade and access corridor; Section detail; CENTRE: Laboratory interior; Plan; BELOW: View from southeast; Overall section

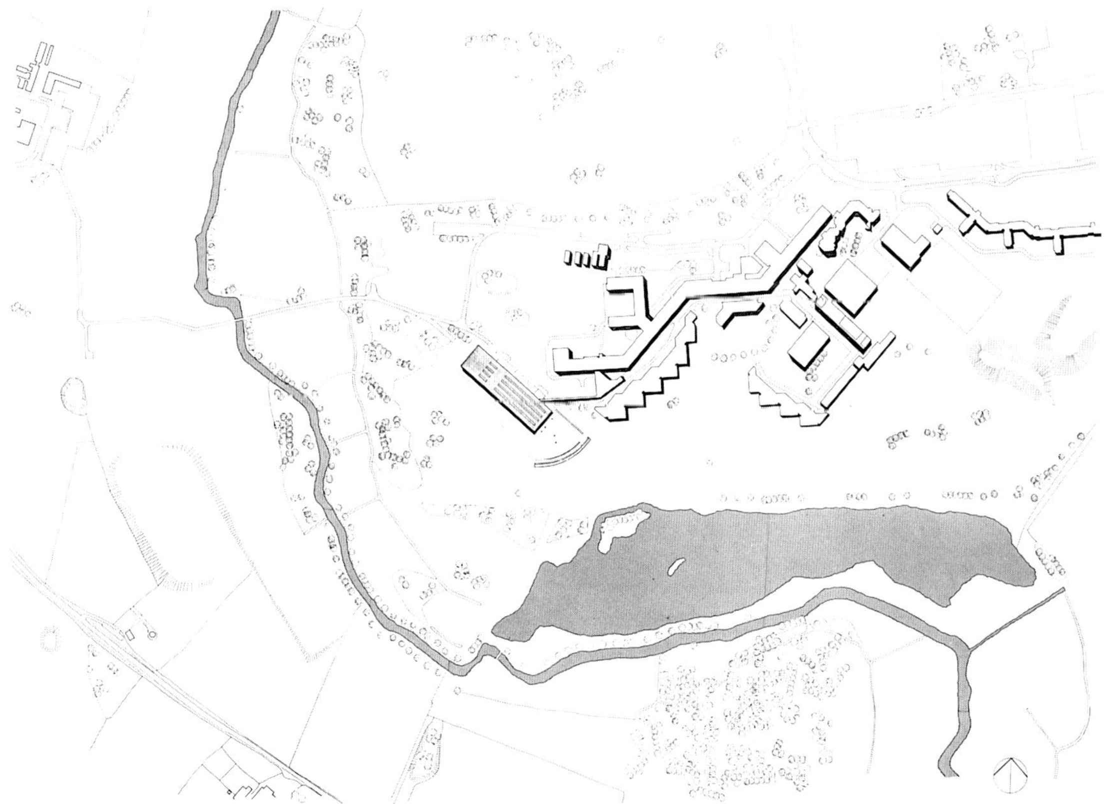

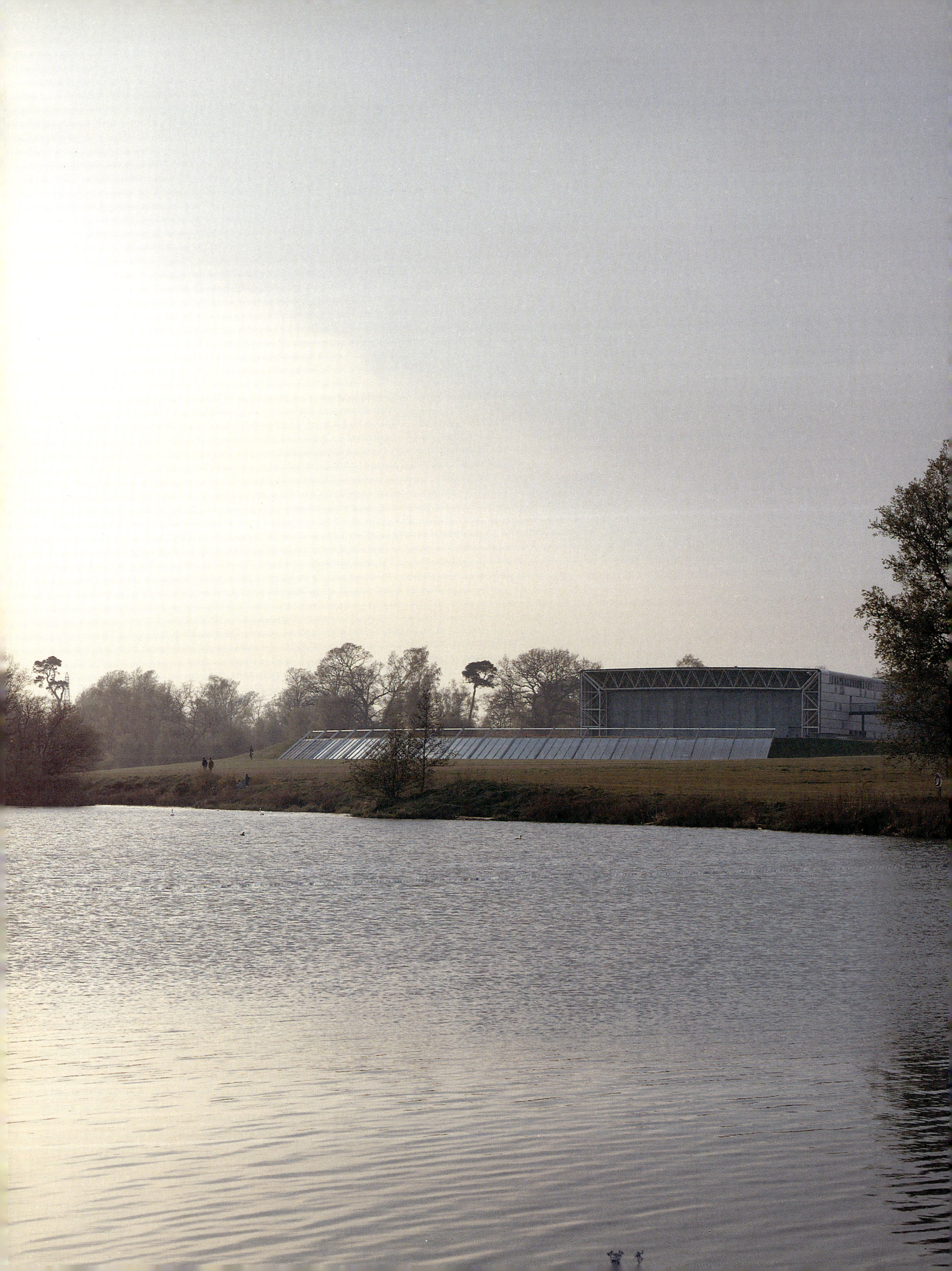

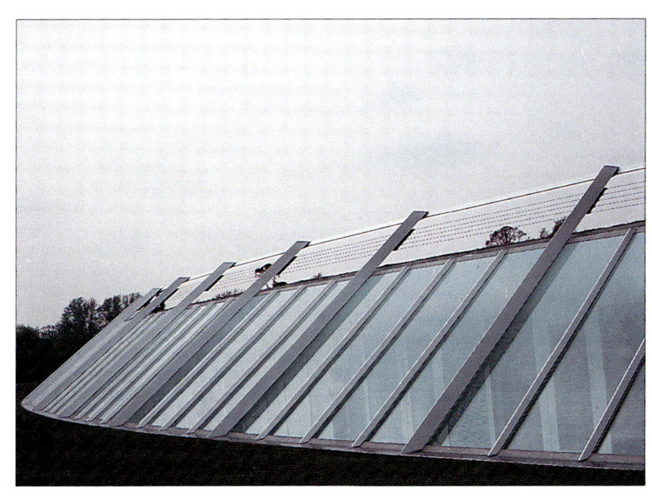

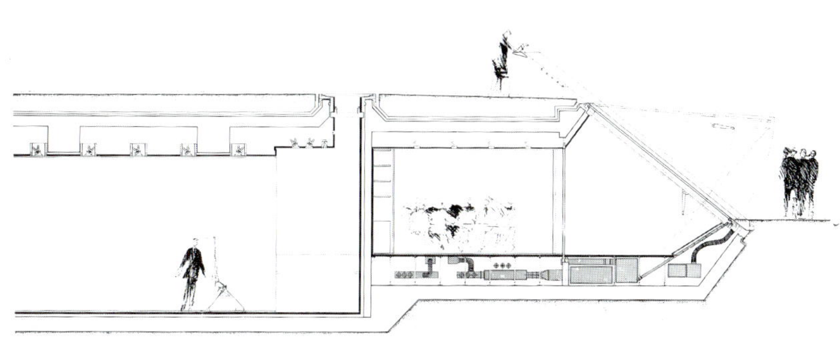

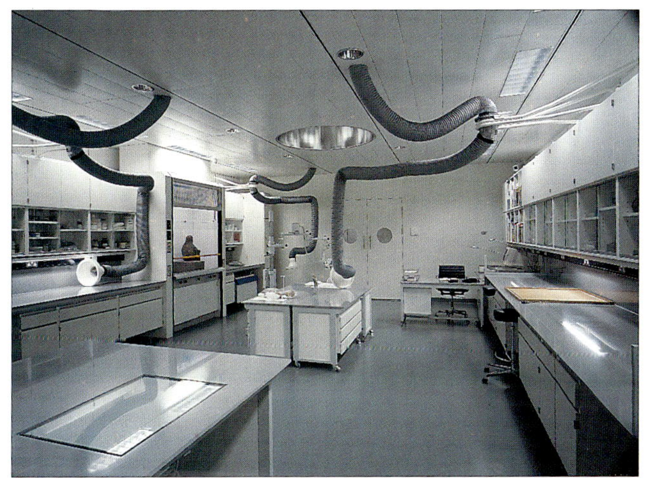

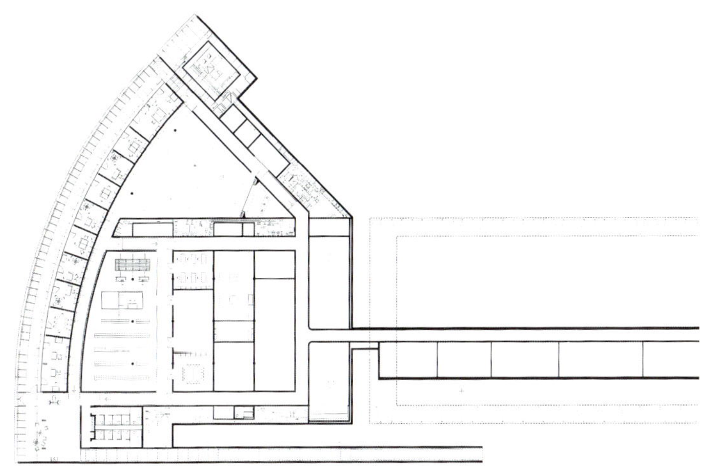

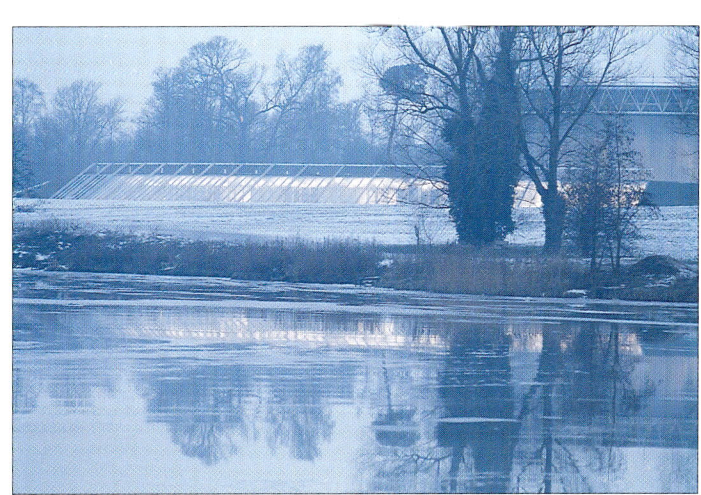

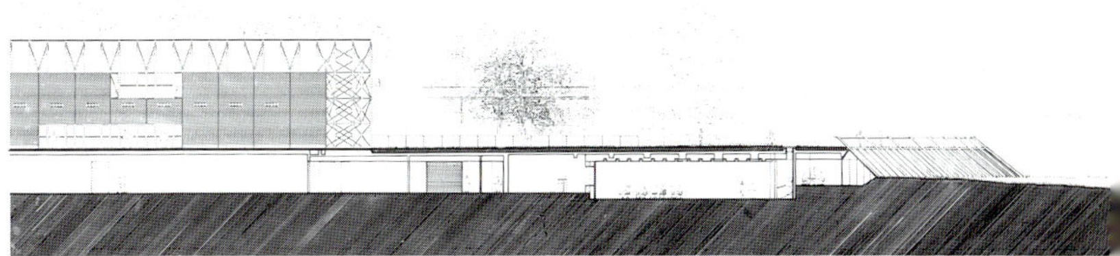

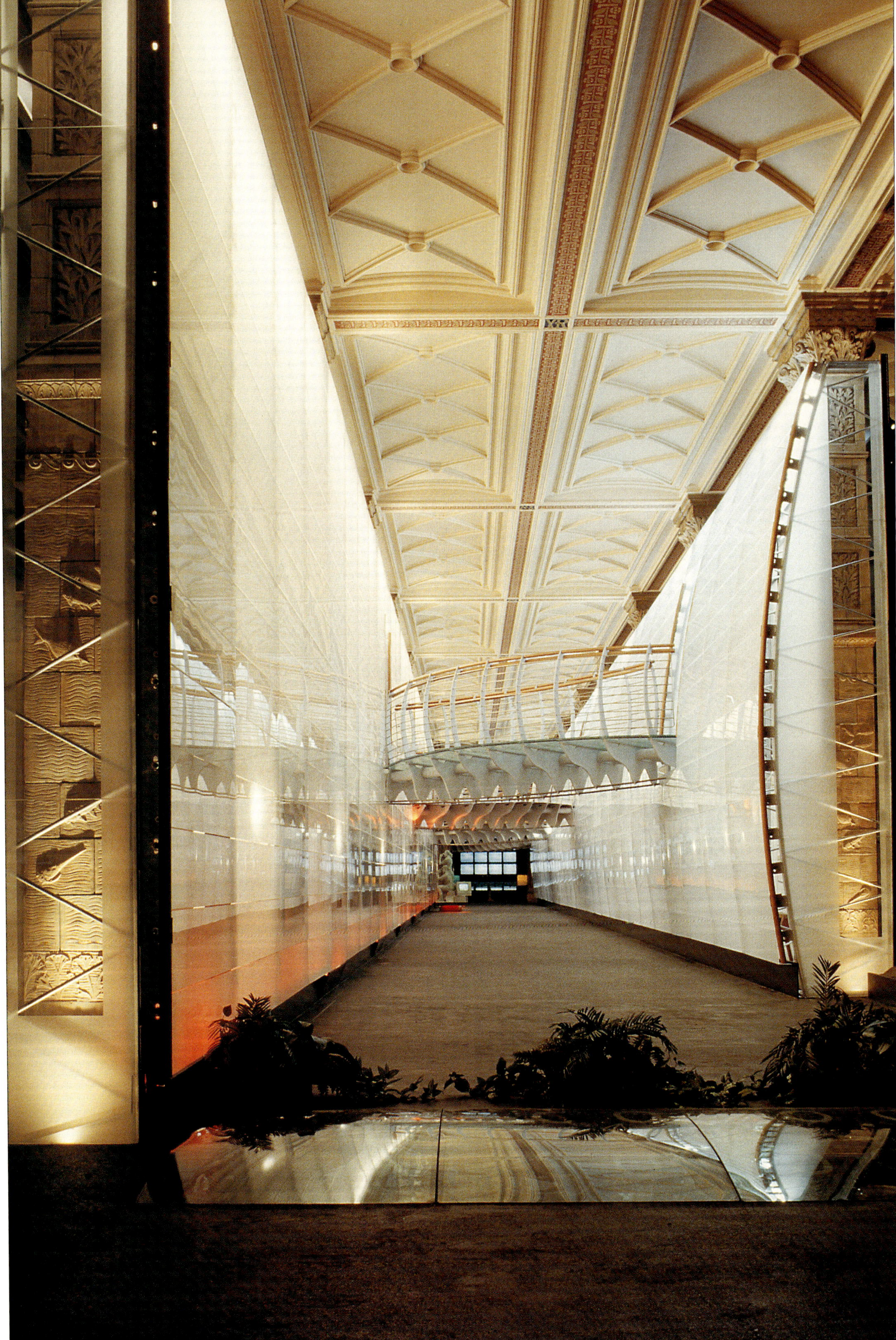

IAN RITCHIE
AN ARCHITECTURAL DESIGN INTERVIEW

Following the International Symposium at the Royal Academy which discussed the subject of New Museology, Ian Ritchie, who has just completed the alterations to the Reina Sophia in Madrid, talks to Maggie Toy about the concept of New Museology and his work in general.

– What kind of art inspires, for you, a New Museology?
An area which interests me in art is cybernetic space. I feel that the evolution of telematic art is the big field coming up, as against the on site installations field which dates from the early 60s and has been going on ever since then. They rejected the gallery, but it is only when the art becomes a collection that it is moved into galleries, when knowledge of the pieces that you are trying to design for exists. So, the New Museology of contemporary art for me is cybernetics, electronic space; whether it's virtual reality or what's actually happening now amongst artists, which is telematic art, a field which very few curators, gallery owners, are actually familiar with and yet it has exploded within the last five or ten years.
– How would you then design a gallery space for this type of art; is such a space necessary?
Exactly, how do you design new gallery space for uncollected art of a contemporary medium, that is a very wide subject. I think the first probable way of dealing with it goes back to a thing called EAT or Experiments in Art and Technology in the late 60s, early 70s: the technology then was robots, to use an image, but today's technology is invisibly transmitted in waves through the air. The end results are often screens or print outs from screens, the real art happens live as an interactive collaboration between artists on the screen.
– The real art *is the process?*
The art is a process which has an end product that is happening before your eyes and it can be captured whether it be on film or video or screen print out. The actual collaborative venture which one creates is where the art is live and interactive. This questions whether the two artists should ever actually be in a room together, with the public, or whether one artist sits in a black room, with a screen and a spotlight on him communicating transglobally with other artists, whatever they want to explore.

We did a project for a monument which France was going to give Japan based on the *Generateur Poïetic*, which comes from Plato, *Poïesis*. These are the things that make other things happen, and it was based on software where you design your own hieroglyphic out of four colours. You phone up the Generateur, through your national network telephone system, have your own minitel or screen, and join in what is a global painting happening all the time. Our proposal originally was for a screen 15m by 80m. The subsequent one was a one and a half kilometre walk screen, wrapped around a ring of that dimension. The finished product is what is happening on the screens. It seems to me that media will be exploited. It hasn't started yet but you will end up with channel 12 or 28 that will be the art channel, where artists work live, and one day we'll have latex screens where you can put your hand in and you can manipulate virtual image and become the artist.
– But then perhaps we won't need galleries for that type of art and thus we bypass the problem?
Except then what happens, as happens in all sorts of art, is that someone decides that they want to collect it. They may collect discs, which is the end product and the process, which then become, if you like, an art library, and people go in and pick a work of art, so work and collections appear. Instead of a collection of physical objects, it's stored data.
– So the gallery of the future then becomes a video viewing room?
Yes, a bit like Hutchinson going into encyclopedias on video discs. In the same way you will get art works on disc. The question is how do you design for what is happening now, before there is a collection. It is happening, at the moment: the gallery is irrelevant. It's the same as site installations, earthworks and Land Art. They couldn't do it in galleries because the galleries didn't exist, so they went out into the Arizona desert and did it.
– You say that Museums have become such big business that it is inevitable that some of the larger ones will lose all sense of direction and their intrinsic value. Why is this inevitable?
Because of competition, there is a growth of leisure spaces. Although we talked in the 60s about going towards a leisure society and having lots of free time, you and I don't feel it; a lot of people have it, but they don't necessarily have the money to go with it. But there *is* a lot of free time, travelling is a lot easier and this has led to an emergence of facilities where people can spend their time. The cultural institutions are now in competition with themselves. In South Kensington, where the government is pulling the rug out financially, you have all the museums competing against each other for the same visitor. I had a discussion with a director of the Natural History Museum and suggested that they should have a family ticket for South Kensington, but nothing came of it. People cannot go and see all of the museums because they can't afford to. I have a strong belief that to place that sort of culture into the economic market place is fundamentally wrong and I believe that the basic cultural collections should be public and free, subsidised by taxes. The individuals who want to create their own galleries will have to charge to maintain their galleries, and of course I understand that. The National Museums are becoming elitist because of the financial implications, and they shouldn't be.
– What in your view is public architecture?
Public architecture is that part of the building which is permanently in the public view. In other words the facades of all buildings are in the public domain and are ironically public property. There is no escape from that.
– Does that mean that you have to please the public? What

Ecology gallery, Natural History Museum, London, '. . . I believe that the basic cultural collections should be public and free, subsidised by taxes'.

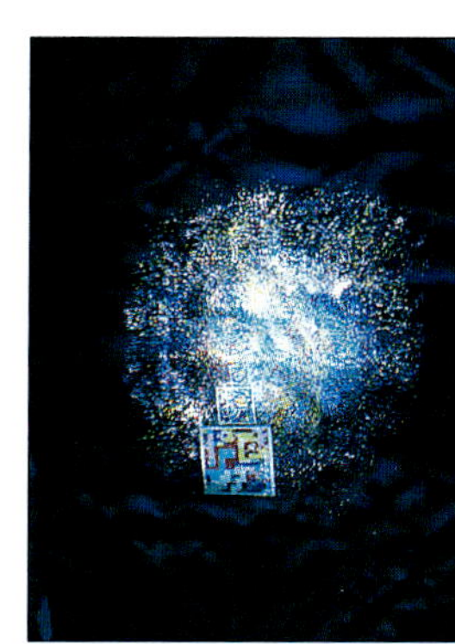

Telematic art, '. . . the real art happens live as an interactive collaboration between artists on the screen'

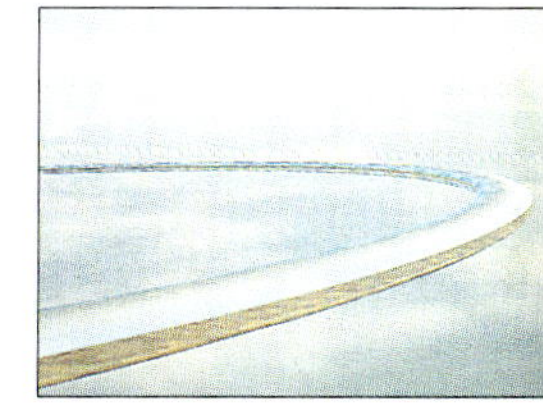

The Generateur Poïetic, 'You phone up the Generateur . . . have your own minitel or screen and join in what is a global painting'.

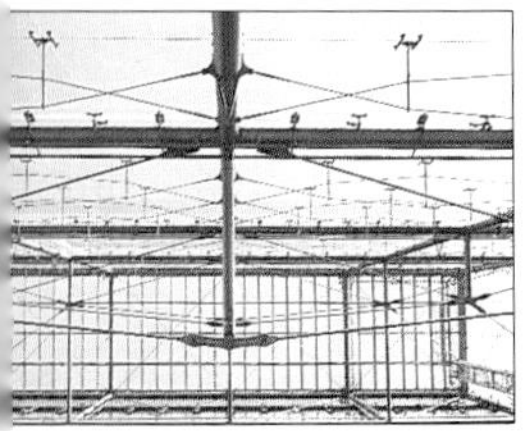

Supporting structure at La Villette, '. . . the complexity of each piece increased so that, as your eye approached, you became more interested in the stainless steel bearings, the casters and the details'.

difference does this acceptance that the facade is in the public domain make to your architecture?

You can be subversive with your facade, you don't have to please necessarily, you can be antagonistic, you can be reflective of society, you can be banal, you can be all sorts of things, but recognising that part of the building is permanently public is actually quite important. Depending on the nature of the brief of the project we are doing one can take an assessment of how the concept will be interpreted as a public component as against a private component. For example at Reina Sophia the parts we did were totally public, day and night; there was no private domain. But at Stockley Park, even though it is a private park, there were public buses coming in and it was seen from the golf course so the facades are public. The inside would be used by members of the public, but it is not what I would term the public side of that building. Our view of the facade and the inside was a dialogue about light and therefore we created a very different feel between inside and outside. A lot of architects do not think the facade is in the public domain – you only have to look around the docklands in London to see that.

– What makes you say that these architects may not be pleasing the public but are making a public statement with the facade which they create?

It is a measure of the selfishness of a designer to decide who designs the building he would like to see on the street, as against the person who designs thinking not only of his personal but also of the public interest. An example I would use is the Modern Movement, where there was no difference in the hierarchy of scale and interest, whether you were 400m away from the building to when your nose was up to it; nothing fundamentally changed. This in turn produced Post-Modernism which is a great smoke screen, but what it actually did was to force a lot of the Modernist thinkers to ask themselves what they were doing. One of the questions which appealed to me was this hierarchy of shifting scale and perception of interest in the facade. I do not turn to classical history books or Walt Disney to find out what I do about it. What interested me was looking at fractal geometry, chaos, hierarchy and developing a new way of looking at facades rather more mathematically. In the scheme at La Villette, the structure was originally analysed using non-linear analysis which is akin to chaos, and as you drew closer, the basic 32m and 8m square became 2x2m right down to the four fixings which formed a square. The complexity of each piece increased so that, as your eye approached, you became more interested in the stainless steel bearings, the casters and the details.

– The outside as a Mandelbrot set with spiralling interest as you approach?

Yes, like bifurcation if you like. The elements are not the same, but they are similar. They are based on a square but the pieces change quite dramatically and, though the facades from 400m away just look like squares, they increase in complexity as you approach. That is one way I deal with the public facade, making a statement about a further understanding of the complexity of nature and saying it is worth communicating that knowledge through the form of the building.

The Deconstructionists, I believe, have a particular approach when they talk about chaos, as they do occasionally. I think they have taken the literal sense: the decentralisation of man; man is not at the centre of things and therefore you can do buildings without a specific human purpose; man is irrelevant. That is a statement. I do not think that it is necessarily architecture but it is valid as a statement, as a piece of art, in that it is responding to the human need to be challenged mentally. But I don't think it performs what I think it should do, which is to serve a human purpose.

Take Tschumi's galleries at La Villette, where RFR worked with him. He decentralised the lines of axis of the structural members so that they don't come in to nodal points, which is not how nature behaves or tries to behave. Removing the axis of things for the sake of deconstructing results is an enormous amount of gymnastics to hold it up. I do not find much mileage in that, I find it quite naive. However I can look at Coop Himmelblau's roof extension in Vienna, which goes along with a lot of the Baroque corner rooftops there. In that sense it is related to its context and it actually works.

But you find that people at the AA pick up Deconstruction and you get a large amount of trite copies which appear in much the same way that Post-Modernism sprouted all over the place, and because it is not underpinned by a fundamental philosophy behind it and died as soon as it started. Deconstruction in that particular context requires the protagonist to work particularly hard at pushing those frontiers and then working at them, because they are going to be faced with a number of copies appearing and it depends on how strong they are as to whether they can actually carry on evolving them. I have my concern that the philosophy was stillborn because of the ability of the rest of the world to copy. I don't think the literalness of the interpretation of Chaos or big number theory in the work of the Deconstructionists is deep enough. The Deconstructionist label was unfortunate because of its link with Constructivism. Where Constructivists took a material which was of its age – steel – and actually bent it and did things with it, Deconstruction, in the contemporary sense, should be playing with biogenetic coatings, materials of our age and using that which is much more appropriate to the complexity of nature, as opposed to playing with static materials such as steel and just moving axes apart. That is very banal to me. Their philosophy is literal but not profound.

– What are the other uses of Chaos theory within your work?

The images of, say, an oak tree or human beings for that matter, where genetically we are the same material, but yet are different, fascinates me as a subject. When it comes to realising architecture, and not conceptual or preconceptual thinking, you are starting with similar materials which everyone else has but using them intelligently and often in a completely different way. Why? It raises basic questions about design, and the approach to architecture.

We are exploring that hierarchy of scale and interest. The area that interest me is nature in the wider sense, in the areas we don't even know about yet. Particularly in genetics and photonics as researched and understood by me and finding an interpretation of that. That is an art. It is beginning to appear slowly within my architecture, it's something that takes time and I'm still quite young and working hard at it. But that's one area of research – and it's not about looking at oak trees and saying how I have designed a column based on a tree.

In the classic way of looking at architecture where the Greeks copied the timber construction but in stone, my interest is in finding out why they used stone. I presume because they wanted more permanence in honour of their Gods, in other words there was some religious or philosophical reason that underpinned the move. In a way they are copying and reinterpreting, not like a fax machine but they are copying, which interests me but only on the basis of the philosophy of our age.

– *Light also seems to play a large part in your work.*

Yes, we happen to do a lot work with light – it is a pretty fundamental material. One interesting project we did was an experiment to control light three-dimensionally. After discovering lasers and being absolutely fascinated by them, it struck me that no one controlled light three dimensionally, so we used a vacuum tube and eventually controlled bird forms of light going up and down the tube. We haven't been able to do anything with it since, and we don't quite fully understand the phenomena that enabled us to make this happen, but we have managed to arrive at a rough idea of how we were doing it. What the application is remains to be seen. But it will have its application I have no doubt probably initially in space whether as a practical or artistic application.

– *How do you use all of the incredibly varied thoughts that you have in your architecture?*

Where most architects start with concept, we start with preconcept, which has nothing to do with building or architecture. It has to have its roots somewhere else. This is the art component. It might be a political view of the context that we are going into which we would like to express, which is arrived at by discussion and thinking in bed at night. In Reina Sophia the architects wanted to achieve minimalism, which for me almost had its end game when I worked on the Ipswich building. So when they, 20 years after the Minimalist Movement, come around asking for minimalism, my reaction was to find expressionism out of minimalism through each individual piece. The combination is complex, so that when you look at the images of it, it's very rare that it looks simple or at all minimal. But, if you look at the reductivist nature of each piece it is quite minimal. Form follows desire as opposed to form follows function.

– *You always refer to 'we' when you are talking about your design, do you work very much as a team?*

Yes, I hate professionalism at the level of professionals: they didn't exist before the industrial revolution and they were only invented in order to defend a domain. The final result of deciding to have professionals is a cult of the individual so you end up in the late 60s, 70s and 80s with media hype and a creation of heroes. It is an absolutely natural end game from having set up the idea of the individuals as professional in the mid-19th century.

– *So you work as a team of mixed disciplines?*

Everyone who works in this office is in fact a qualified architect although some are also engineers and we have also an anthropologist. We also tend to work with two or three structural engineers who will become involved with preconceptual thinking.

We have a Quantity Surveyor as well, because if you're doing real architecture it has a cost attached to it. And there are one or two we work with who have sideways thinking minds because architecture is not just about the building.

– *What role do you think architectural magazines should play today?*

I give a lecture in which I say that all students should leave architectural magazines alone for two years. In a world without an architectural magazine there would be an opportunity to visit something and 'discover' it, which is now very difficult to do. That is a problem of the media age. I would like to see a magazine which is slightly more philosophical about the basis of things. It's not the glossy pictures that bother me, it's the profound thinking that goes in and whether or not it is profound! Very few architects are very literate but they can be helped to write what they are trying to say.

Good minds are great fun and I love to be out of my depth mentally because I find it an absolute challenge, and I think most artists are exploring body and soul beyond where they are at the moment. What I can't stand is prejudiced and closed minds.

I strive for original thinking, not necessarily originality.

– *Do you consider yourself a High-Tech architect in the tradition of Foster, Rogers, Hopkins and Grimshaw?*

Our architecture, which is still maturing, has a bias towards technology, but it does use real science and physics of materials. It's not about the image or hi-tech appliqué. Structural intelligence is so important to us, whereas it's not as important to Norman Foster. For him other things are more important, which I can understand. In the same way that expression of change is inevitable, which is Richard's thing, and which is why he expresses it all on the outside, I'm interested in the relative speed of change. That literary expression of change is good, figurative architecture, although the consequence of accepting changes in your building ten years on is very difficult to those architects who are precious about what their buildings look like.

In the case of Nick Grimshaw's architecture, his strong bias towards the details, often beautifully executed in themselves (and using new materials) somehow manages in the scale and hierarchy of the elements to create a whole which to me, can be visually disturbing. Michael Hopkins is quite interesting visually, and our architecture appears to be more like him than any of the others. But it is our philosophy and scientific research which is at the heart of our architecture, we still have a great deal of research to do. I think the measure of that is the motivation of people here. If that energy isn't in the preconcept and how it is conceptualised then you haven't got a hope in hell of having a happy time – and we have a happy time here. It is a hard working but very relaxed office. I have a particular view that we don't have a style; no one can point at any of our buildings and say that's by Ian Ritchie Architects.

– *Is that something that pleases you?*

Yes, we have in the past been strongly advised to develop an identifiable style of architecture in order to obtain clients. So ironically this confirmed my resistance to it. The Natural History Museum, the Louvre and La Villette came to us because of our knowledge of glass and the engineering of it. Certainly Reina Sophia came to us because of this, and I don't mind that. It's not that we are against having a style, it's just that our minds don't produce one. We don't know what we're going to do for the next project until we get our grey cells active. If we did, I'd get annoyed. It would lose its interest. It's like going home to your girlfriend. It is nice when you go home and it's new every time, but that's something you have to fight for and its hard work. Because we know about glass, it is an extra security for clients; when we say that we can do something, they are confident that we will deliver. One of the symptoms of our approach is that we haven't built as much as we could, because you end up not getting on with clients, not on a human level but because confidence isn't created. We cut out if there is no confidence; it's not worth it because life has too many other pleasures. There has to be a shared joy in the work.

– *Don't prostitute yourself for your art.*

Don't prostitute full stop.

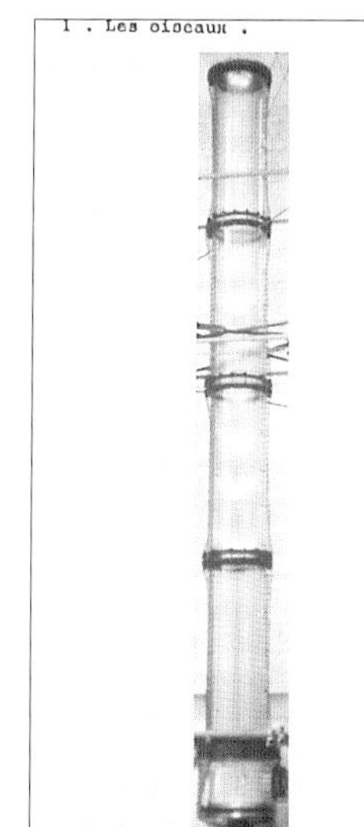

Experiment in the three-dimenensional control of light, '. . . we used a vacuum tube and eventually controlled bird forms of light going up and down the tube'.

Reina Sophia Museum, Madrid,'The shape of the key stainless steel glass fixing tied in with the shapes from Guernica, *with arms holding the torch and the hair . . . They look like birds sticking on the glass'.*

– Which would you say was your best building so far, or is each one better than its predecessor?

If there is one building that probably surprised everyone it was the Eagle Rock house. It's almost deconstructionist. It was purely sculptural, influenced a lot by the paintings of Moholy-Nagy. It was finding a dynamic, an original concept for design, which avoided a conventional solution on such a beautiful site.

– Is that something that pleases you then when people are surprised at a building?

Well it surprised me that people were surprised. It was the first building we had done in England. In a way for me it was very experimental. It became a question of how you make a sculpture livable. It was very much a sculpture. Because I didn't want a building on the site, I wanted sculpture. The present owners think it's heaven, they consider themselves custodians of a great work of art! If someone asked me what I would have done with it when the lady owner died last year, I would have said dismantle it because it was very much built for her. She was very much the protagonist spirit for the bird. It wouldn't suit me, it's not what I would have done on that site for myself. Maybe we're just not as precious as other architects about our work.

– Are you optimistic about the future of architecture?

Oh yes. I think one thing that makes me very optimistic is the Paternoster Exhibition, because its the end of a culture, they have actually shot themselves in the foot, I think.

– Please describe the development of Reina Sophia.

Our involvement was really Red Adair! In Spain, once the contractor has the project he is the one who is contractually obliged to deliver the goods and the architects are not the technicians. The contractors actually said that they wanted La Villette. They explained that the Minister of Culture was coming down and unless they were pouring the foundations for these elements, the project would become a political football. They asked us if within a few days we could give them a drawing telling them how much concrete to pour and where. There was no lift analysis, nothing telling us how many people were going to use this building. So we took a margin of error. All of this was done ever so quickly. Every single piece we designed was a plane as we weren't into tubes. The only reference to round objects were the bars on the windows of the hospital which I thought would be quite interesting to pull out as big bars, in the sense of a different scale; everything else is in planes, planes of glass, planes of steel, planes of concrete. As *Guernica* was the key painting that was to be housed here, many of the shapes came from that collage approach.

The shape of the key stainless steel glass fixing tied in with the shapes from *Guernica*, with the arm holding the torch and the hair. It was about holding something towards the future and the fact that it ended up there was just ironic, but it was there in the back of our minds, probably. We had to go back to minimalism to do it. So as you come out of each level of the museum you expect to see Madrid. We said no to this. We put up a 'hedge' so that you are sent to the side and then only when the lift doors open do you see Madrid.

One of the minimalist things we did was to say, we'll hang the glass on the outside and to stop it flapping about in the wind we'll resist it from the inside. The idea of a didactic role people can understand and get intrigued by was something we had intended at La Villette, but it was so subtle that it was difficult to perceive. So we tried again here. The structure works and yet it is also poetic. They look like birds sticking on the glass. I think the lighting at night is not great. One thing you don't do with glass is to light it, you should light the building, then everything about is transparent and comes to life. The halos on top are for maintenance cradles but they are rather 'catholic'.

Reina Sophia. Architects: Jose Luis Ifiiguez de Onzono and Antonio Vazquez de Castro. Engineers: John Thornton and Bruce Gibbons. Architects (Ian Ritchie Architects): Simon Conolly and Jon Buck. Contractors: Huarte and Pilkington

Generateur Poïesis. Software: Oliver Auber. Artists: Jean-Louis Lhermitte, Guillaume Pratz, Ian Ritchie and Peter Rice.

3-D Light Control. Physicist: François Bastien. Artist: Jean-Louis Bastien. Research team of EDG Clamart, Paris and Ian Ritchie.

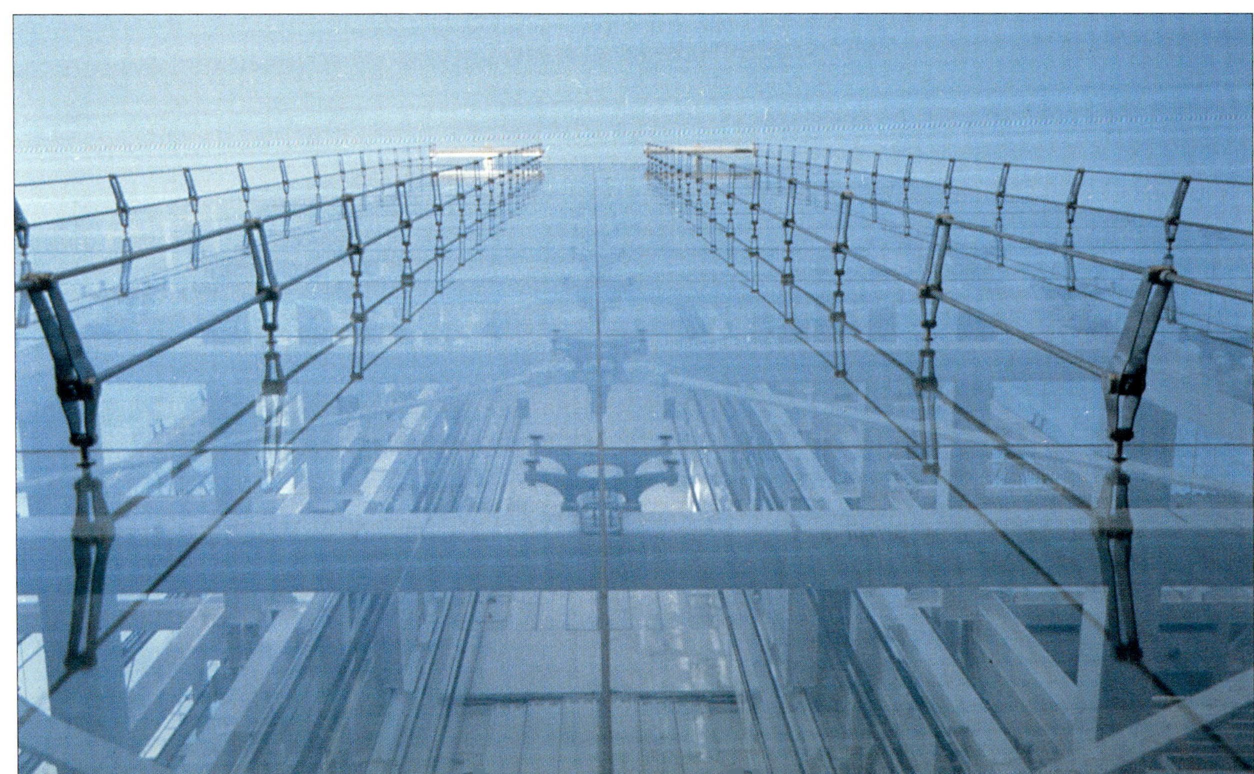

IAN RITCHIE

REINA SOPHIA MUSEUM OF MODERN ART, MADRID

The project takes the following guiding principles as its basis:

Minimalism – The reduction of each component to a very simple form. The juxtaposition of these elements to create a rich and legible composition.

Modernity – The visible expression of current and forward-looking attitudes to design and technology.

Performance – In addition to ensuring effective movement for thousands of visitors a day, the aim is to achieve a degree of transparency that reduces visual impact from outside and allows uninterrupted views from inside, both when waiting and, more spectacularly, when riding in the lifts – a pause to make visual contact and reorientate yourself with the world outside the museum.

The Design – A hierarchical composition from large to small scale of vertical and horizontal planes in concrete, steel, stainless steel and glass. The intention is to articulate clearly the functions of each component in this composition, and to ensure the legibility of the load-carrying system.

The basic principle of glass support is to separate clearly the external system carrying the weight of glazing and the internal system which restrains the glazing against horizontal wind loads.

The entire glass envelope to each tower is suspended by stainless steel rods from roof level. Each panel of glass is individually supported, so that differences in thermal expansion between steel and glass can be spread evenly across all joints between panels.

Wind loads are transmitted through connectors to adjoining panels and back to the main structural frame. Secondary vertical structural members resist wind loads between floors of the link to the building. The size of each panel is determined by wind load, economic glass thickness, structural module and heights between floors.

Given the demands of a rapid programme, the glazing method uses an established and tested system of glass fixing. The method of suspension is more innovative, but uses simple components designed to allow easy monitoring of quality and rapid manufacture in the quantities required.

Interior view of lift tower

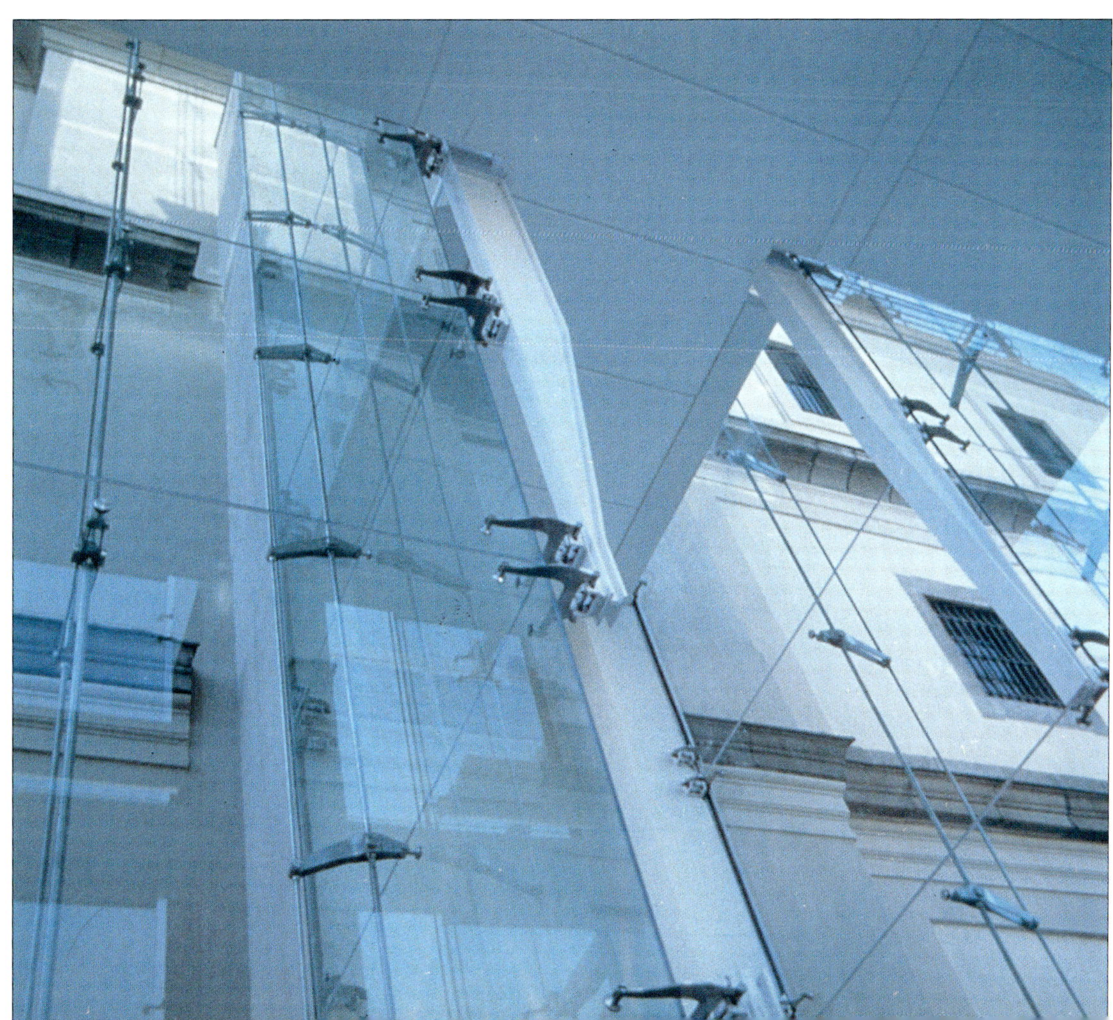

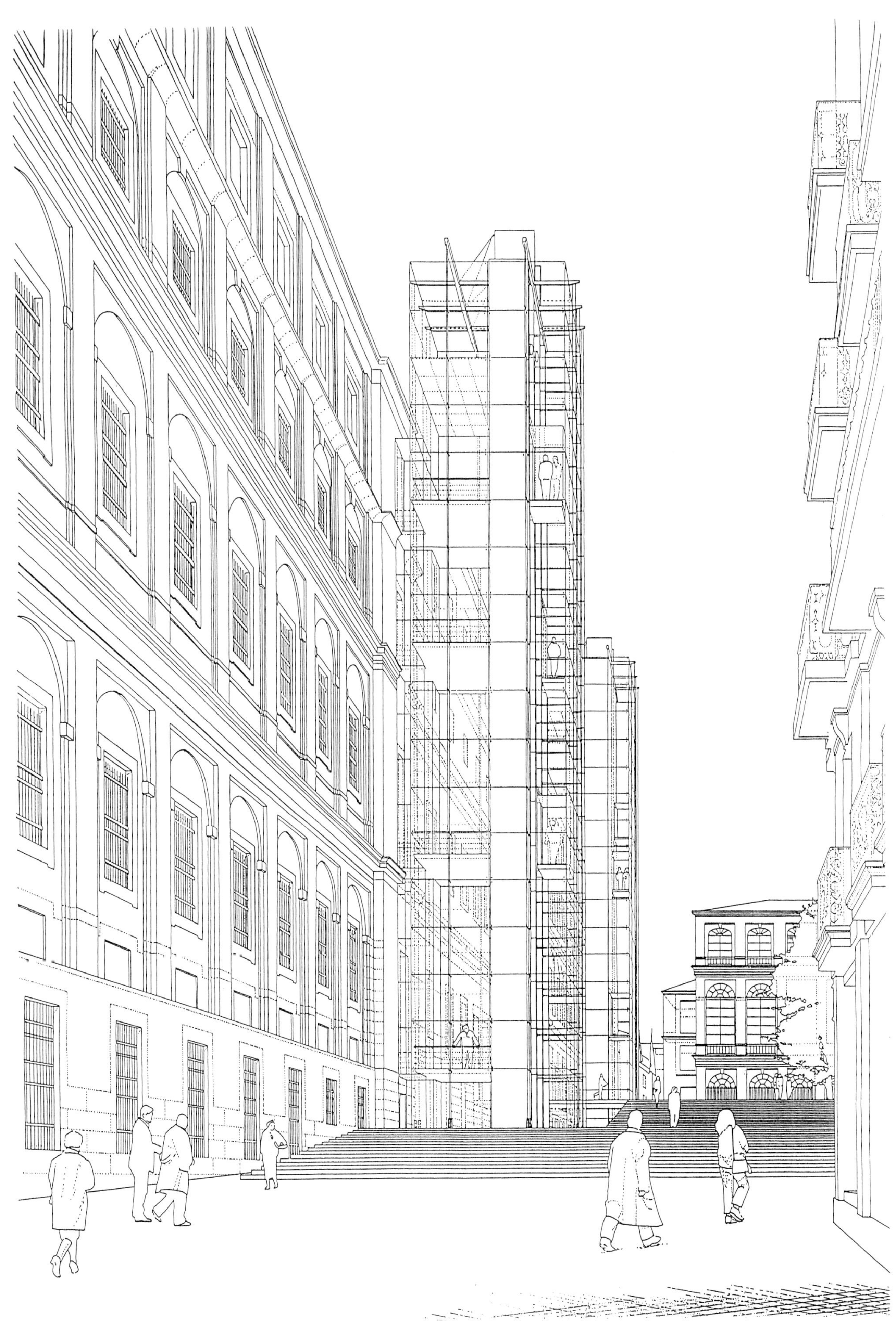

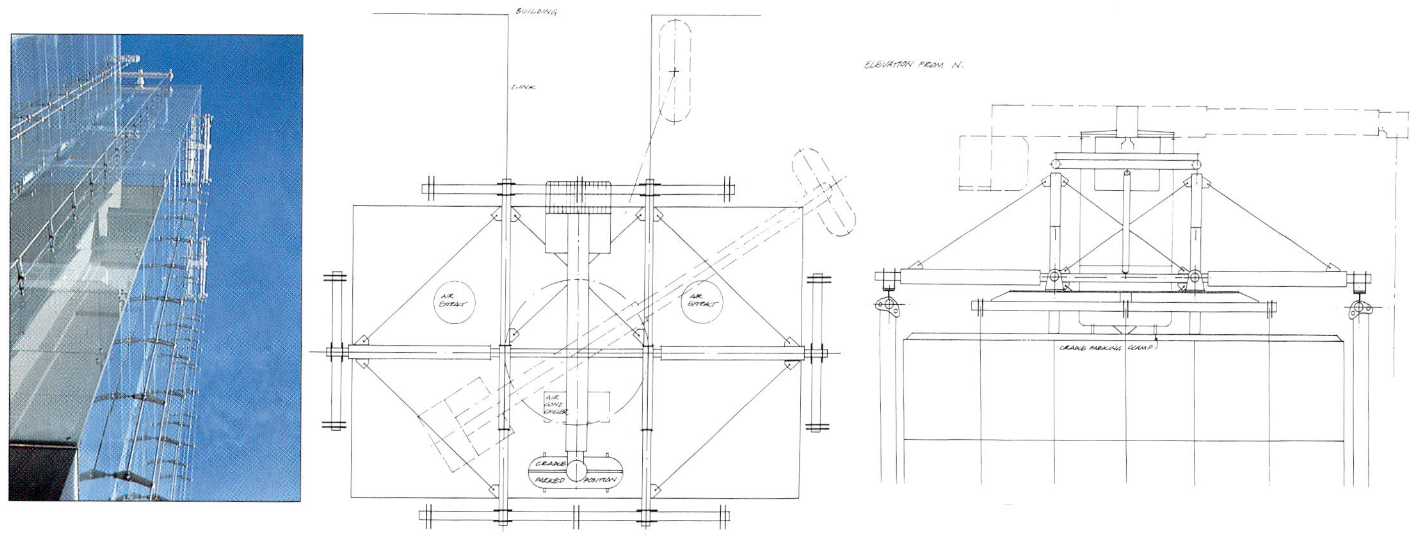

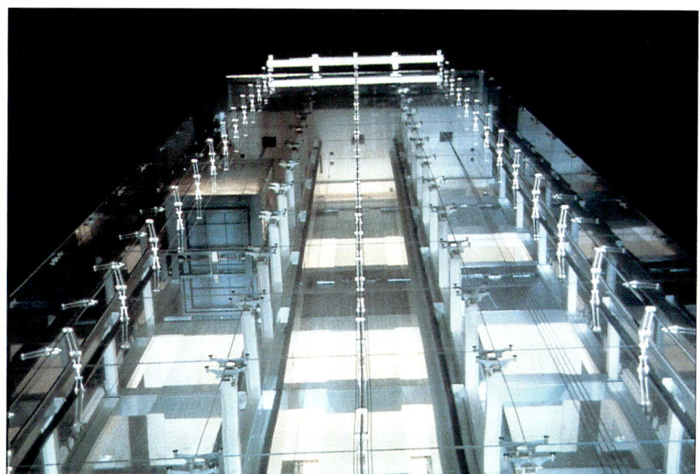

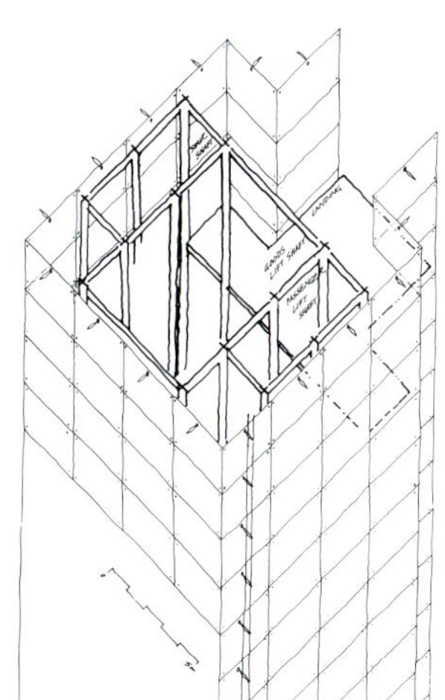

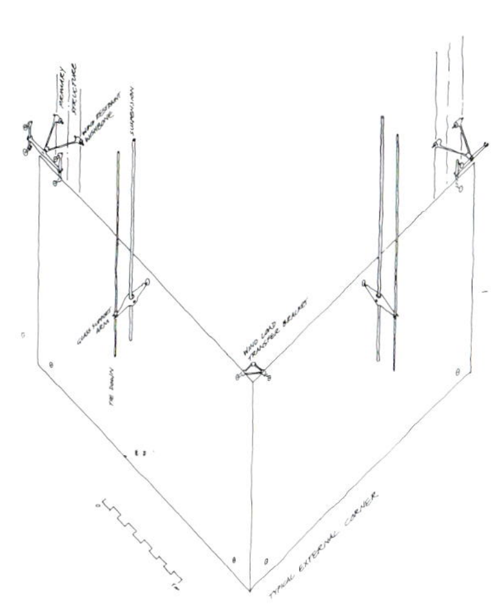

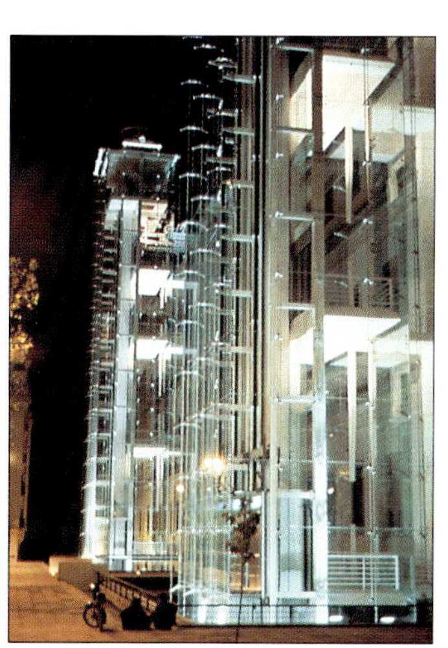

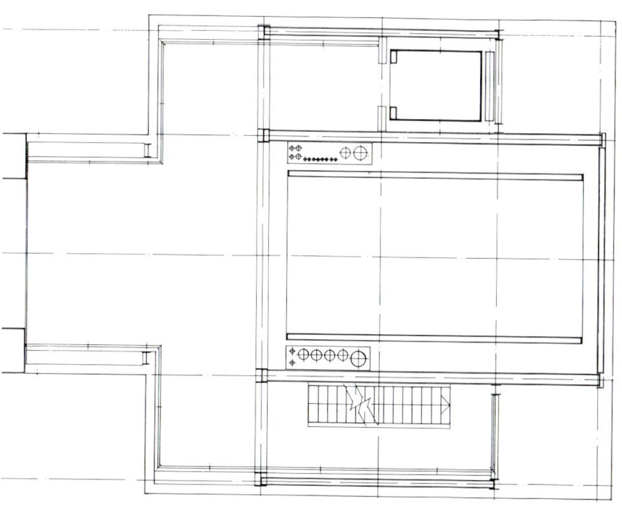

OPPOSITE: Drawing of two lift towers showing connection with museum
ABOVE: Side view up lift tower showing stainless steel bearings, plan and elevation of tower rooftop
CENTRE: Night view of lift tower and glazing attachment to tower
LEFT: Night view of two lift towers and plan of tower floor connection

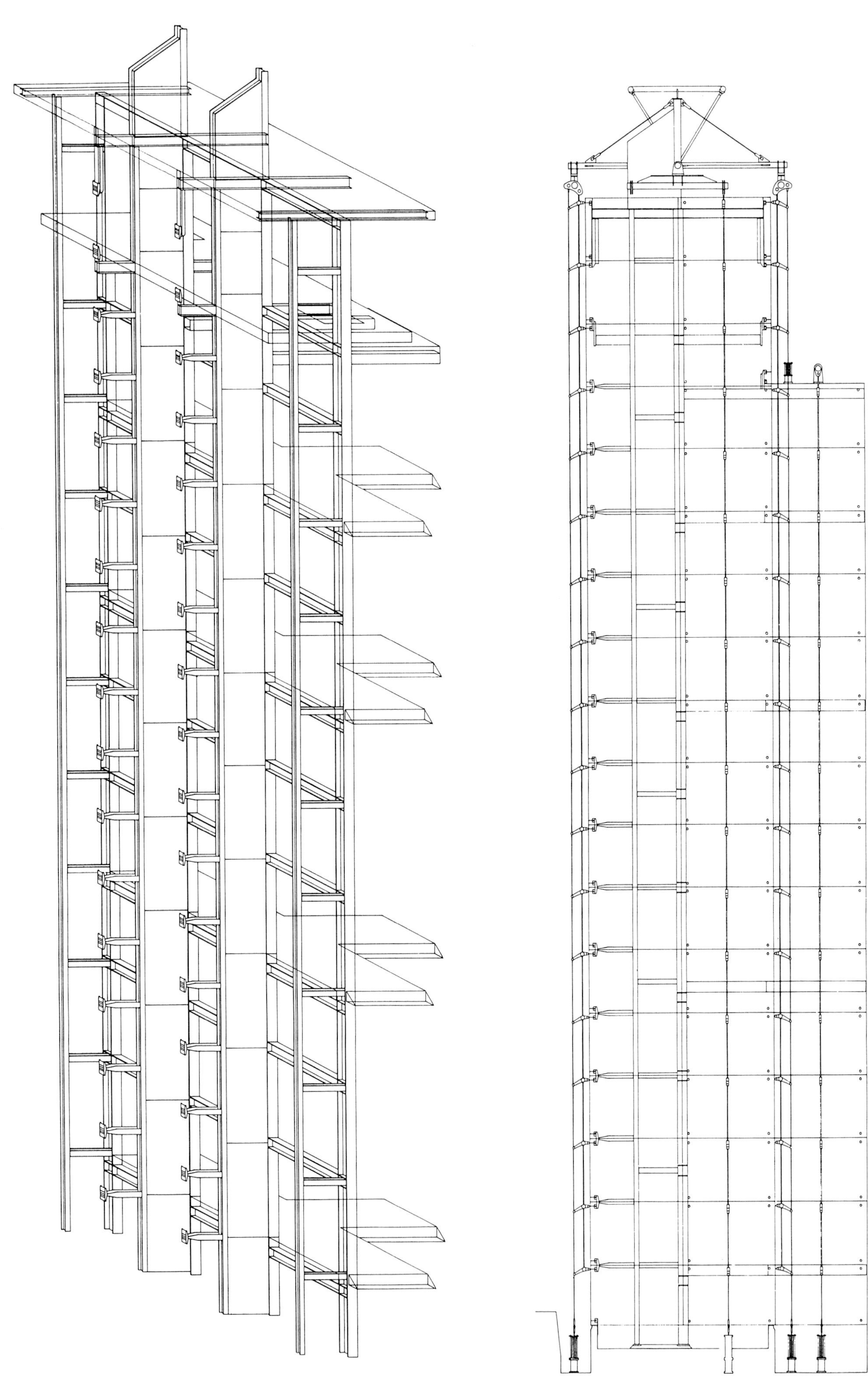

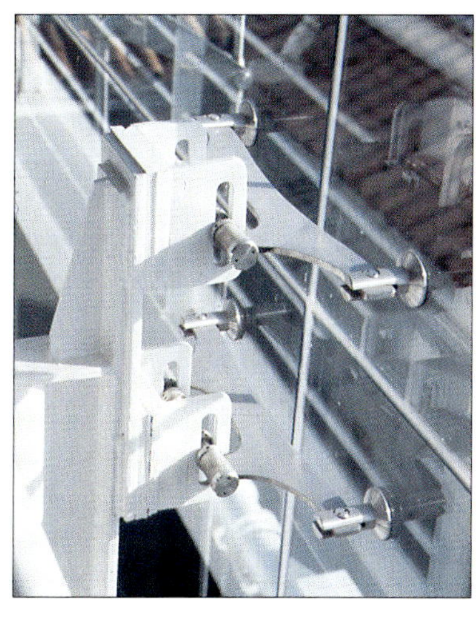

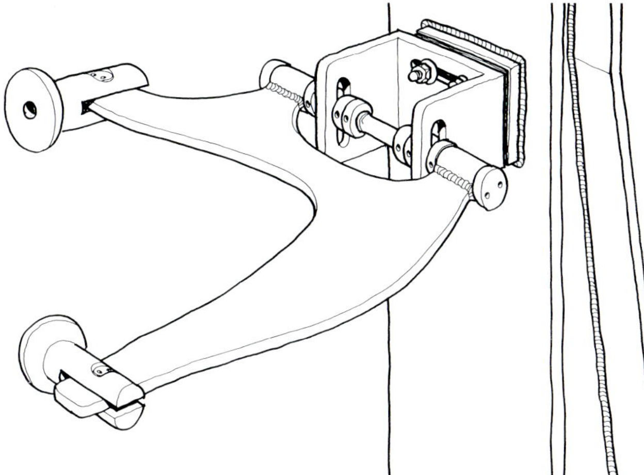

OPPOSITE: Drawings of lift tower support frame
LEFT: 'Bird' and 'Guernica' shaped stainless steel bearing, external corner tie and re-entrant corner post
CENTRE: External view of tower top showing 'halos' supporting maintenance cradles and glazing support arm
BELOW: Tension springs at base of lift tower and standard wind tie

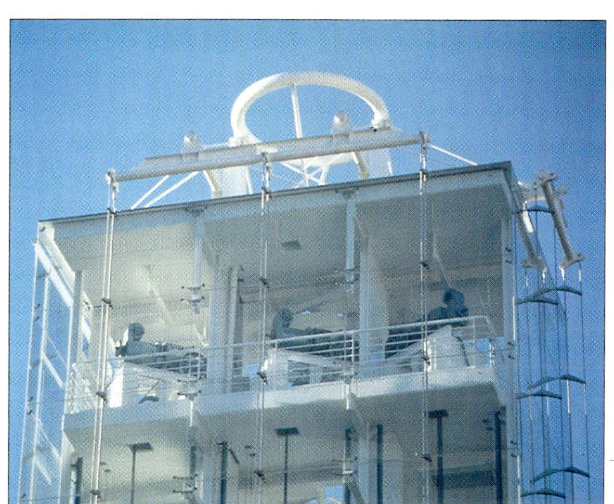

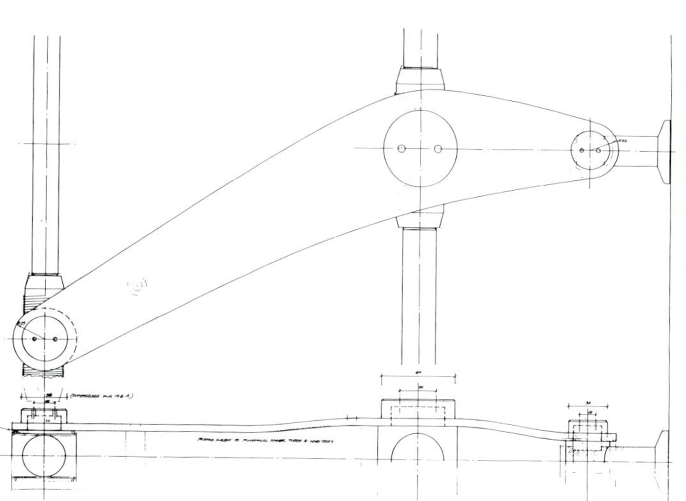

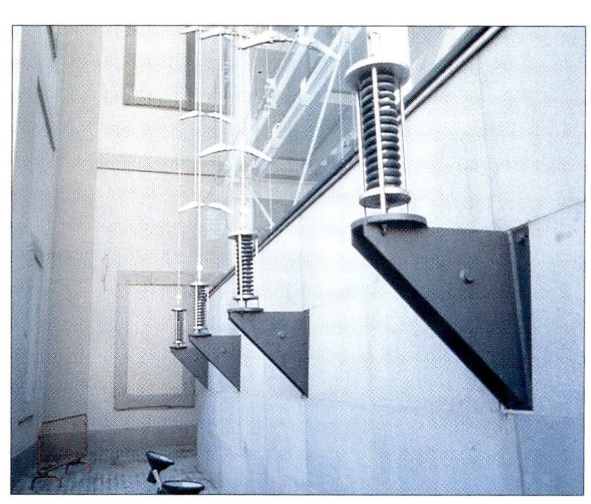

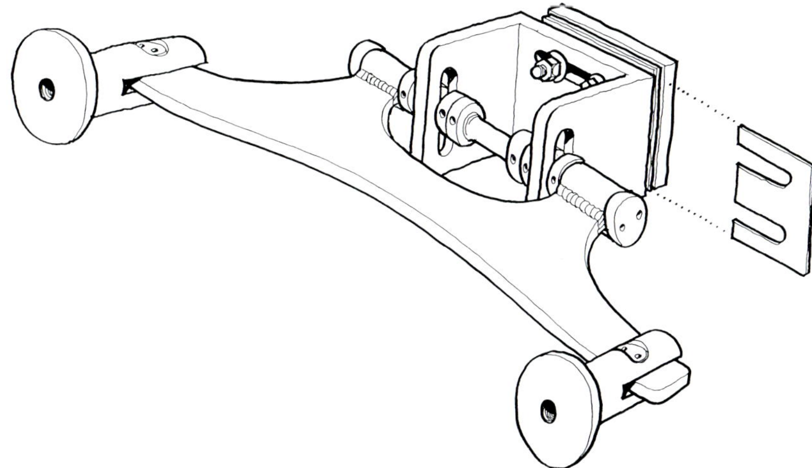

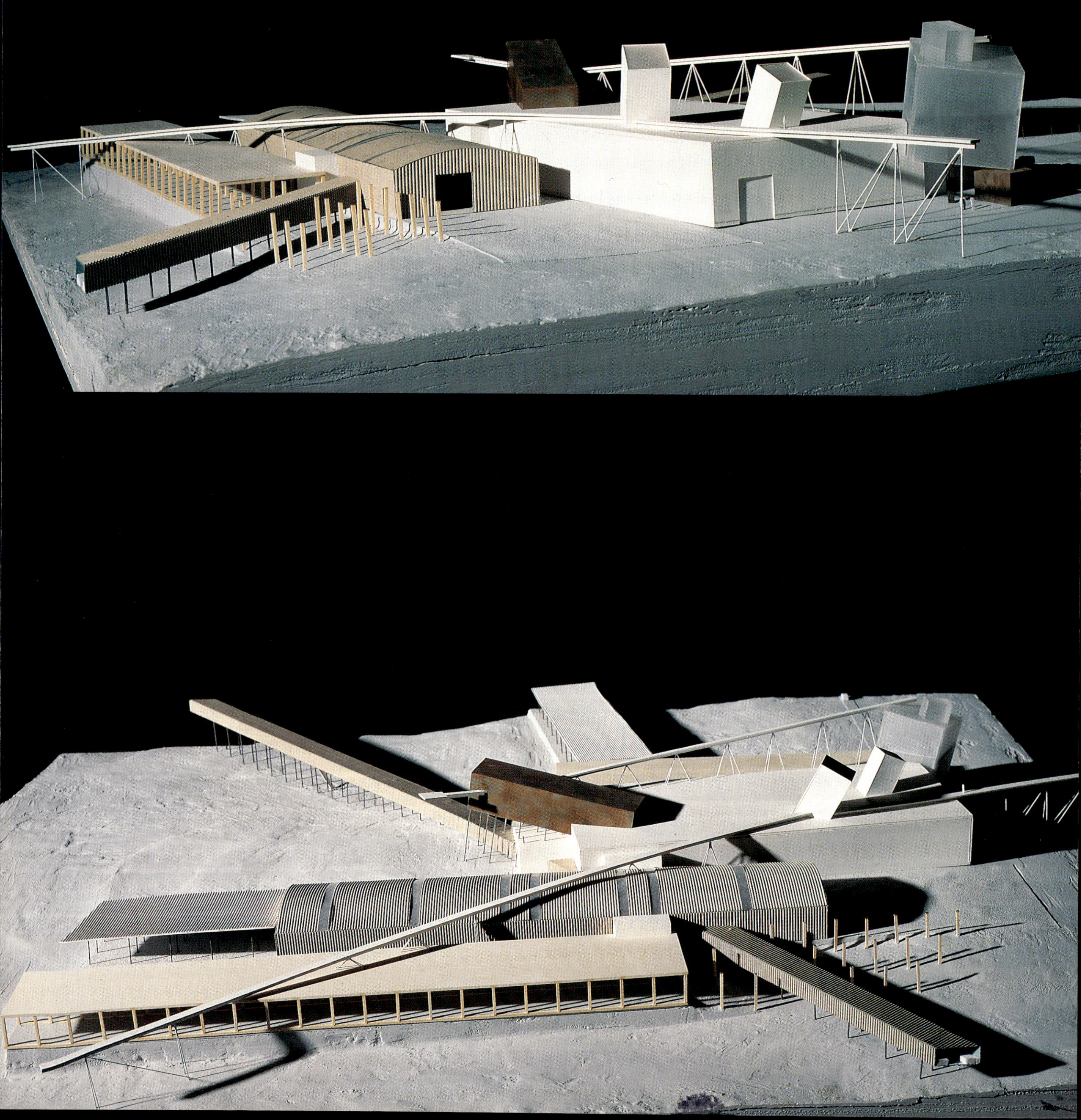

WOLF PRIX, COOP HIMMELBLAU

AN ARCHITECTURAL DESIGN INTERVIEW

Wolf Prix, who participated in the New Museology Symposium at the Royal Academy, discusses his firm's design concepts with Vivian Constantinopoulos. We illustrate the interview with images of Coop Himmelblau's new project, the 20,000 square metre studio for the artist Anselm Kiefer in Buchen, Germany.

– What was the climate in Vienna in 1968, when you began your practice with Helmut Swiczinsky, and the background which made you decide to begin the Coop?

Actually we started exactly in May 68 but nothing was happening in Vienna at the time. One of the major issues of Himmelblau is that we never looked closely to the Viennese tradition, politics or architecture. We always work to go beyond the Vienna borderline. However, we didn't look towards Eastern Europe – Prague or Budapest for example – as many others, poets for instance, were doing at that former time. We were always more interested in what was going on in the West – Paris, London, Los Angeles, New York. 1968 was really the time that architecture exploded, and we decided to form a team, at the same time as a lot of architectural and artistic groups were starting all over the world as well as Vienna. A role model for our name was the rock 'n' roll groups of that period; so rather than calling ourselves 'Prix and Swiczinsky' we decided to give ourselves a group name.

– It's interesting that you say that everything was exploding at the time because you have mentioned that you freeze a moment in your architecture, so that you capture something. Given that you are a 'cooperative' and work in a team, I wonder how you synthesise this 'moment'.

Well, I would also use the term imploding. This method of a cooperative can be an advantage if you use it properly because it's not so important which idea is from whom, but rather the importance lies in getting the project complex and working. So it's not a fight between two people but rather a play where we are very interested in exploring each other's argument. Therefore the project becomes more complex as it continues as there are two personalities putting things into it. It's not only a line but also a plane. This does not mean that the process becomes aggressive; but sometimes old structures are in our way, and, in order to create new space, the old has to be destroyed, erased, taken away.

– When you begin a project, how do you conceptualise spatial consequences of the finished work?

I think I should explain what is behind the whole concept. Firstly, we do not design spaces as the foreground of our work. This is not what is in question in our work; rather it is to design the imprint of the space, the *emotional* imprint of the space. Later, it becomes exciting to actually create that space, whereas initially it is to build the imprint of the space: what we call the emotional psychogram of the building. We can draw parallels here with Cubism where Braque and Picasso explored how to achieve three dimensions on a two-dimensional area. What we try to do is to go from two dimensions onto three. We think that architecture will be the art of the next decade because only art is capable of catching the complexity of the world around us. So we have to get rid of an additional way of thinking and seeing, and develop new methods of designing in order to achieve this. And this is to *mirror* what is around us rather than being a teacher, dictating one's point of view. We call our architecture 'Open Architecture' which means that there should be freedom in the work. This is not neutral work, but work that has a confidence in itself, with differentiating spaces within it due to that emotional imprint. We have developed a very specific design method which allows us to explore complexity more fully. It's not a frozen thing but rather a cut through life – like cutting through a cable with many different wires within it – where there is tension, ambivalence, aggression and friendship: a complex structure.

– Your work appears to be very expressionistic and spontaneous. How do you see the other part of the architectural enterprise which is involvement of the user. How do you allow for the spontaneity of the user?

We use our subconscious when designing in order to exclude as many things as possible at the very first moment. When we get the feeling that something is right and it begins to hold together – which I should stress is not a rational decision but an emotional one – it becomes easy to organise all the elements of architecture such as structure, function, programme, materials, etc. Of course, you have to feed the computer which is your brain. . .

– But also in your subconscious, as you say, there must be the client.

We communicate a lot with our clients, but never about spaces; we would rather talk to them about their emotional needs, what they feel about light, sun, colour, etc. This gives us the chance not to deal with architecture at the very first, conceptual stage. Of course, we sometimes have arguments with the client, and there are certain things which we refuse to work on – prisons, bunkers etc.

– I am interested in how you, as architects, control the effects of your design.

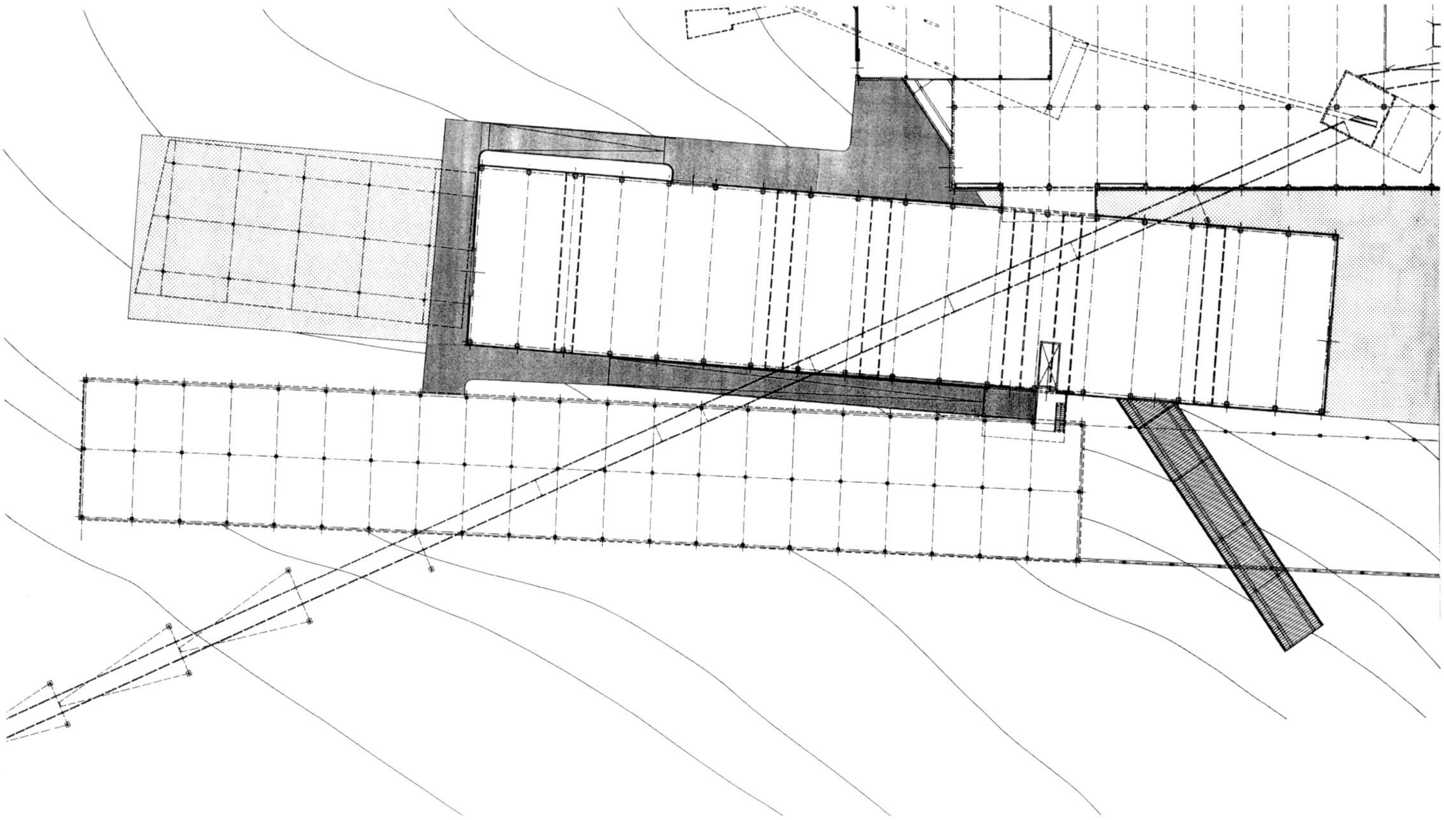

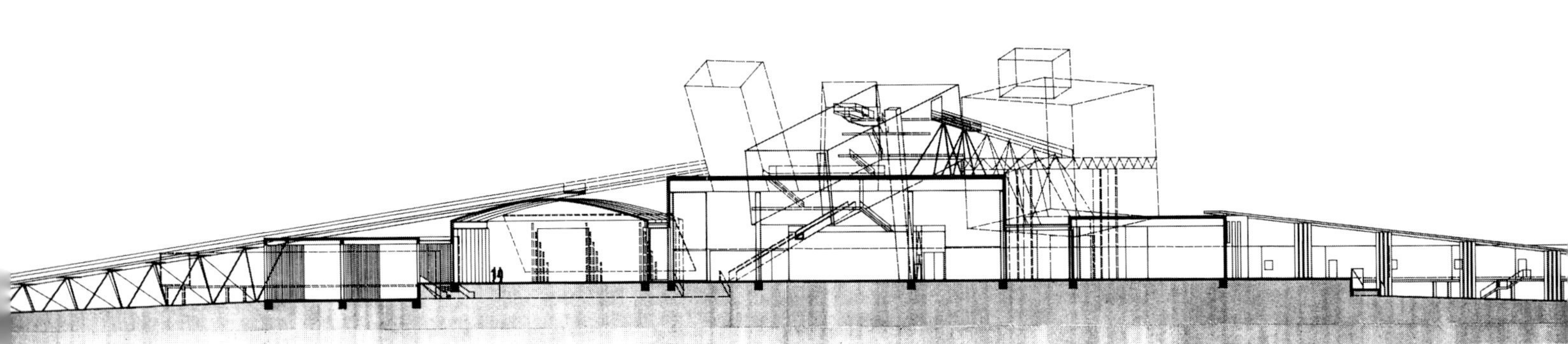

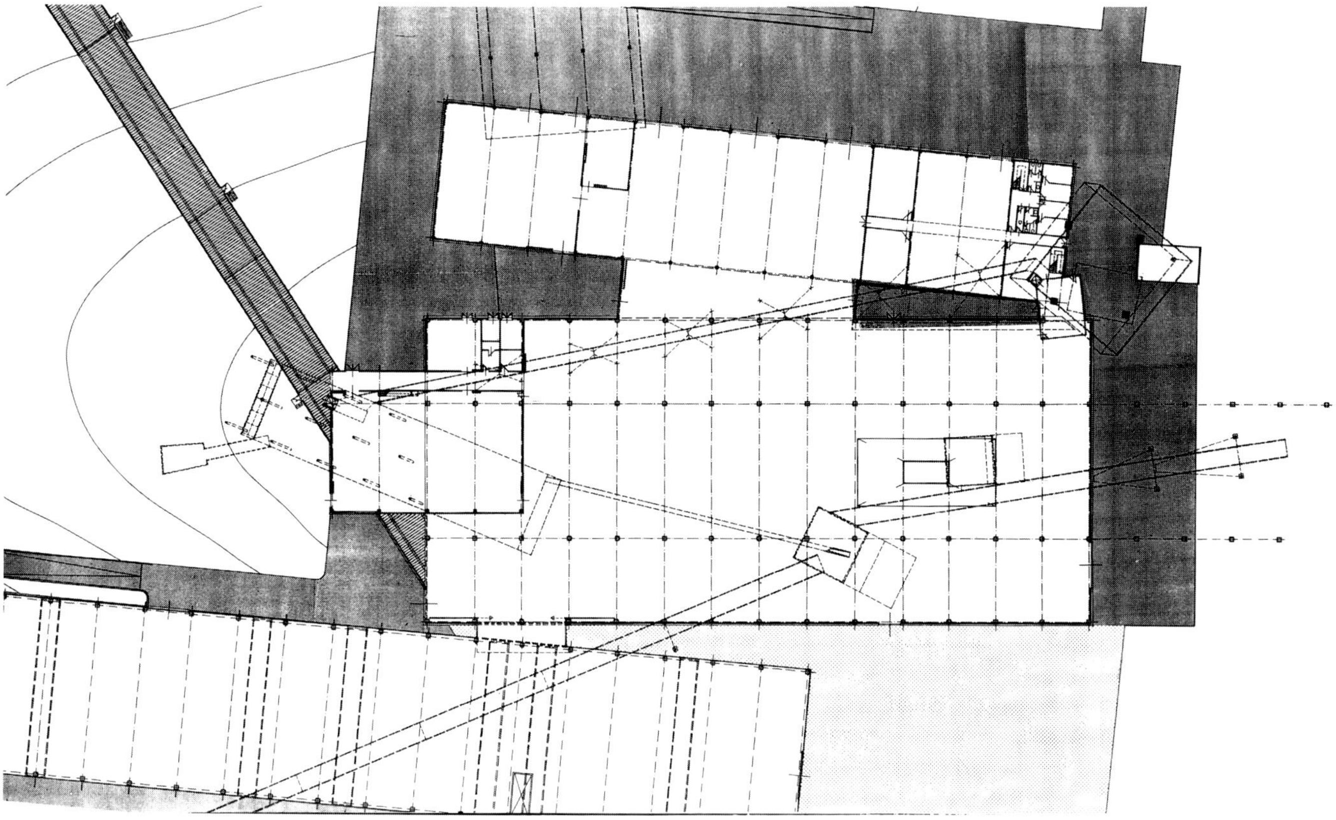

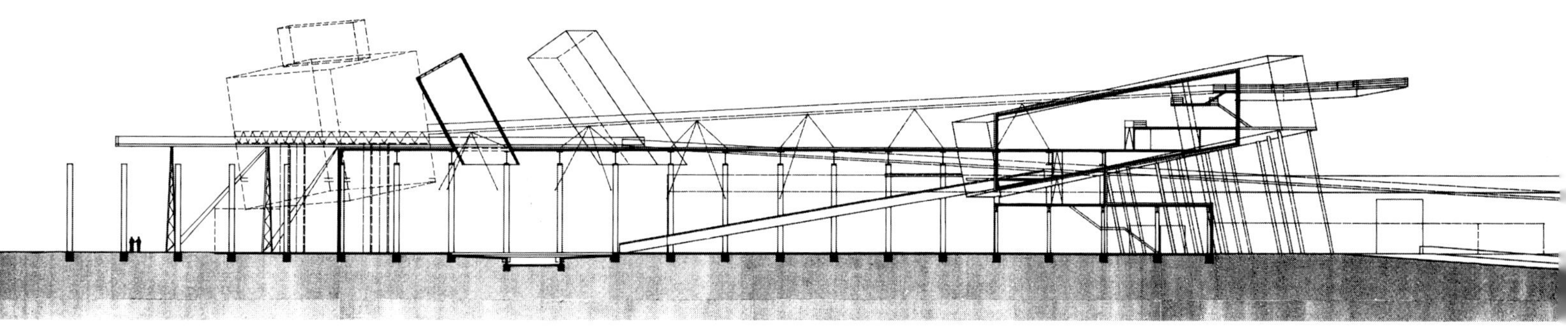

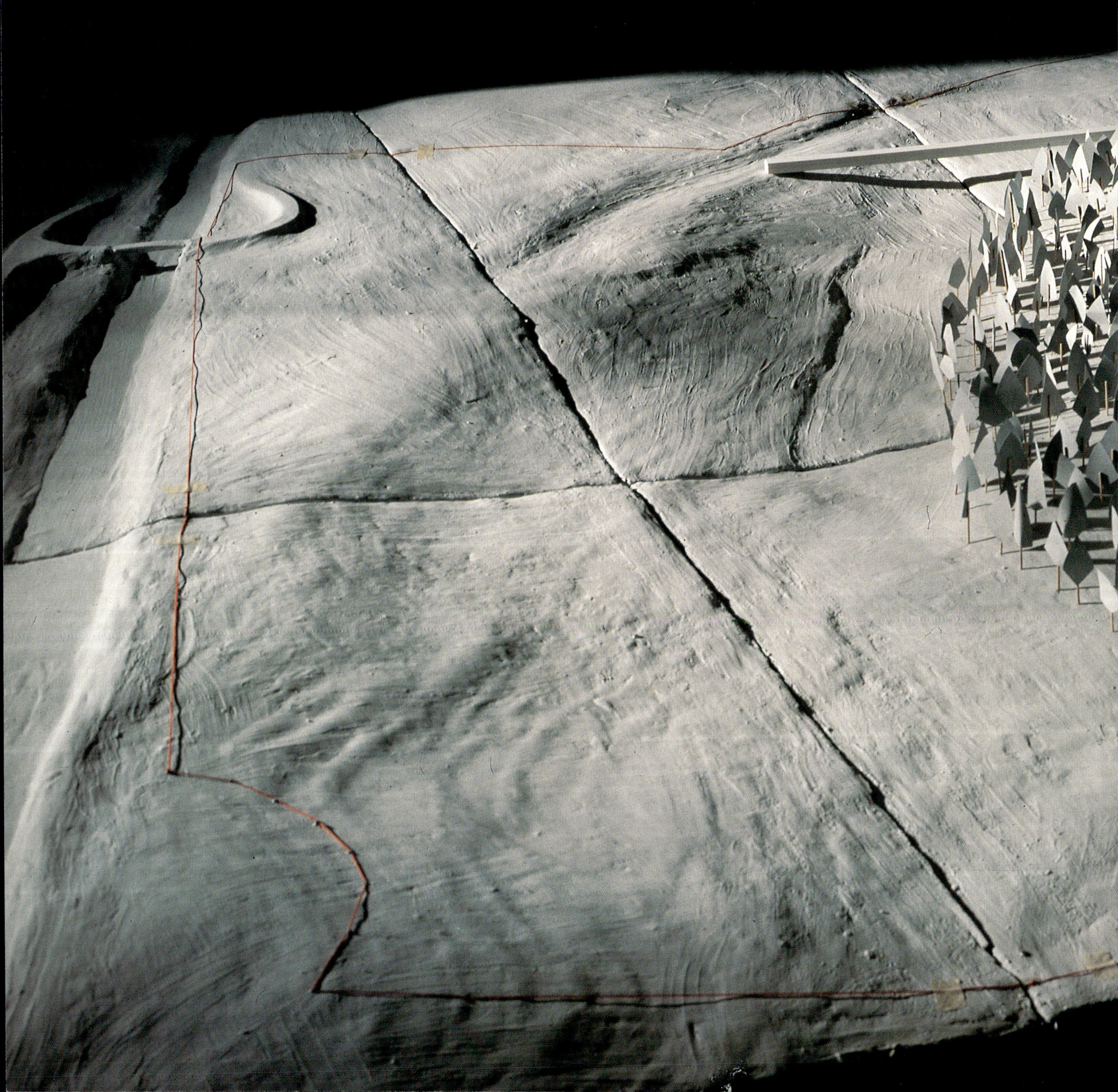

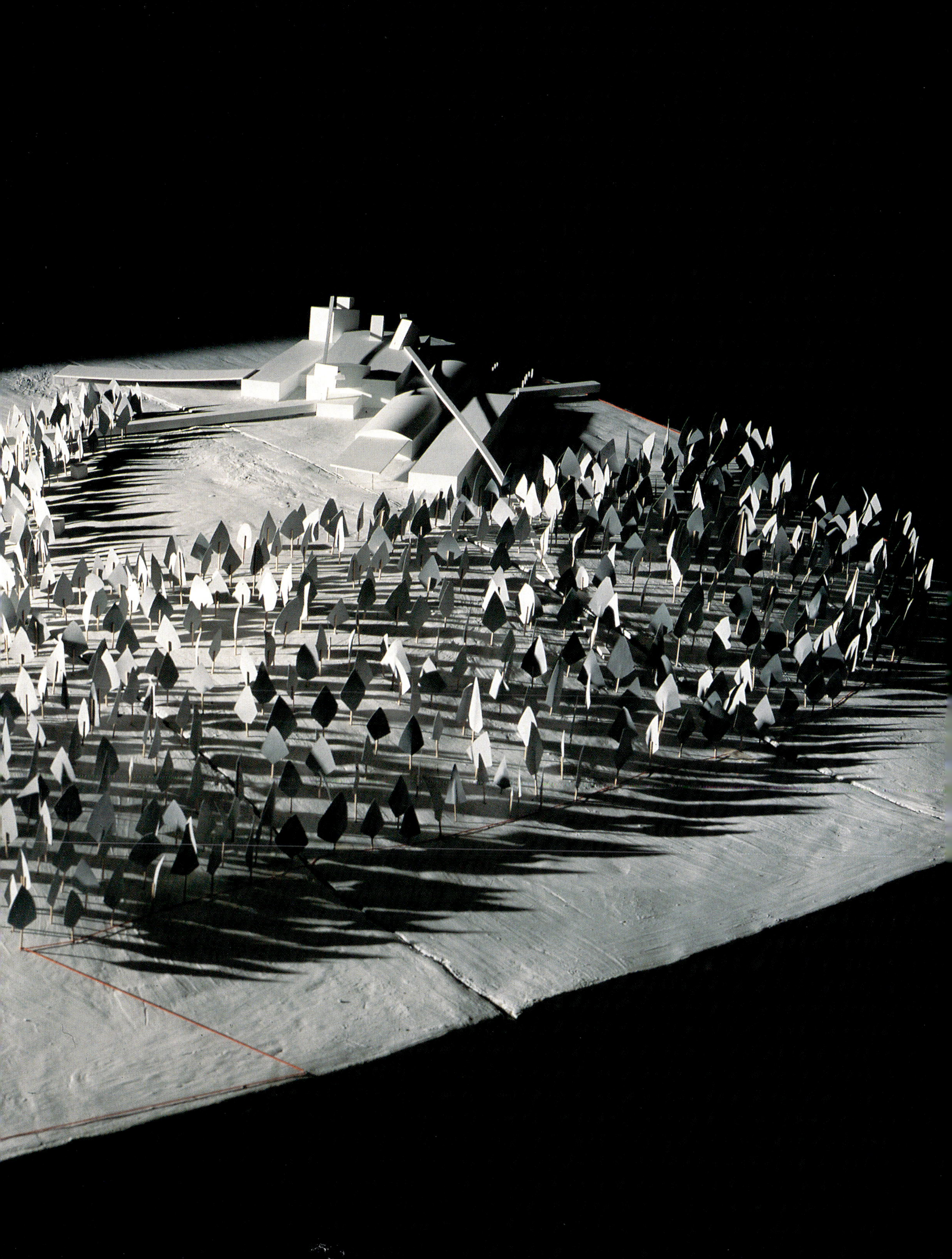

We are not afraid of *not* controlling the effects of our architecture.

–Yes, but if you don't mind not controlling don't you think that the architecture is not seen through? Perhaps the object is forgotten, and with that the initial aims of the architecture: how the user is going to exist in the building.

This is not the main issue in architecture. I think that if you create an exciting, emotional environment the client will take it and be touched by it. So he is touched by the light, by the surfaces and spaces. The doubt that one may feel on looking at the model is because one can't imagine how the finished product will work.

– At the New Museology Forum you were talking about the studio you are designing for Anselm Kiefer. Despite the fact that I have found that you talk about your architecture in a very subjective way, with Kiefer you seem to be designing very closely with him. Indeed, he seems very specific about what he wants.

He is, let's say, able to play in the team. We took his line – that which he had created as an initial conception of the studio space – and from this developed other ideas. We have had very open discussions with the artist, sometimes we can convince him that it is a better idea to continue something in one, rather than in another way, and we can quickly come to a final decision. I must add, however, that this is a particularly unique project. Also, he knows our work and likes the materials we use, therefore it was okay for us to develop new materials in this project. We could be regarded as sort of specialists. We know how to deal with light for example as it is something that we have been concerned with for the past 20 years.

– Yes, but I am wondering whether the major part of the architectural experience – using the actual work – is outside your own design strategies since you pass your own, very personal, expression onto the client. That is not that you want to dictate an effect, but rather leave your work up to another.

This depends on the project and who is going to be the user of the building, whether it be a family or the theatre-going public. I feel that the more people are around you, then the more you have to decide what you want to do.

– Does it then become more subjective and/or more controlled?

I must say here that it is not a shame to make 'subjective' architecture and I feel that it is impossible *not* to make subjective architecture. What we try to create is a variety of differentiated spaces, like landscapes. This way, the user is able, immediately or eventually, to find something he wants to have within the whole building. Comparing this to a landscape, you can say that in a landscape you can find both desert and mountains, but what we try to do is create a lake as well.

We do not, for instance, design furniture because we want to user to take a grip on the space. Here, of course, I am talking about residential projects, but, say, in a theatre where there are a variety of users and plays the building is used for, the same idea applies: namely that the work has to have an open system and an open concept.

– I see your architectural technique as being based on the abstraction of the body, with you using the body in a diagrammatic and expressionistic way – as lines in space.

This procedure took us ten years to develop. Around 1975, when we first began doing this, we did objects, sculptures and environments for museums. We tried to intensify and shorten the actual moment of conception so as to get rid of circumstantial pressures and get right to the point. We did not know where this would lead, but we were concerned in dealing with the *moment*. We discussed projects for ages but without considering their consequences; getting the feeling of how objects or spaces transmit a feeling to others, and what the imprint of the feeling was. In order not to be led astray – not even by the graphics – we tried to develop a special design method excluding as much as possible. We have realised in the last few years or so that we talk less between ourselves and find that we describe things with body language, with our hands for instance, which are then drawn by the other. Our *own* bodies, therefore, started to be involved in architecture. In 1969 we used machines where body functions were translated into spatial signs; the heartbeat, for example, was translated into light and sound.

– But the body as you see it is precisely something that becomes translated*, and the architecture is about the body language but not* of *it. The real thing is consequently cut out as the work is about the real thing but not the thing itself.*

Yes, but I would say that our architecture is the most 'body' architecture in the world, except maybe Frank Gehry's. And I mean here that it is touchable, movable, that your body can feel exactly what is behind it, ie your body can feel our excitement as architects in building spaces. We do not exclude the body; this is extremely abstract. Perhaps someone like Eisenman or Libeskind excludes the body from architecture. I personally am excited by the materials used, by seeing and touching welding seams, which I feel to be in contradiction to what you are saying about our exclusion of the body.

– I do not disagree that you draw from the natural, the physical, the immediate and vital, but it seems to me that this is located and mapped out, and then becomes a series of abstract lines between points.

Yes, I agree, it disappears. But it becomes real when the space is built. I would say that the *feeling* returns when the space is built and when you step into it. This is very important.

If you were to ask me how we design I would not tell you, and it's not necessary to tell you. It is just to give an explanation, and one of many at that. One explanation is that we are developing completely new concepts, therefore exploring where what we are doing now could lead to and, as a consequence of this, we do other things. Our procedures come in waves: thoughts are developed, cut off, fall and rise again – they *move*.

To dictate would be a most scientific way of doing architecture. Po-Mo architects dictate in the way that you are suggesting. I feel that there are different ways of looking at architecture. Compare this to a rock concert where there are different musicians in the band playing different instruments: playing the music is so different from your feelings which are receiving it. On top of that there are 250,000 people at the concert experiencing different feelings; but basically it is a good feeling. Similarly in our architecture I would say that there is a good feeling, a good vibration. I believe that the more fun we have designing a building, the more the people who use it will themselves enjoy it. So, everyone is right but nothing is correct. . .

The complexity we work towards is that of joints between function, programme, structure, forces, spaces, light for example; you can't isolate light from the rest of our work; you can't take away a piece of the structure as the building would break down; you can't take away a programme as this would change the whole thing. However, I feel that open architecture, say, in our lawyer's rooftop office, means that the building could be changed into apartments immediately; and this is one of the goals of our architecture.

– One final question. You have said of contemporary architecture: 'the devastation of the city is transformed into fascinating landmarks of desolation.' You therefore talk about an unfriendly, urban and desolate environment, and yet your architecture (and your discussions of your work) is vital and immediate and enjoyable, that is, optimistic.

What we mean is we know well enough that people hate the city and yet they live in it. What we challenge and try to say is use your city, don't beautify it.

What we said above was specifically aimed at the complacency of Po-Mo architecture which tried to escape back into the former century, saying that a city has to be beautiful: don't touch anything as the old city is beautiful while the new structures are so ugly. We say: *use* it; do whatever you want to it but make sure you use it and identify the usage of the city with your own lifestyle. The time we said this was at the high point of medieval city-planning thinking, of Leon Krier for example, and a wrong romanticism, a 19th-century way of thinking which I feel to be the most dangerous century we have – let's not forget that two world wars arose from this century. We said don't believe this complacency and these beautifying issues; just use the city in whatever form it is. And using it means not being afraid of the city, not hating the city and consequently not hating yourself.

– But you want to change it.

Well, if we get a commission to do a house on a corner for instance and the brief says create new space, we have to erase what was there already. An issue that came up at the Museology Symposium was why should we replace the old with the new? This is precisely our issue: we say *replace* it, because every good architect has done exactly that.

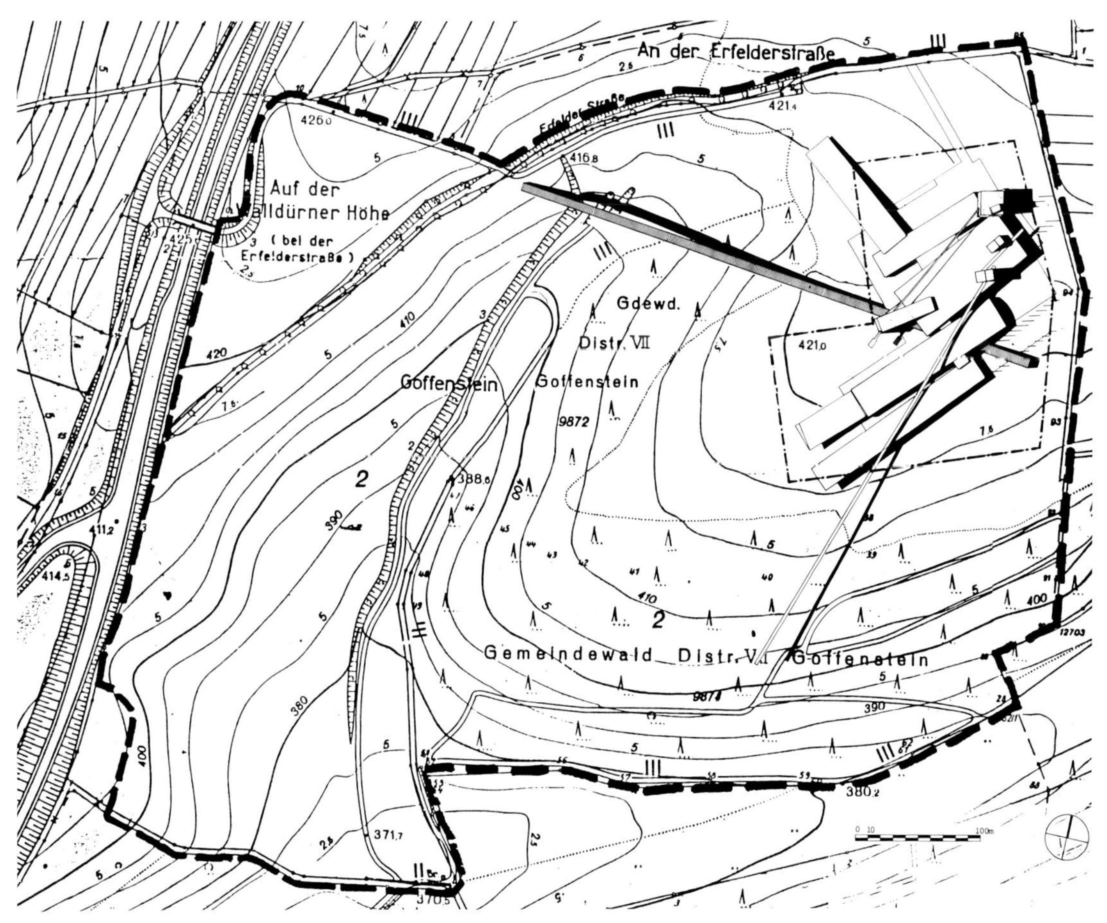

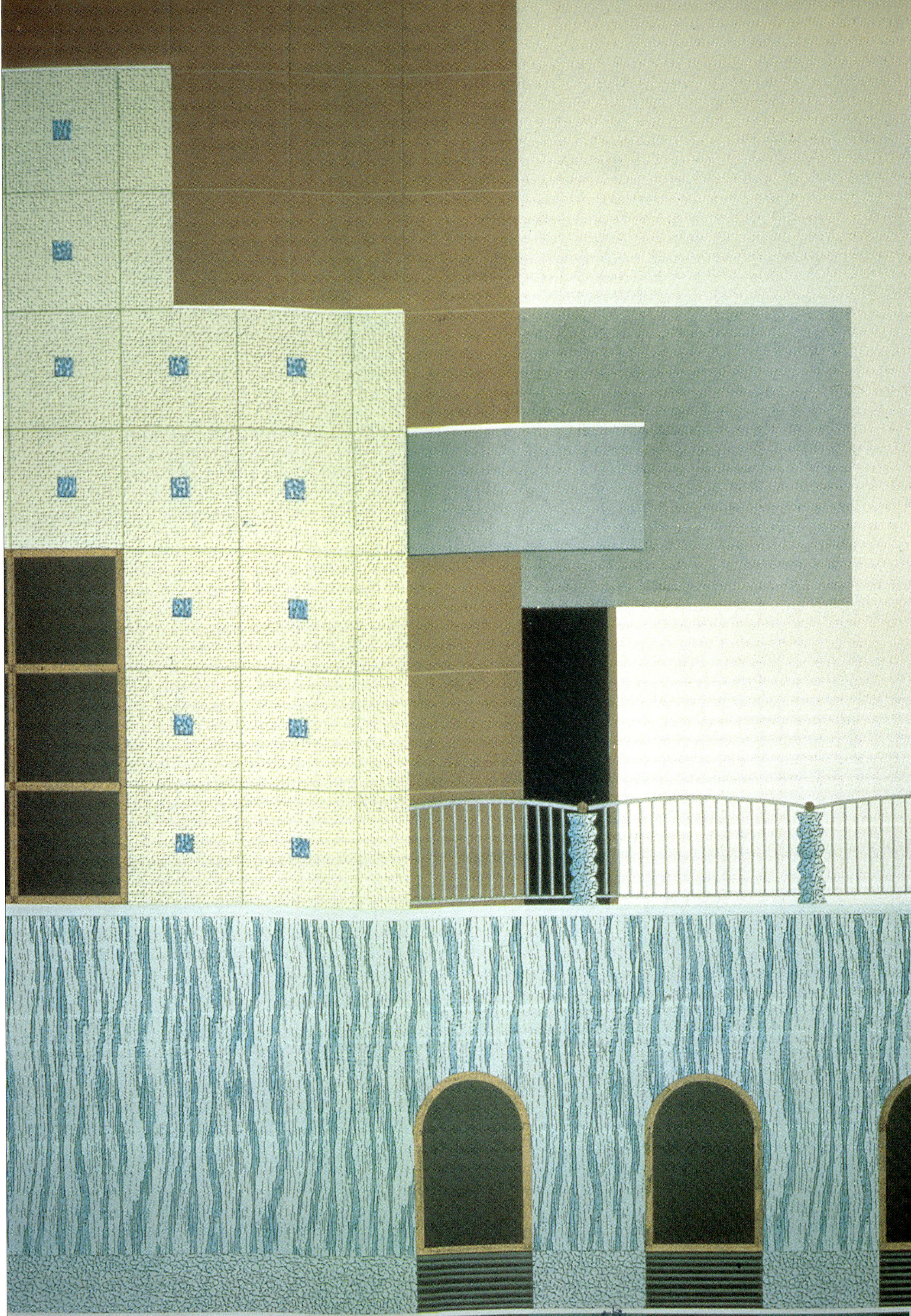

ALESSANDRO MENDINI
THE GRONINGER MUSEUM

The Groninger Museum developed out of the concept of 'artistic architecture'. Within that concept the actual architecture is intimately interconnected with other ingredients of the project such as painting, decoration, installations, new sculpture and diverse media of visual expression, but especially design. It does not adhere to the traditional idea of a synthesis of the arts. Rather, it is a mixture and exchange of methods among these disciplines, the intention being to achieve an 'object-phenomenon' with a high narrative complexity. There is no interruption between the building's self-museumisation and a living museumisation of the works exhibited in it. Thus the building will in itself be a system of museum works, while the exhibits integrate with and interpenetrate the architecture that receives and expresses them.

The appointed places for the exhibition of art today are manifold in their nature and structure – streets, gardens, fairs, galleries, private homes, churches, showrooms, department stores, amusement parks, temporary shows, periodical megashows, major itinerant exhibitions, etc. Among these the Museum seems to establish itself as the ideal home of art, as the clearest and most emblematic place, the symbol and synthesis of hope for art in the world.

And we refer to art as meditative entertainment, to art as a record and accumulation of experience, and certainly not to art as a necrophil depository of cultural power. The formula for a museum is the fruit of two reciprocally necessary projects of equal importance: the architectural project and the organisational one. In the case of Groninger the organisation is gifted and subjective, the museum being envisaged as invention and not as a neutral place. On the contrary, it is seen as the ideal place for a continual staging of artworks, with a particular sensitivity towards very young art of every type, to be sought in every corner of the anthropologically interesting world beyond the centres of gravity of official knowledge. The intended effect is intimate and introverted, but also happy and cheerful, domestic and gentle.

The architectural project treats the Groninger Museum as a possible urban utopia, as an ideal place abounding in surprises, an organic mental labyrinth that only indirectly demonstrates its courtly and didactic purposes. As an instrument appointed to 'create while making art', the museum cannot deny itself a mini-monumentality of its own; and as an instrument appointed to preserve it, the museum must respond to the needs of a mini-academy; it must be perfectly functional and scientific. To accomplish these various objectives the Groninger building – its most explicit feature being that it rests on water like a ship – has a symmetrical, ancient, sharply iconic and ritual plan, the fruit of its structuring by typological sectors. In its elevation it is transformed into a macro-object of design, a multi-textural sculptural and pictorial architecture whose aptitude for telling a story, for linguistic differences and self-representation is heightened by the work of guest architects: Michele de Lucchi, Philippe Starck, Frank Stella; as well as by Coop Himmelblau and Peter Eisenman, whose works turn the museum proper into a 'museum of life-size architectures'. The scenic rendering of this Object-Museum as an event plays therefore on two theories of interpenetration: between the principal visual disciplines treated as equal (as already mentioned), and between architectural genres treated as ambiguous (museum, house, theatre, church). On these bases the architecture is intended as art, and art as a spectacle of pure, political and metaphysical vision, as contemplative activity without any ideological message. The museum as 'total art' realises the utopia of man's highest spiritualisation and cosmic imaginary.

This outlook on the condition of architecture, on a grand temporal and humanistic scale, is seen as the problematical junction between academy and avant-garde, and it seeks its best solution through the most archetypal notions that man can refer to. Visitors to the Groninger museum island, after crossing the bridge, will find themselves unveiling an acropolis/secret forest, and will be induced to assume a utopian behaviour in it, the fruit of a hybrid chain of meanings amplified by the descriptive sequence of signs – an example of the eternal search for rebirth, for new attitudes and territories still unknown to man.

As regards the urban context, the new building is intended as a signal in a very important spot in the city. Situated on the axis between the station and the centre crossed by the canal, it is an emotively fundamental spot for the inhabitants, but is so lacking in urban identity that the presence of a new, calm but clearly visible, secure and characteristic feature is actually necessary to it. The pieces comprising the construction are: a bridge with two squares linking it to either side of the canal, with the feeling of a rampart somewhat redolent of the Enlightenment; the gilded tower, the pre-eminent volume of the whole museum, which exalts instead of hiding the storehouses containing the works of art, intended as 'treasure'; the sector that houses superimposed temporary exhibitions, modern art and a gallery of classical art in an elastic, uninterrupted sequence of strong and polychrome external expressiveness; the sector devoted to ancient ceramics and to regional archeology/history, which reflects its contents from the outside; the multipurpose central sector with entrance hall, theatre, library, cultural services for public and scholars, and administrative services.

On the outside, the architectural complex can be appreciated at two levels. From a distance the view is more synthetic and compact, whilst from close-up the

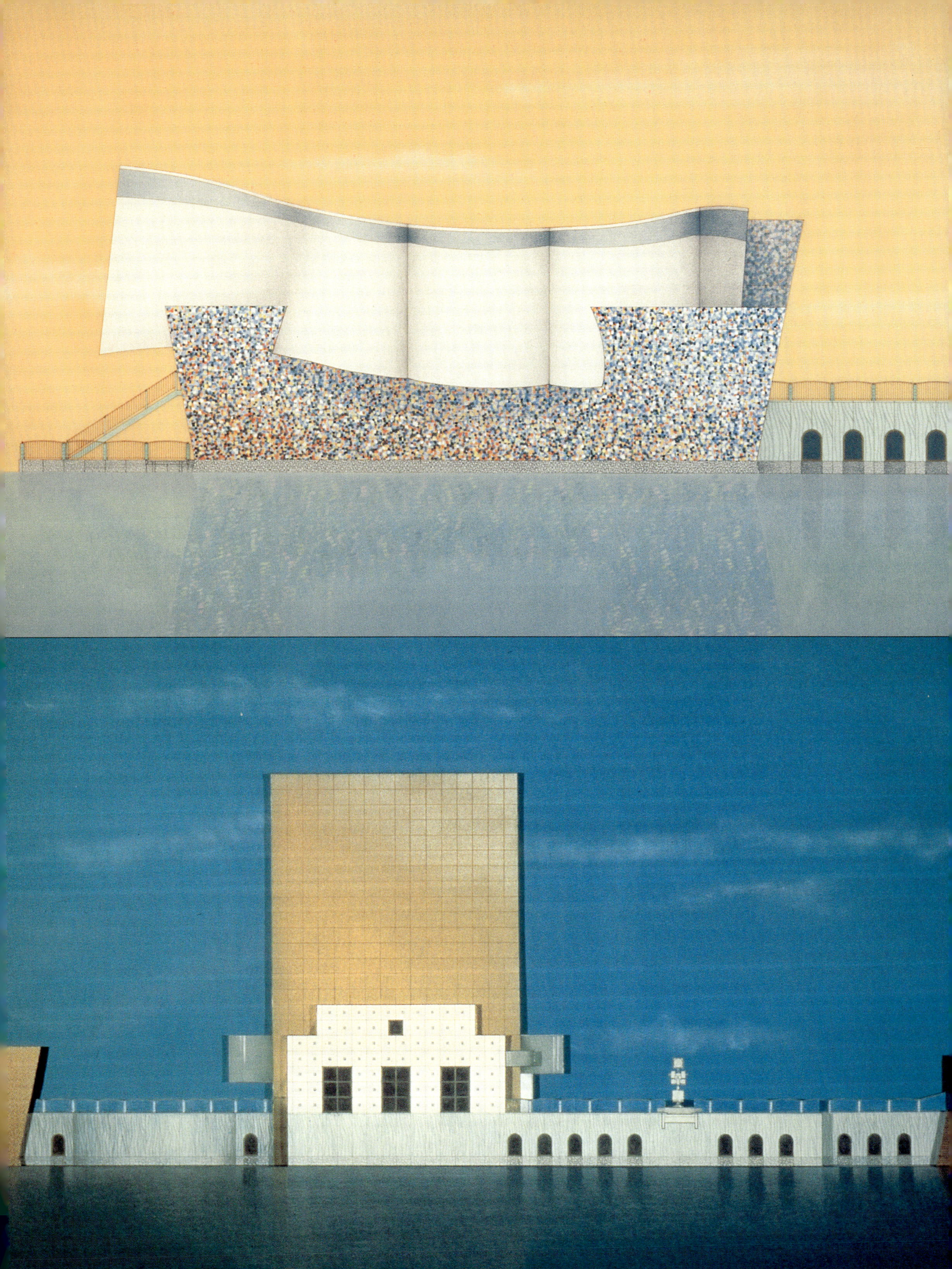

surfaces reveal occasionally out-of-scale textures, brightnesses and particular arabesques that enrich the details, while also lending a touch of evanescence to the ensemble, associated with the idea of a jewel, of a mirage and of floating. Often the materials and the elements used are those 'of design' and 'of sculpture' and bear no reference to the iconography of architecture. The materials and colours (pale blue, gold, silver, black, ochre, yellow, pink) are delicate but very diverse, used together in an unusual way reminiscent of cubism: golden laminate and polychrome silkscreen, cement with pasta-coloured modelled caissons, brick with a medieval feel, vacuum-shaped: aluminium panels, mosaic, bronze-type shutters, squares and landing-stages in ceramic and wood, iron balusters and concrete columns, cloths, alcoves, sculptural and pictorial elements, electronic panel writings to 'reverse' towards the city the museum's inner contents. The nocturnal illumination of the building heightens its effect of incorporeity, artistry and suspension.

From the museographic point of view, the standard room in the museum's contemporary art and temporary exhibition sectors is rigorously windowless and entirely equipped with stage lighting, so that scenes can be changed as and when required. The problems of the wall/painting, floor/sculpture, small room/installation relation have been reconsidered and re-framed from scratch: the standard room being conceived as a conceptual stereometry, an abstract space, a sensual environment of happiness and mystery, endowed with invisible technical systems. The floors are in coloured linoleum, and the walls are variable in colour, with works hung in rotation. This makes for a more theatrical display of exhibits, with infinite possibilities of presentation, and with a study of the dimensions of individuality and of the relations between rooms, intended to avoid physical and mental tiredness and obsessive repetition.

The three sectors entrusted to the guest architects in their turn respond to these same criteria, but on the basis of their own interpretations, and of the necessity to show the permanent collections. Hence Frank Stella's classical art gallery sees for the first time the exhibition of classical painting by a great modern painter; the east/west ancient ceramics sector by Philippe Starck brings into a rarefied and emblematic climate the physiological issues and the magic of the minor arts; the regional archeology/history sector by Michele de Lucchi expresses in a sequence of 'three dimensional squares' the spiral of history, running backwards as far as prehistory.

The Groninger Museum is not a specialised museum, but rather, its sectors are each characterised to the extent of requiring precise and diverse specialisations in themselves. In a sense, it is a museum made of various smaller museums. In reality, therefore, it is the possible example, the simplification, of a 'universal museum', of the general formula for an imaginary place in which to show and to reinvent all knowledge. As such, the ambition of the Groninger project is to achieve a universal sociability. It proposes this ambition through three ideals: that of the cosmos intended as an aesthetic totality, that of artistic creativity as the prerogative of all men, and that of asserting itself as an anti-monument, as a message against cultural terrorism.

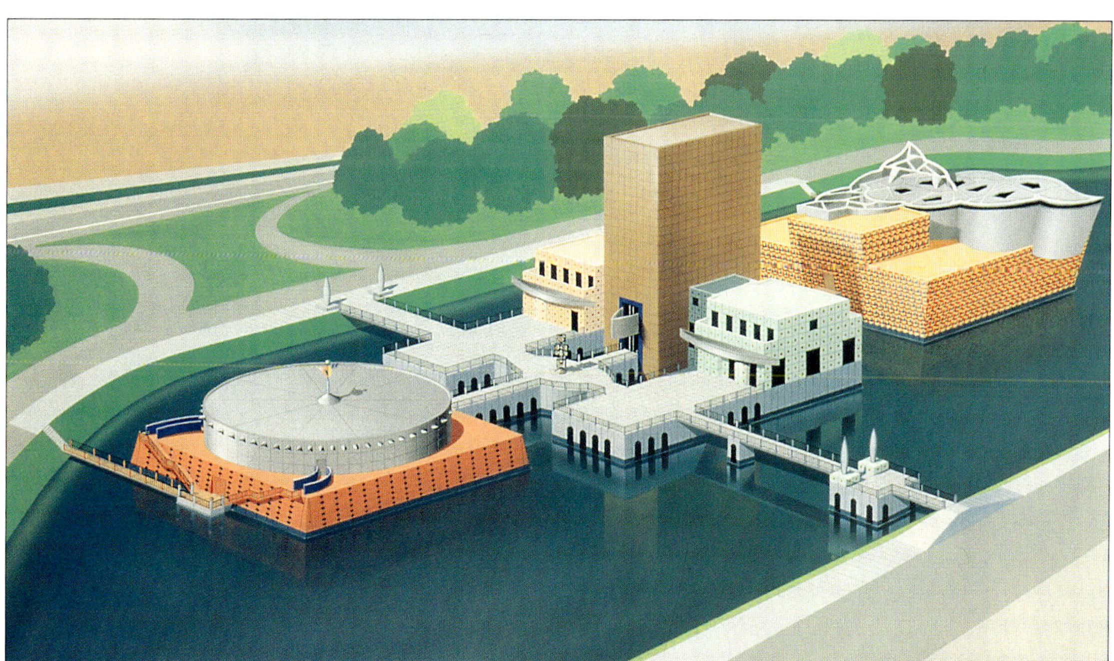

PREVIOUS PAGE: Elevational detail
OPPOSITE, ABOVE: Elevation of central galleries; BELOW: Elevation of museum
ABOVE: Aerial view

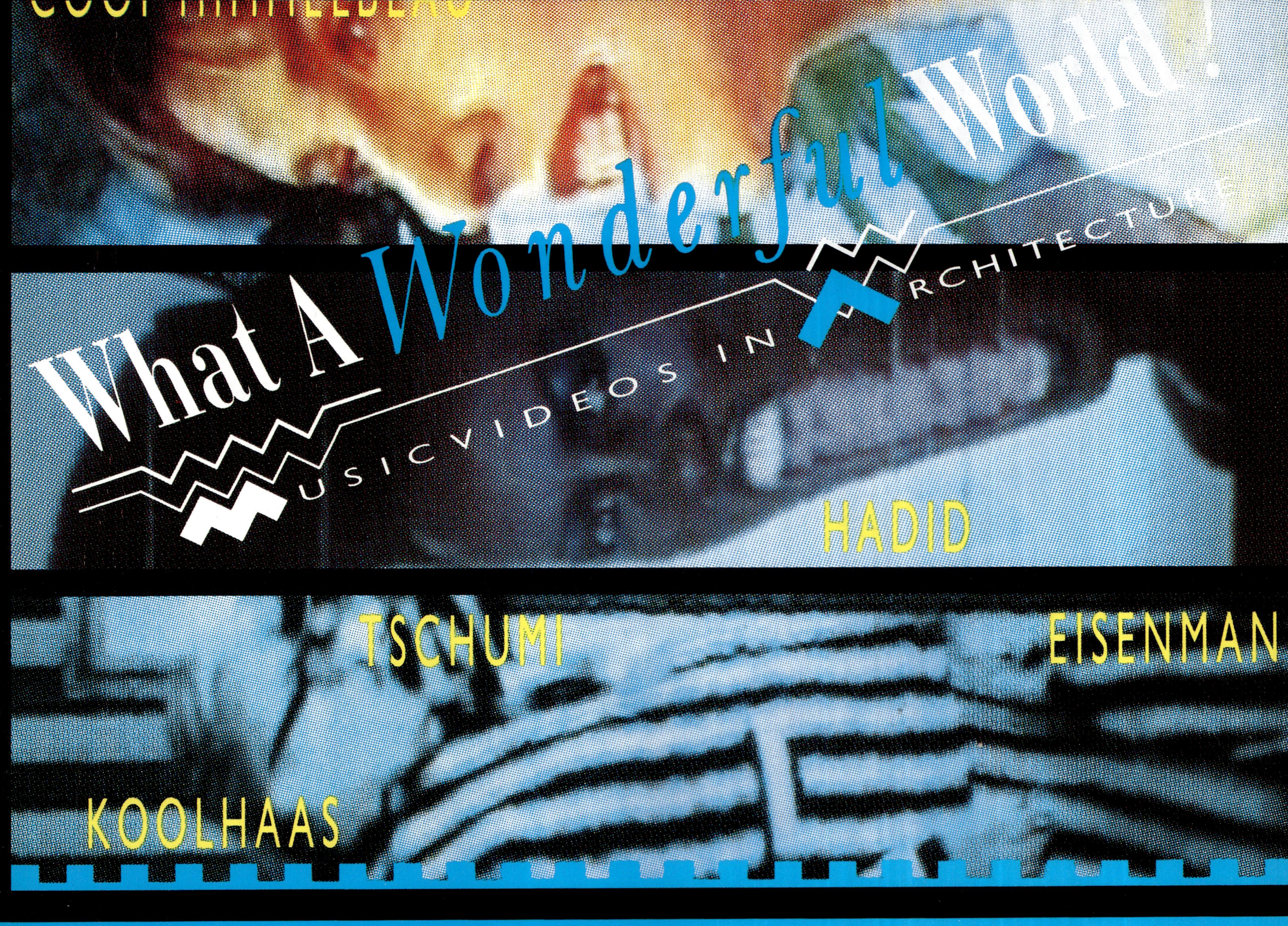
What A Wonderful World!
MUSICVIDEOS IN ARCHITECTURE
HADID
TSCHUMI
EISENMAN
KOOLHAAS
ARCHITECTURE

WHAT A WONDERFUL WORLD
MUSIC VIDEOS IN ARCHITECTURE

The project 'What a Wonderful World' is a collaboration between the Groninger Museum and the Department of City Planning in which an extensive selection of music videos will be shown in five specially designed pavilions. The project was an attempt to work at the image of the city and the quality of public places in an experimental fashion, free from the restrictions of immediate usefulness.

The music video is a relatively young visual category which consists of a blend between image and sound, and which is produced by record companies in order to sell their projects. It is a form of advertising, in which a certain idea, emotion or story is conveyed within four minutes. The short time in which this has to take place requires a special way of selecting and cutting.

After it had been decided that the music video would be the central issue of the manifestation, the question arose in what manner this could best be done. We wanted, in any case, a presentation that would be radically different from ordinary circumstances at home.

The architects of 'What a Wonderful World' were expected to take a clear position on the relationship between form and function. During the manifestation, the pavilions will be used for the presentation of music videos. Each pavilion must be able to accommodate a maximum of 30 to 40 people, who can jointly experience the music videos in a way that is in line with their nature: quickly and casually.

The main purpose in the selection of the architects was to stimulate a more creative approach towards the city, whereby the emphasis would be on greater attention to usability and visual quality. In addition, we wanted to invite a number of architects with mutual affinities, so that a picture of the present developments in architecture would emerge. These assumptions eventually led to the choice of Coop Himmelblau, Peter Eisenman, Zaha M Hadid, Rem Koolhaas and Bernard Tschumi; five architects who were already concerned about the relationship between architecture and the media.

The pavilions, at five locations in the centre of Groningen, represent a thorough disruption of the established relations between architecture, visual art and the city. The museum seems to branch off spatially, dissolving into the urban area. The form and function of the pavilions are not only illustrative of the museum's escape from the established order of the city. The reverse is happening as well: the city is making a subtle re-entry into the museum. City and museum seem to merge into one another, sometimes running synchronously, only to branch off again in the same way as image and sound do in the music video. It is almost self-evident that, for the architectonic realisation of this project, the organisers have engaged only architects who have already spent some time looking for a new sound in architecture, a different tonality which ignores the familiar articulation between composition and programme.

The consequence of this is that in some pavilions the architecture in the physical sense gives up its resistance, stops being only entourage, and exchanges its role of setting for an active intervention in the motions of image and sound, so that it becomes disconcertingly amorphous, a purely dynamic moment in the city.

The pavilions leave all the traditional categories of architecture, the commitment to location, differences between interior and exterior, far behind. Rather, they are miniscule power stations, in which image and sound enter into chemical reaction at regular intervals; where minor explosions take place turning the perturbing aspect of architecture into a permanent phenomenon in the city.

A new museum is more than a temple bearing witness to piled-up treasures in an edifying way, thus confirming established opinions. Today's museum demands, challenges and stirs. And such a museum wants more. If possible, it will also revitalise a languishing neighbourhood, increase touristic allure, enhance the business climate and, with architectural precision, it will mark a spot – in the case of Groningen, gate and square at the same time – that symbolises an urban development policy which is inclined to think in points rather than in lines, and in lines rather than in areas.

Such a museum has no alternative but to leave the beaten track. It has to compete with art – that is, as an institution it should be more than a vehicle, as a building it should enable architecture to make history.

Innumerable collectors – from Durand to Pevsner – have devoted their efforts to the ordering of the infinite number of items produced by architecture. Their catalogues substantiate the irrefutable history of confident and enduring types, classified according to function. A musuem is a museum, a theatre is a theatre, the stabilising principles have been written down and drawn, the line is firm.

However, everyday life could do without the purposeful building. Ships, factories, towers, theatres and living rooms are no less hospitable than deliberately designed museological accommodation. Theatre and film ignore the theatres and cinemas and perform in a museum, a shed, a train, on the street and in the harbour. A cinema that becomes car park, a rotunda that becomes sports centre, these are the transformations which disrupt the order of typological classification. Even more marginal are the pavilions, the temporary buildings, the movable property of history, presenting an amazing performance only to break up again, leaving nothing but an ineradicable impression. It is this deliberate transience that harbours the potential energy of each pavilion.

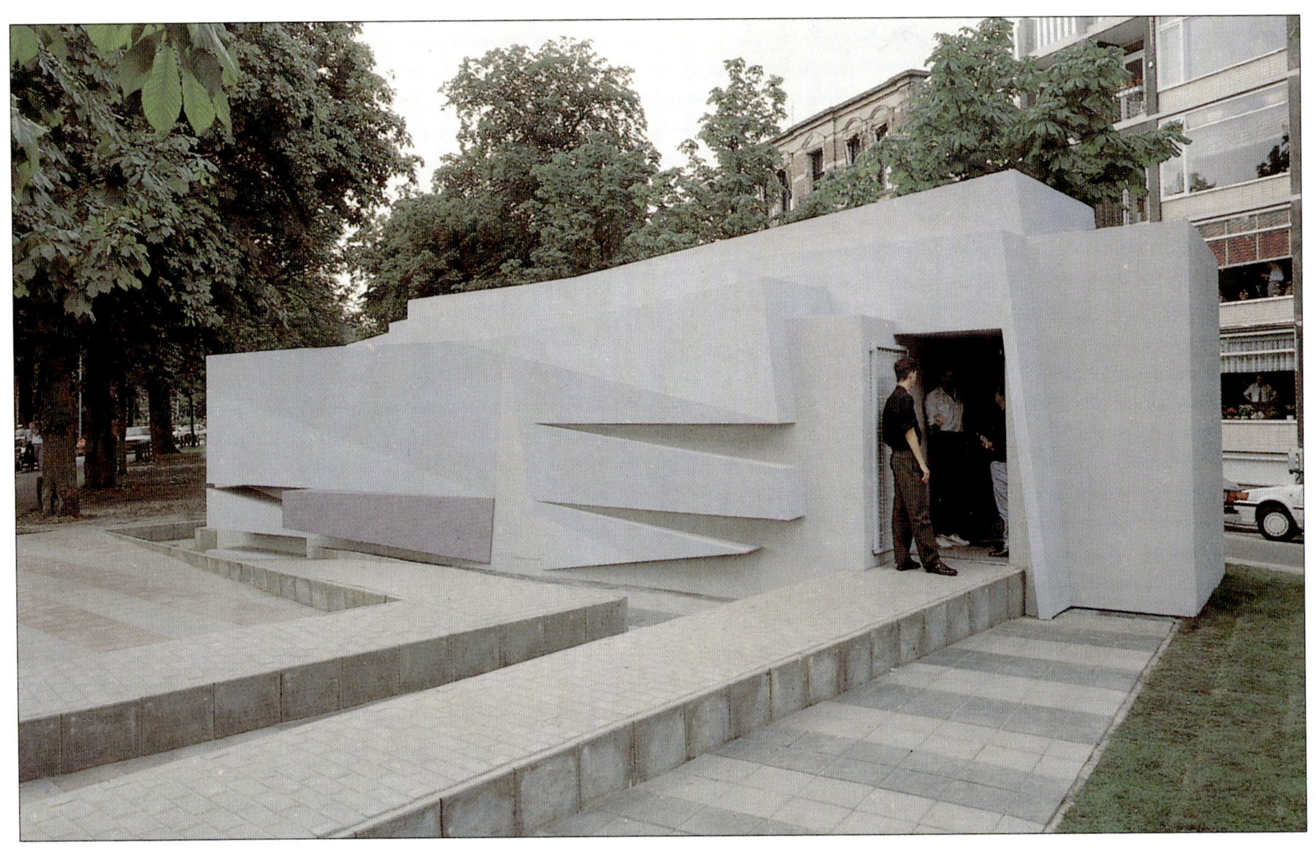

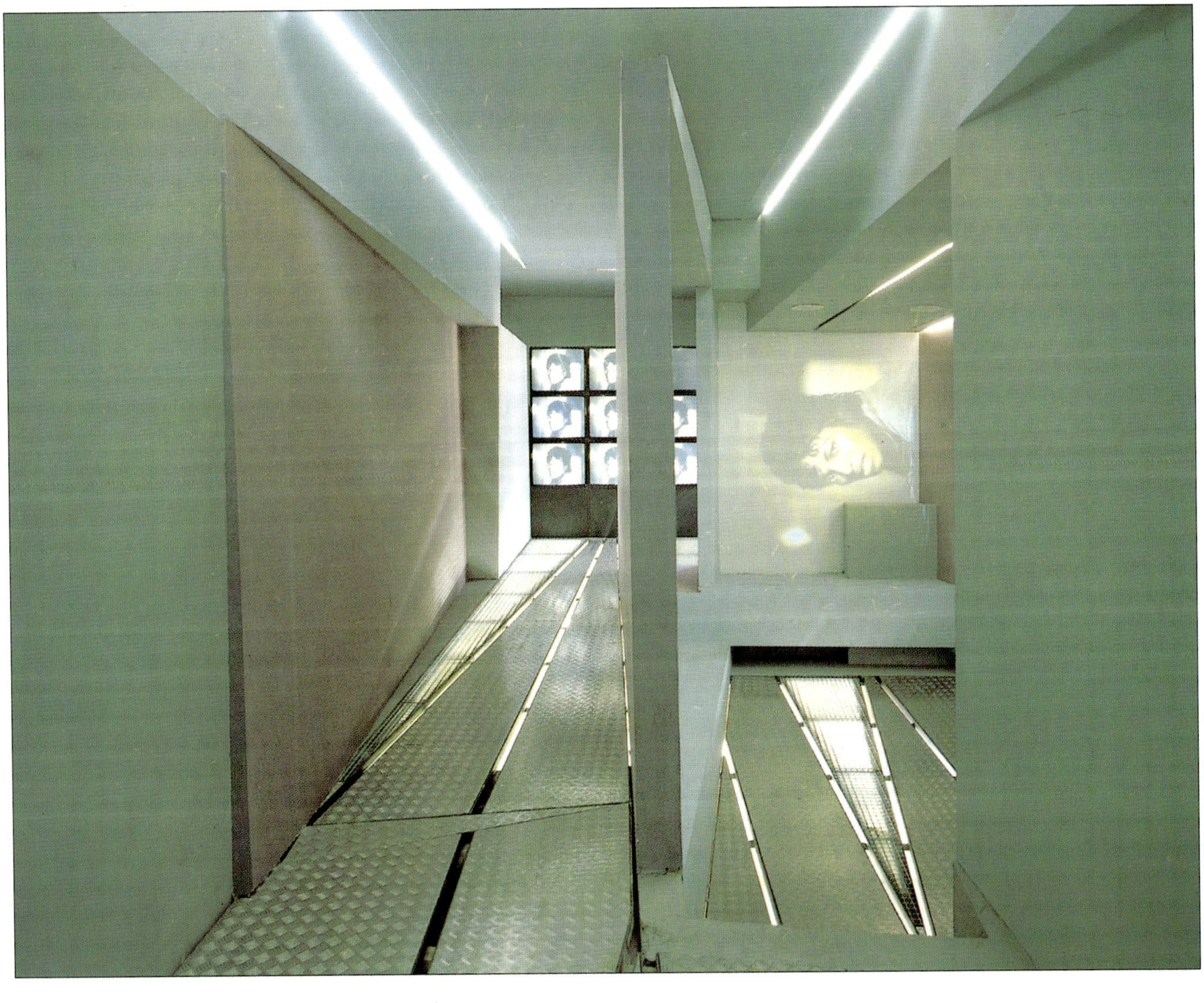

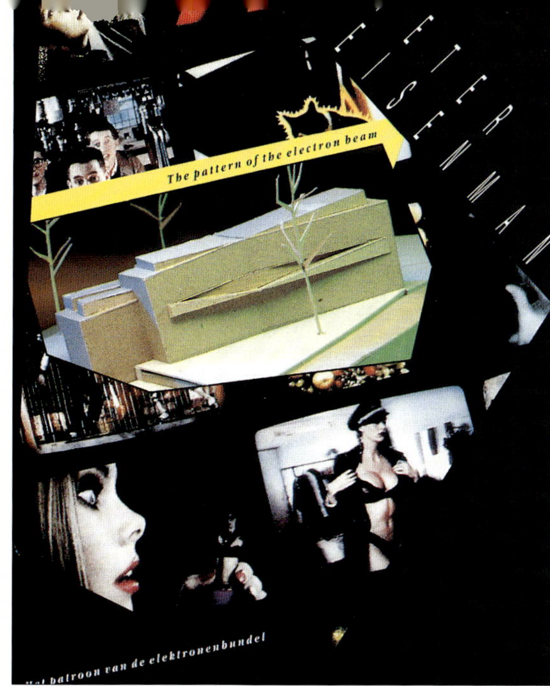

PETER EISENMAN Our project is based on the idea that the new video technology nurtured by the growing home video industry is revolutionising the notion of the moving image. The traditional notions of time and space have become suspended. Our pavilion marks the attempt to redefine the traditional relationship between three-dimensional artificial, man-made, space and architectural time through an immediate contrast with the experience of time and space in video movies.

The structure is based on an analysis of the way a video image is produced on a picture screen. An electron beam sweeps across a screen, moving from left to right, filling in an image point by point.

The visitor to this pavilion follows a path which is analogous to that of the scanning beam - he or she moves along the chevron path, and is constantly repositioned within space. Thus, the visitor becomes part of the medium itself, passing in front of viewing screens and continually crossing through images, shifting his or her position to form images in different ways. Though the pavilion provides neither a traditional auditorium nor a static point of orientation for the spectator, it does allude to the traditional auditorium in its sloping floors.

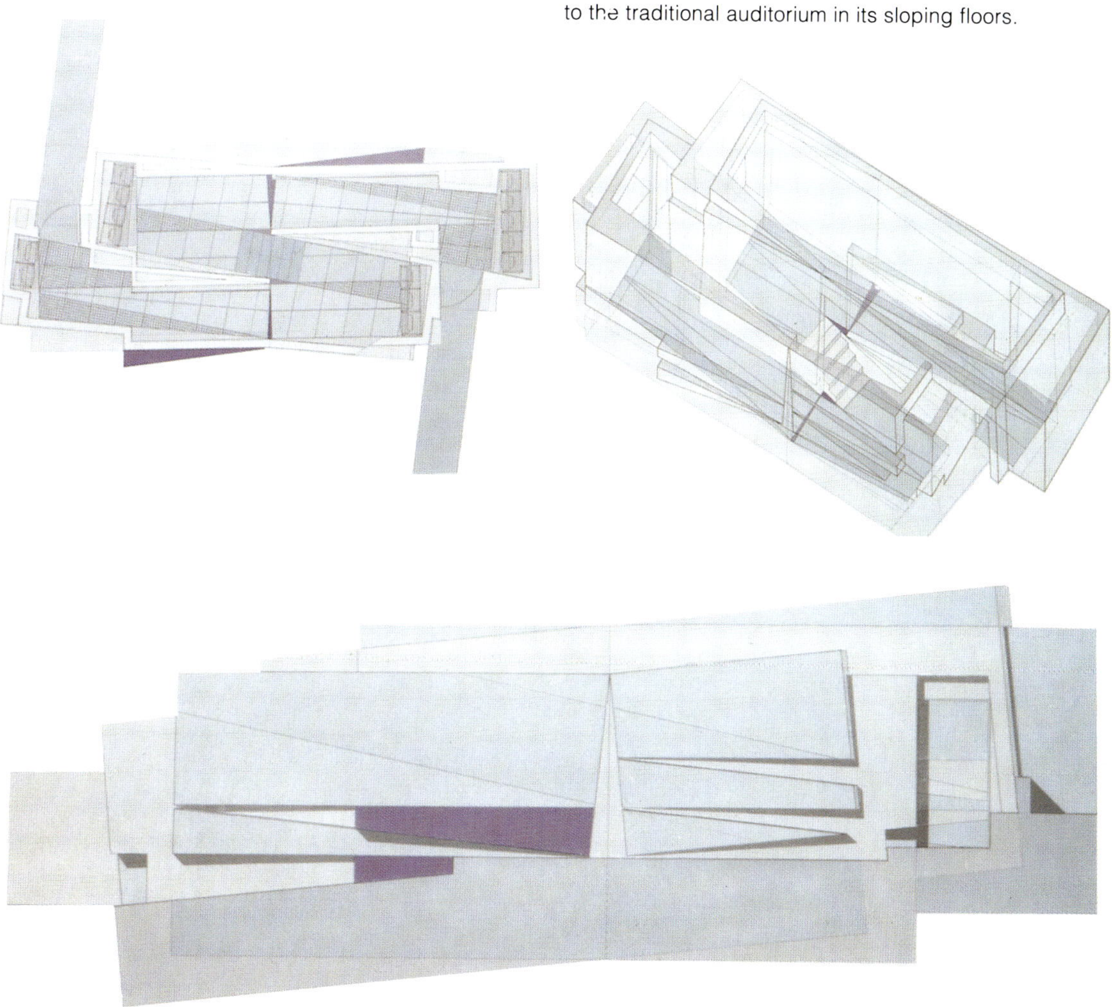

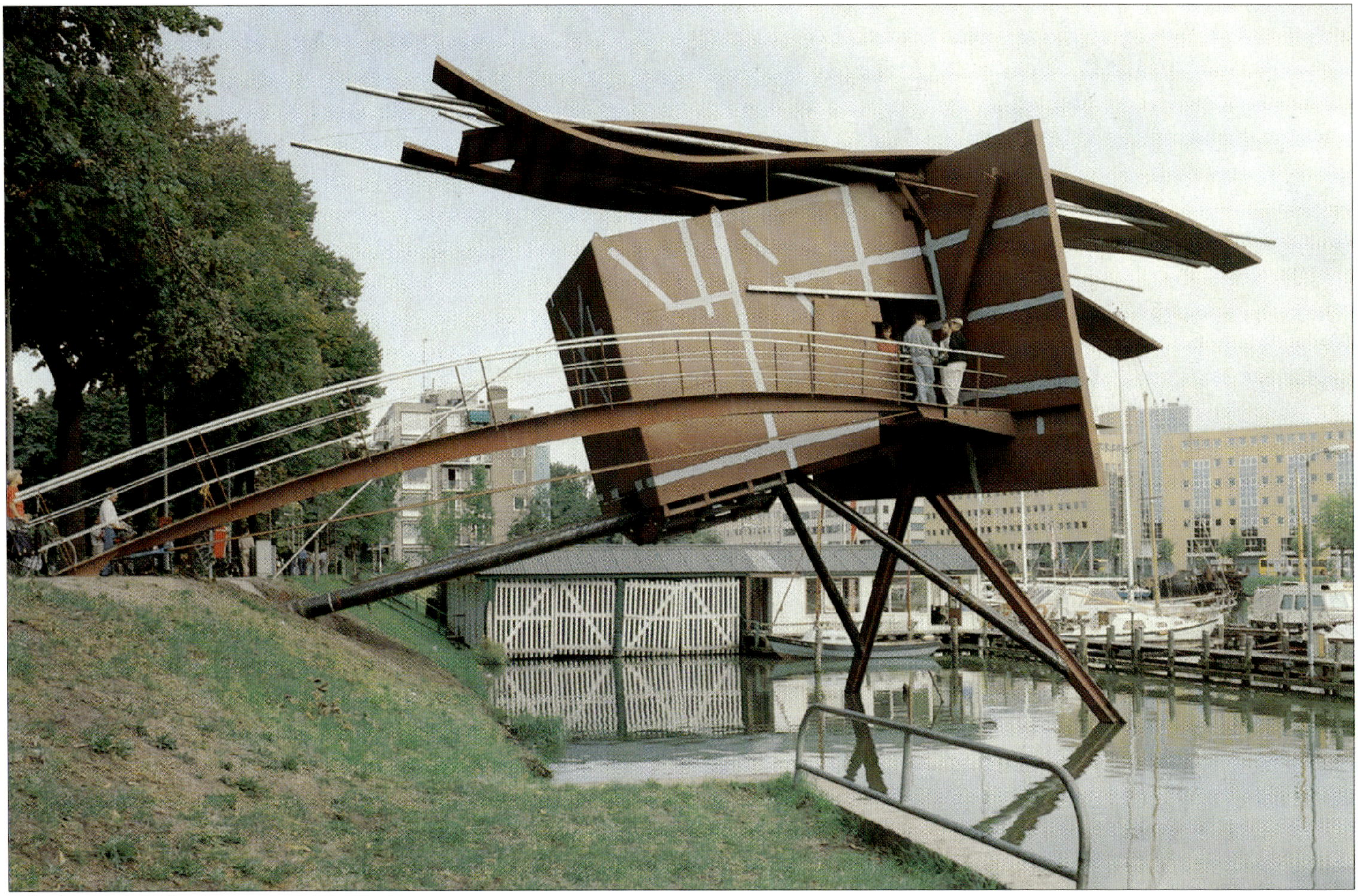

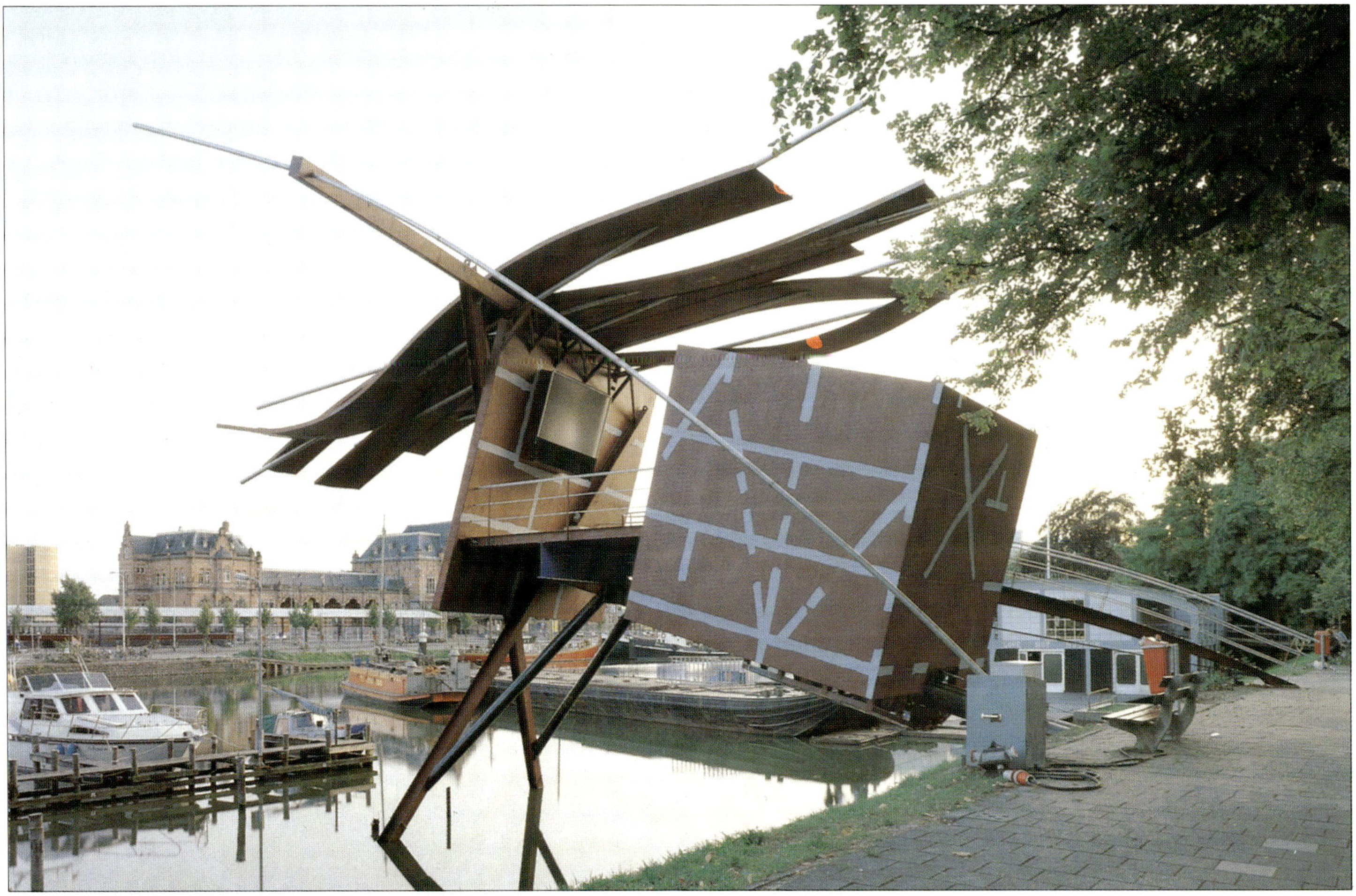

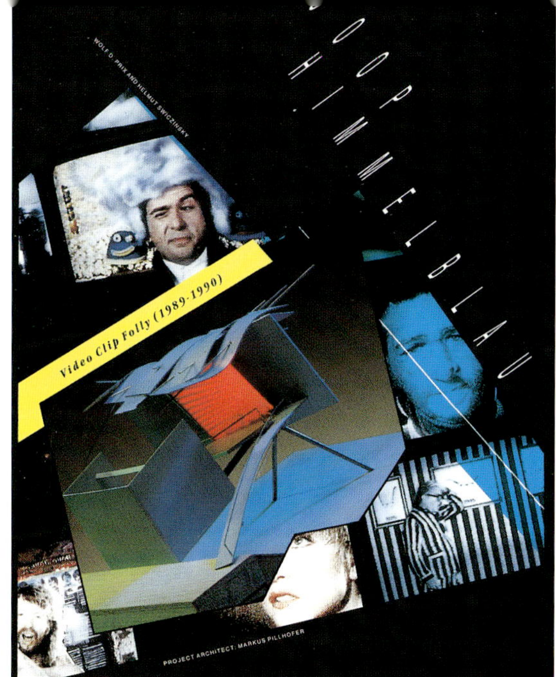

COOP HIMMELBLAU The commission was to design a space in which 40 persons could watch a video presentation.

The design is based on the idea of translating the emotion produced by the video in terms of the movements of the room.

The first drawings show the division of the room into platform and screen, into roof and walls. The platform, the screen and the roof (which has been subdivided into wave-like elements) are floating above the water, separated from the moving room.

The room opens and closes, operated by the video programmes and by the video surroundings.

The video will be shown in the closed room, with the volume turned up.

When the room opens, the people standing on the waterside will also be able to see the erotic videos.

HORIZONTAL SECTION

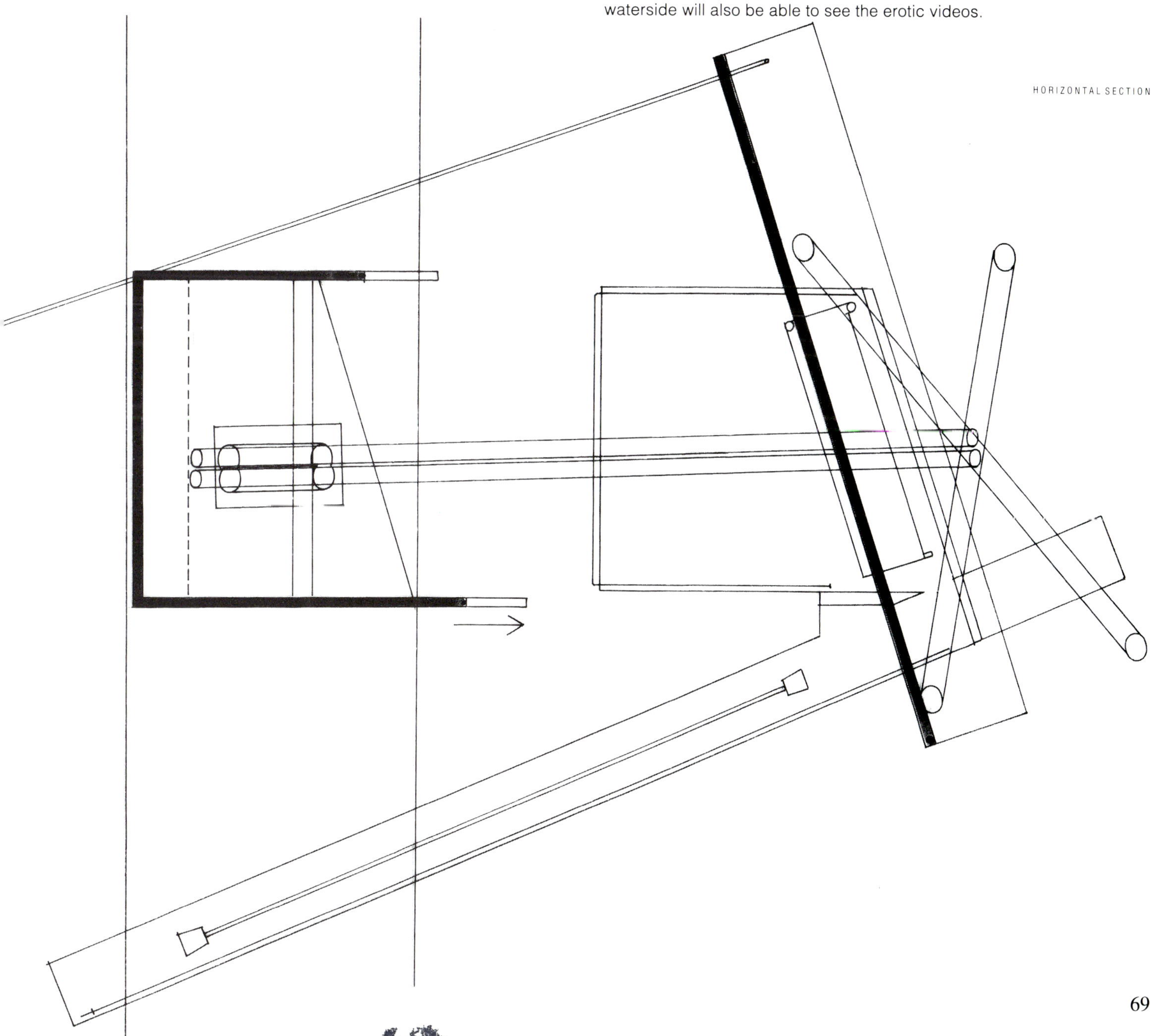

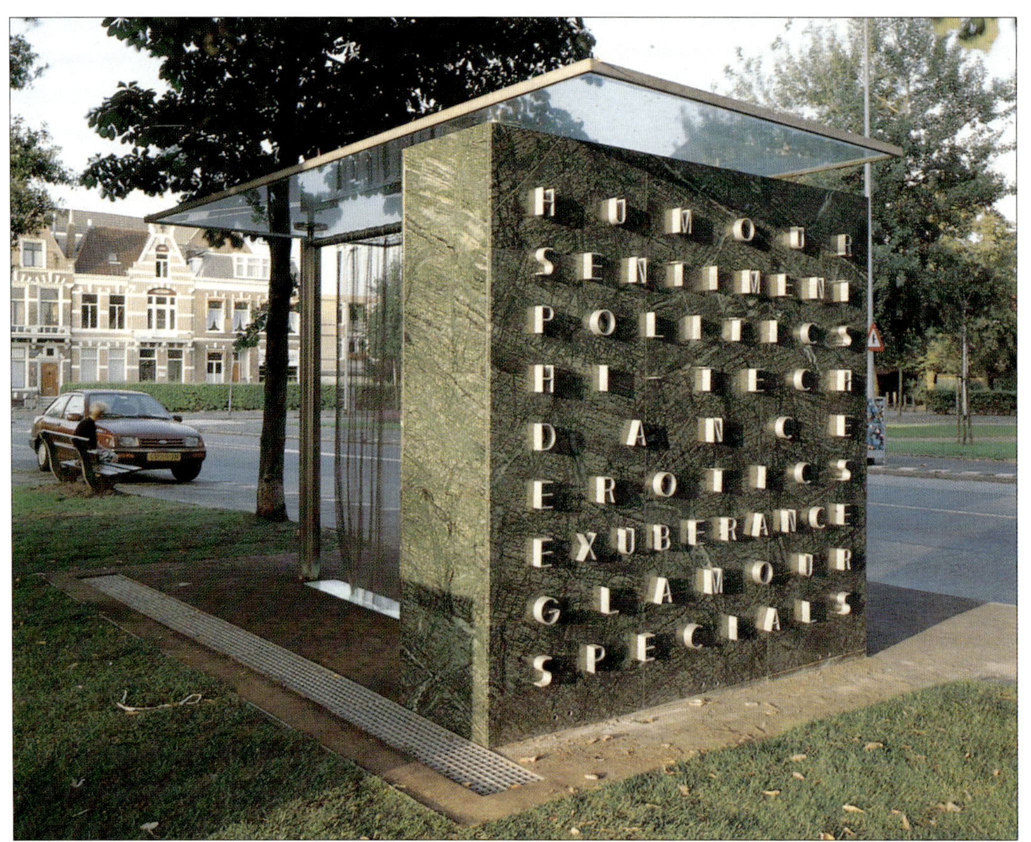
HUMOUR
SENTIMENT
POLITICS
HI TECH
DANCE
EROTICS
EXUBERANCE
GLAMOUR
SPECIALS

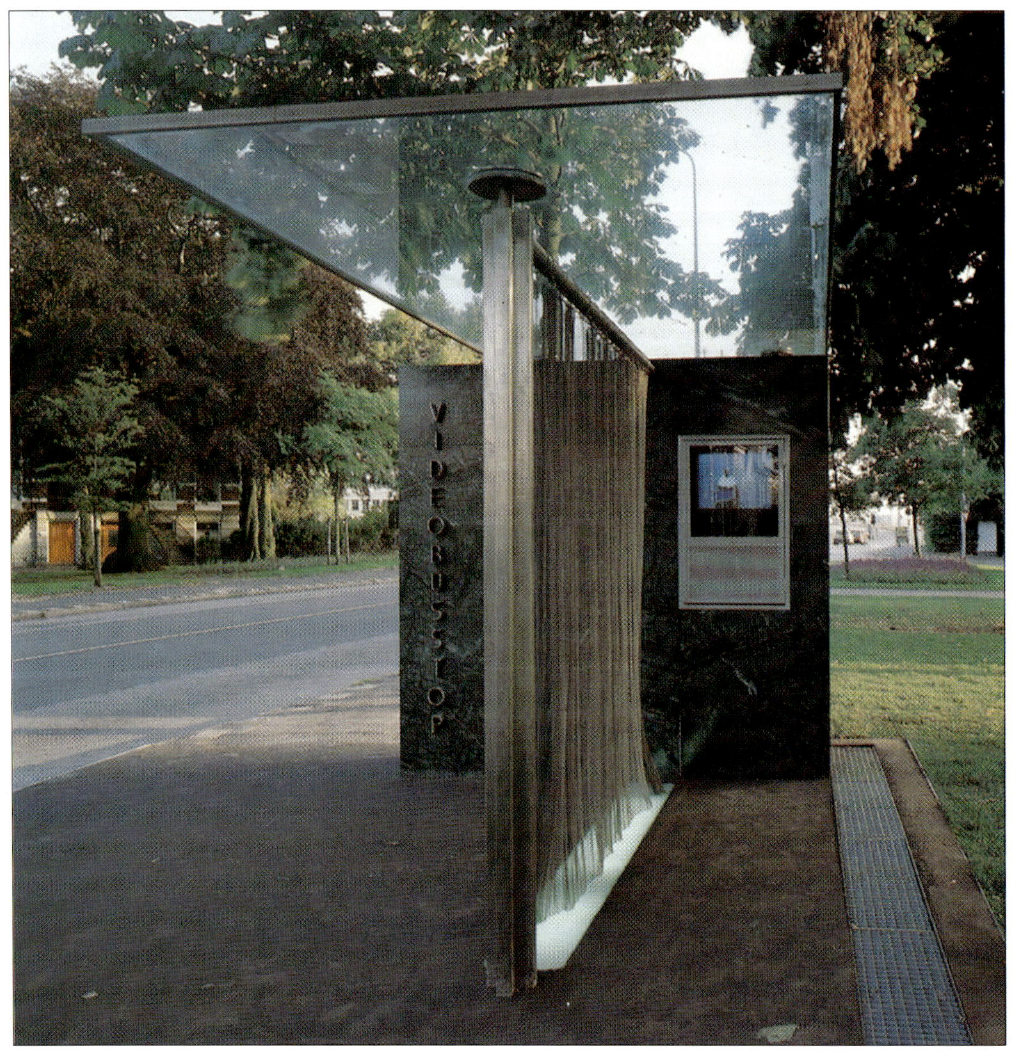
VIDEOBUSSTOP

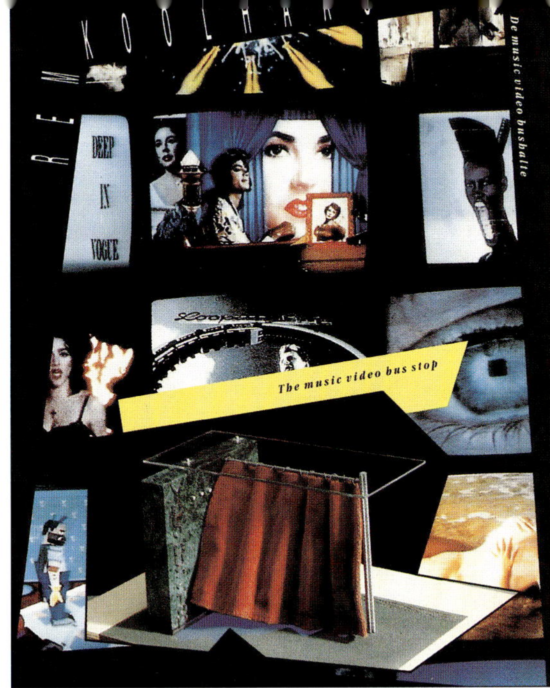

Rem Koolhaas What is the potential of video?
Would it be possible to imagine a bus stop which would be more than the usual prefabricated collision between glass and steel profiles?
From the impossible meeting between Mies van der Rohe and JC Decaux, an impossibly dignified bus stop is born. A marble block and a steel chromed cross column pass through space, a glass plate floats above.
What is behind the curtain? An accidental screen.
The reinterpretation of the Barcelona pavilion as bus stop is also its own demystification.
'The whispers of music' attract the people to the screen, who might occasionally look at a video programme and might finally miss their bus.

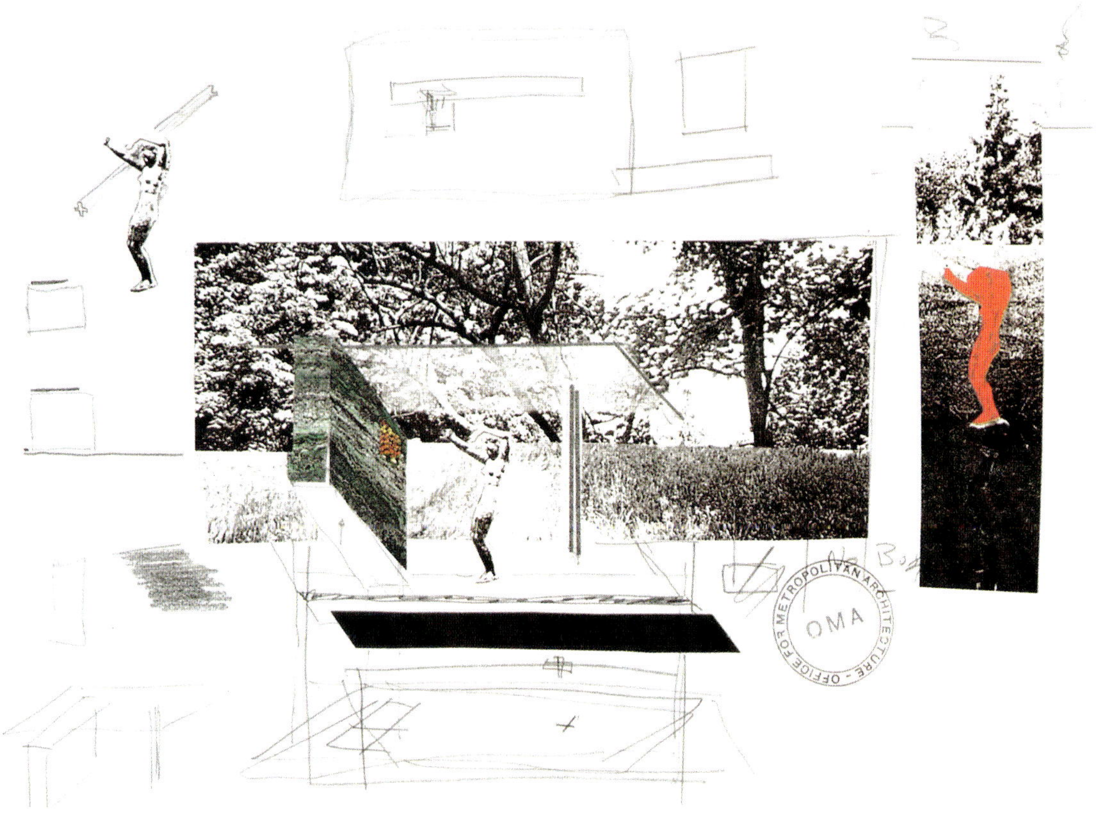

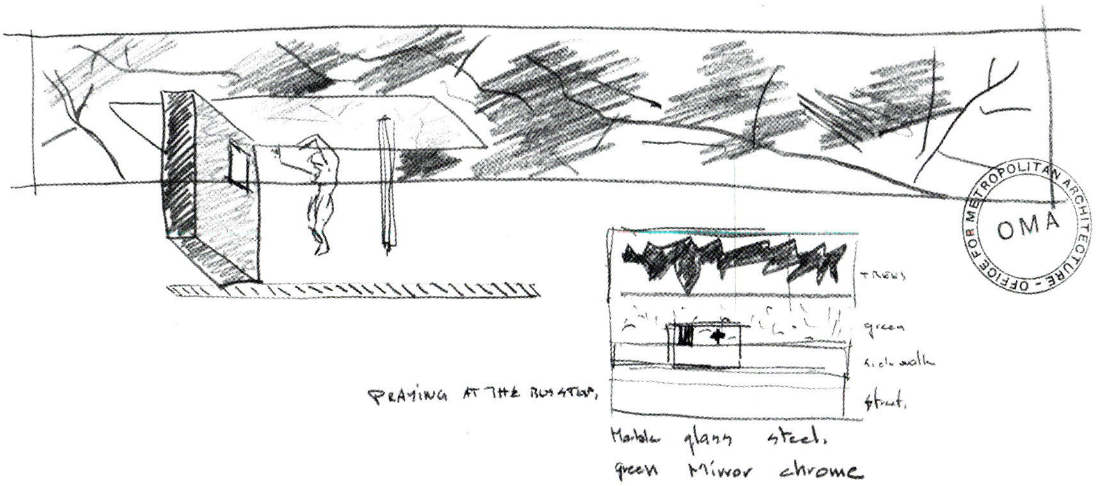

OFFICE FOR METROPOLITAN ARCHITECTURE OMA

OFFICE FOR METROPOLITAN ARCHITECTURE OMA

trees
green
sidewalk
street
PRAYING AT THE BUSSTOP
Marble glass steel,
green mirror chrome

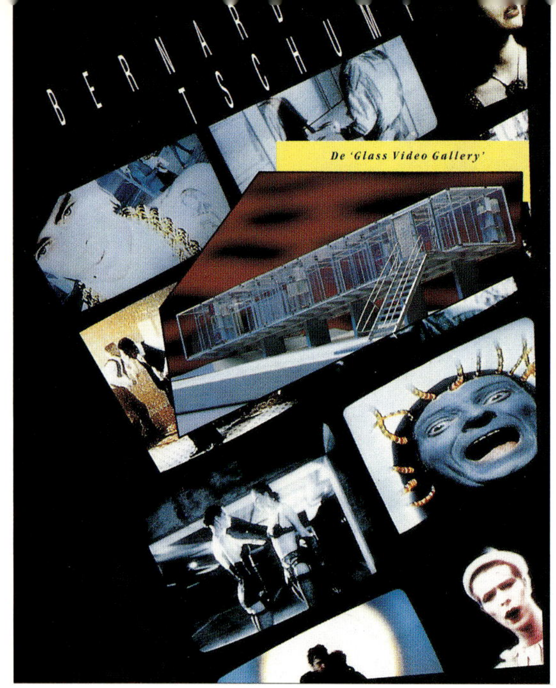

BERNARD TSCHUMI Is the video pavilion to be a static and enclosed dark box, like the architectural 'type' created for cinema; an extended living room with exterior advertising billboards and neon light? Or rather, should we create a new 'type' that brings what was previously a living room, bar and lounge event into the streets?

We propose the inclining, transparent, *Glass Video Gallery* which will contain a series of interlocking spaces defined only by a labyrinth of structural 'glass fins' and the points of metal clip connections. Isolated in this labyrinth are six banks of video monitors for displaying the music videos.

Placed within the Hereplein Medallion the gallery will be an extension of the street condition; except, a street where borders become indiscernible, monitors provide unstable facades, glass reflections create mirages, and derelict space is exposed. The gallery and medallion will contain objects on display like monitor walls viewed through TV dealership storefronts on the street, and objects displaying events like the plastic sex-clip galleries of urban red-light districts. In the Hereplein Video Plaza one will watch and be watched simultaneously.

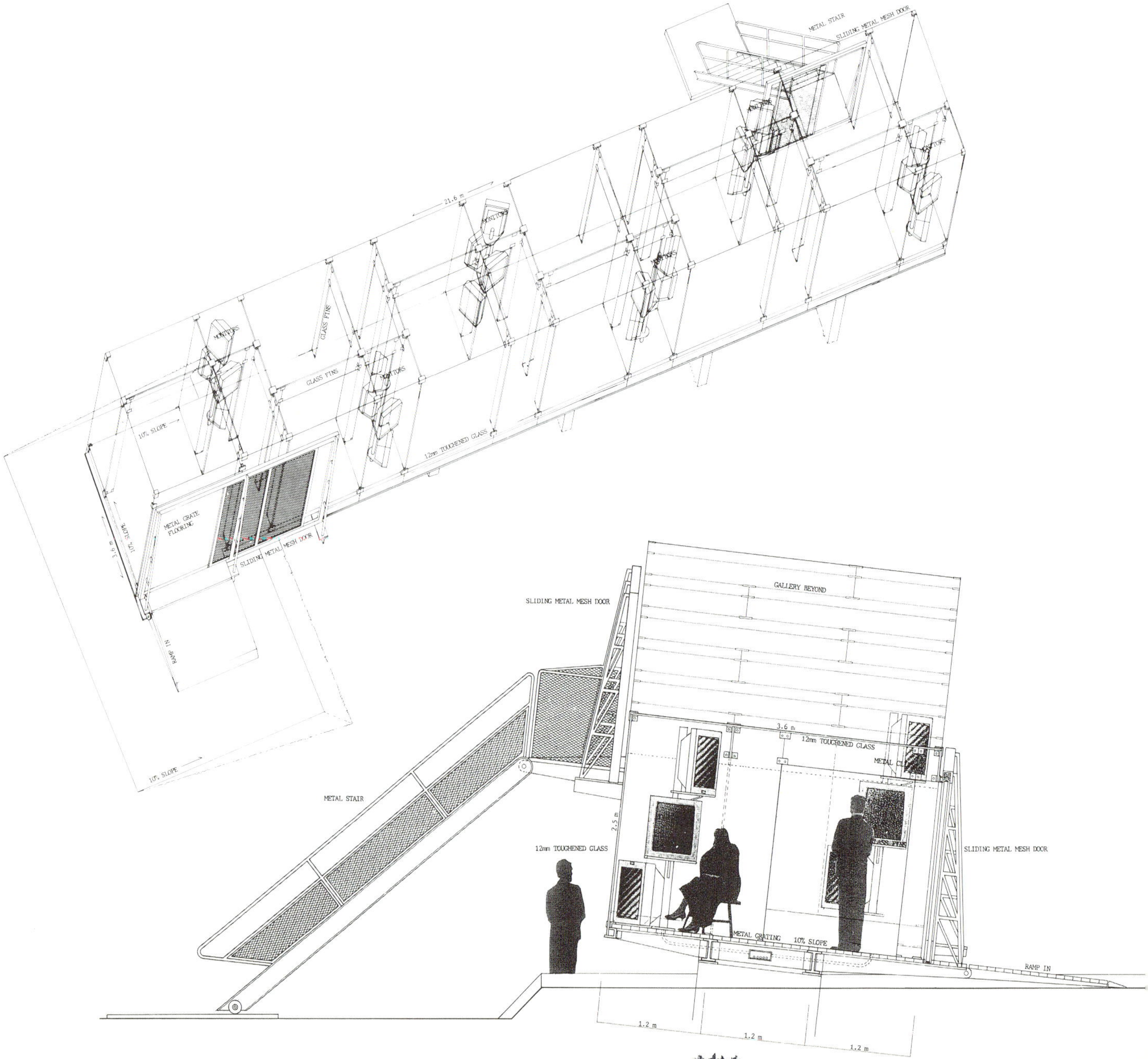

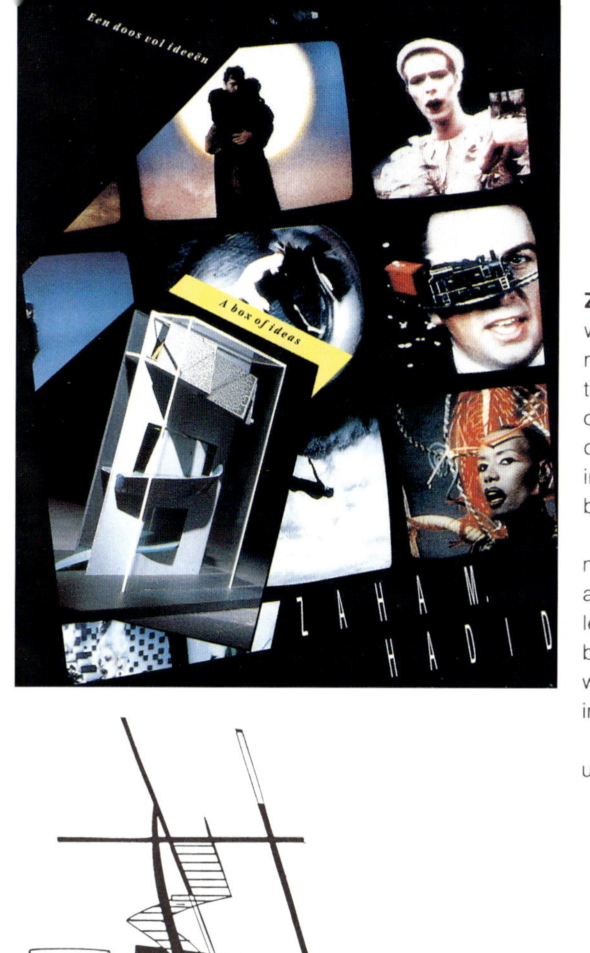

ZAHA HADID The design for this pavilion provides a window to the world, in which people can be seen moving amongst the video imagery, they become part of the performance, the full height of the construction. It is our intention that images are projected from the upper decks down to the mid-deck, onto translucent panels set into the glazed facade, and onto the raised ground finish beneath.

The 'search for a new language of architecture through music videos . . .' is a difficult one. We have looked at the available means of projection in terms of the site selected. That is to say, given the setting, one can use the building itself, adjoining walls, voids and planes upon which to perform, or project the magic of the video image, galvanising the forces to transform the site.

Passing drivers or pedestrians may quickly see the use to which the pavilion is being put.

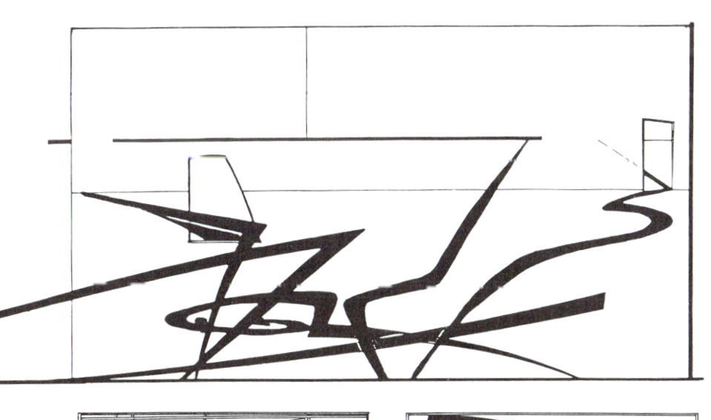

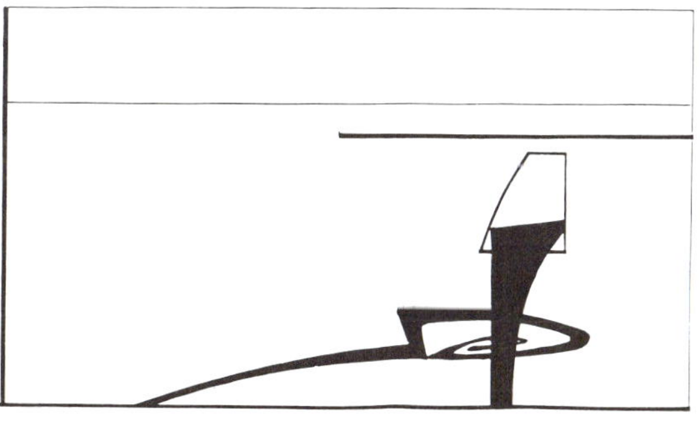

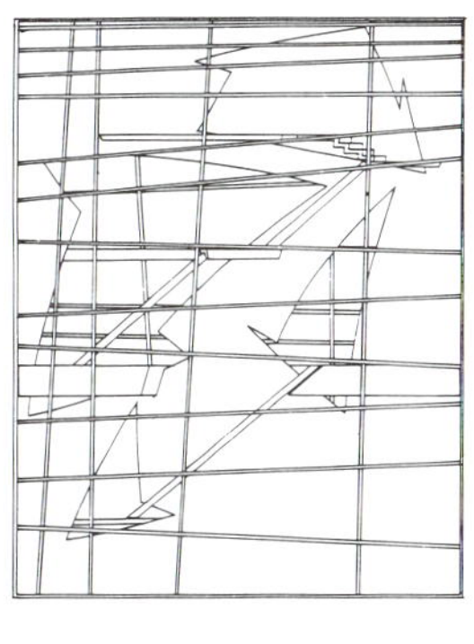

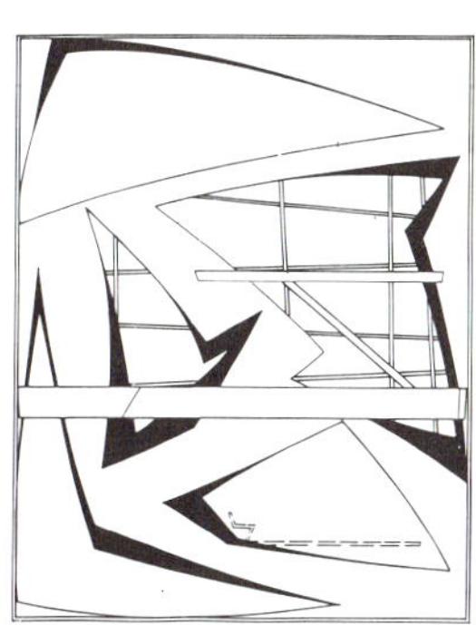

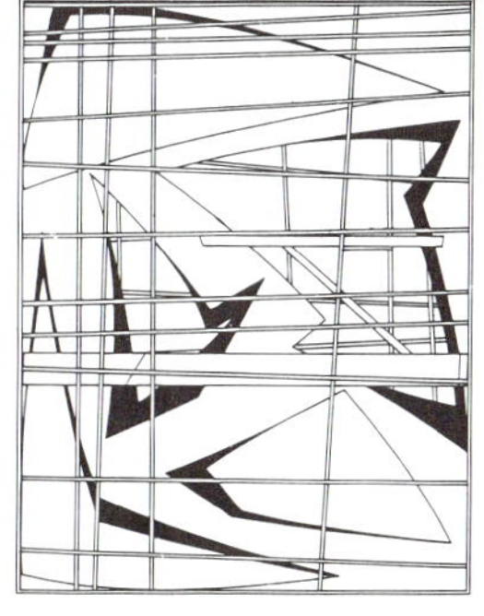

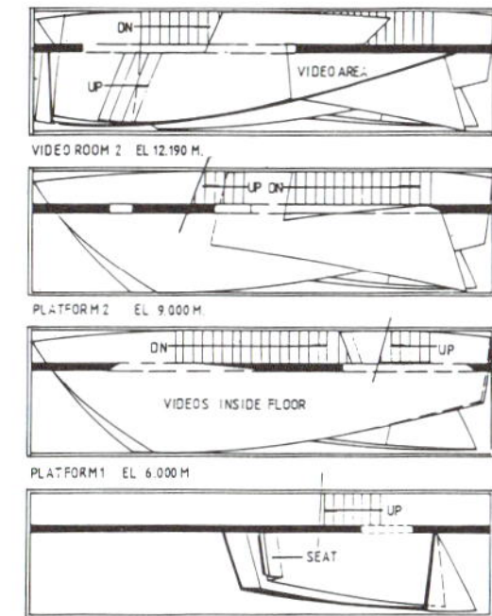

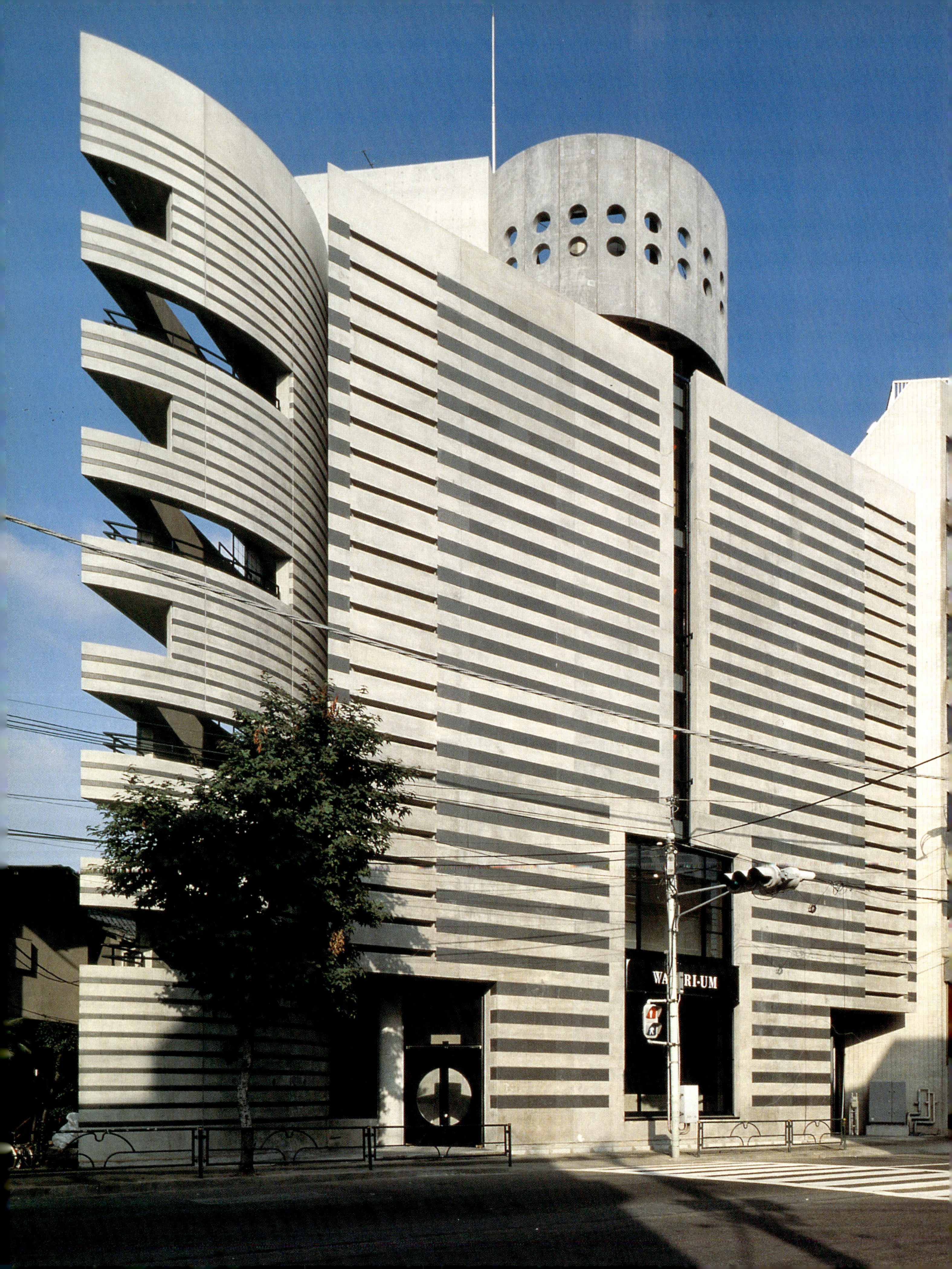

MARIO BOTTA

WATARI-UM GALLERY, TOKYO

The art gallery in Tokyo is now a reality. After years of discussions, projects and disputes, the dialogue with the riches and the contradictions of this enormous city proved to be the reason why I faced the efforts and the discomforts of this project.

I accepted this task as a bet. To build a small building in a big city has been for me a concrete, almost physical way to check my ideas with the imaginary space suggested to me by this metropolis. My impatience, my curiosity, that sense of challenge which is implicit in every creative risk, urged me on and supported me. This adventure allowed me to relive those deepest feelings that are rooted in my culture and in my way of being. I may have come to Tokyo to rediscover myself.

I am an architect born in a small village of the country that extends from Miilano towards the Alps. As a child, when the imaginary was still part of reality, I used to muse in the habitat of my village about the immensity of the distant cities. Today I still love to go after those intense sensations that helped me in my childhood.

During the quiet, long nights spent in the country, it was the life and the hustle and bustle of different people and cultures that came alive in my dreams. I drew comfort figuring out that other men with the same origins as myself had faced the discomforts and sacrifices implied by the search for a distant challenge, with nothing but their homegrown skills with which to face successfully the competition from distant cultures.

The testimonies of these few who had found fortune and had honored their land with their work sounded like signs of great hope for my uncertain future, too. I was seduced by the idea that a 'job' could make a 'mission' possible. It was probably this certainty, this search for an encounter between the real and the ideal, that made me choose this as my job. To build is a way to escape from the precariousness of time passing, it is a way to contain ideas and hopes stemming from everyday life.

The confrontation with places and cultures distant from my daily progress caused me to make clear the ways of seeing and of interpreting 'doing architecture'.

For this little museum I followed a strong and precise sign that had to resist the confusion and the contradiction of languages, styles and forms present in Tokyo. It is probably in this metropolis rather than in other urban contexts that one can catch accumulations of situations and of interests which in their interlacements characterise the riches and/or the poverty of today's city.

Tokyo exacerbates the contradictions of 'modern' cities; the dimensional and spatial break of the pre-existent is perceivable at every street corner: next to the lacerations inflicted by new urbanistic actions, a thick, pre-industrial urban context survives which offers a contrast between a spatial relationship and urban memory.

In the everyday changing 'Babel' of urban languages, I wanted to verify what could be the 'endurance' of a strong and primary architectural sign and image, generated by a reason inside the building itself and supported by natural light and geometry, suggested by the building rather than with regard to the environmental impact.

The result is a building which finds its own proportion through a slight asymmetry dictated by the vertical connections (elevator and stairs). The desire for different answers to the three fronts with regard to their three different urban conditions, finally modelled the different prospects. The prospect on the main front is axial and stretched for its maximum frontal extension (as if it were the search of a maximum wing span for a bird). The front on the little side road is flat and stretched to underline the corner stair as an element of urban appeal. The back prospect turned to the bordering property is sober and almost opens southwards in the high part. It is in such a way – with constant recall of the rigour of that romantic architecture which is very dear to me – that I dealt with the objective difficulty of this building.

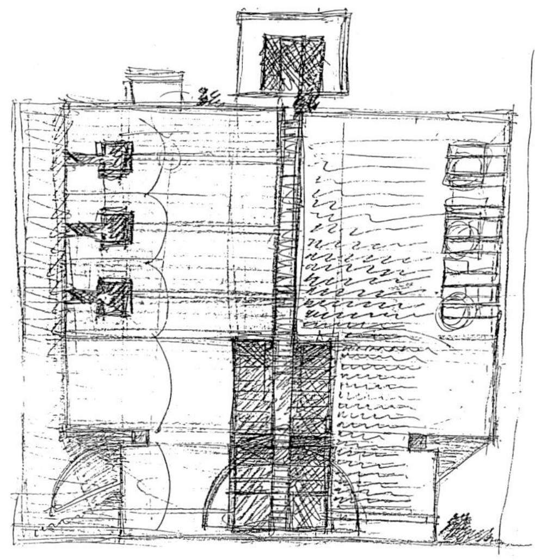

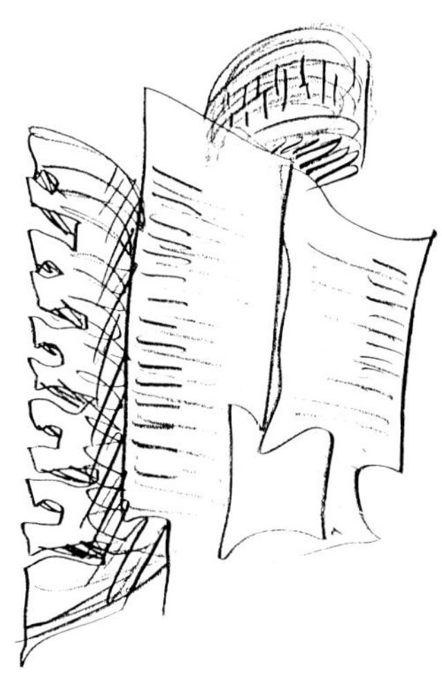

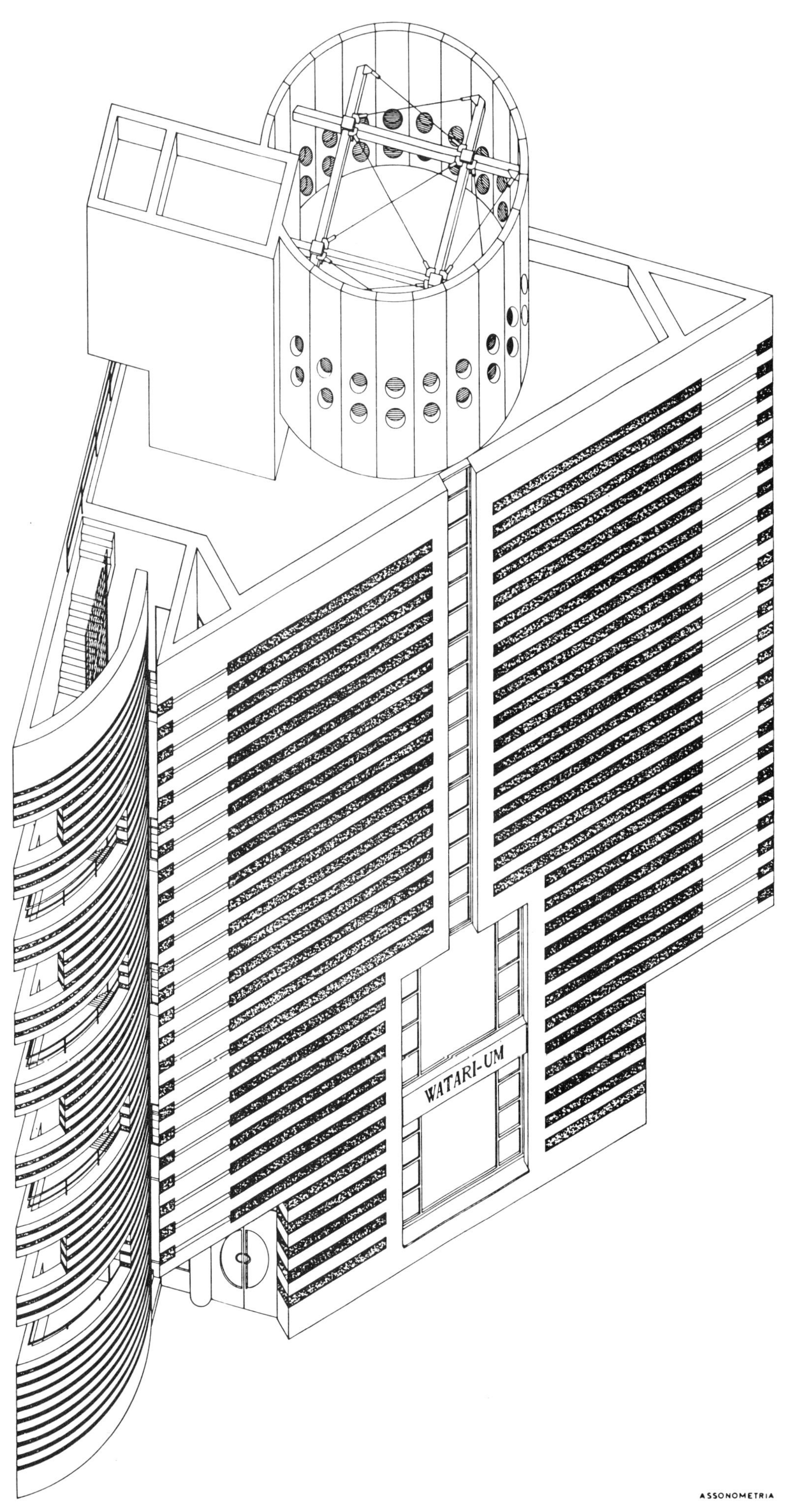

ASSONOMETRIA

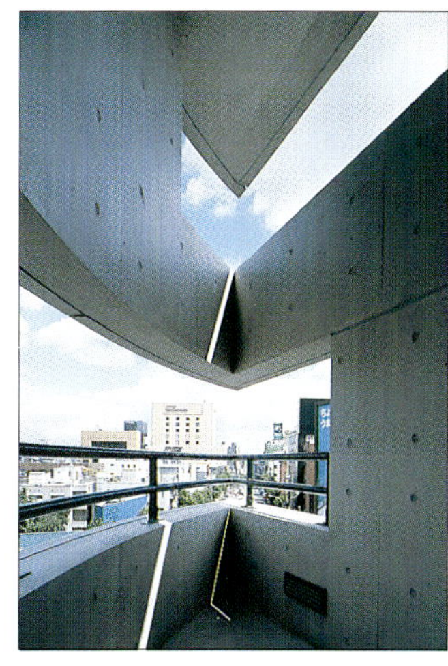

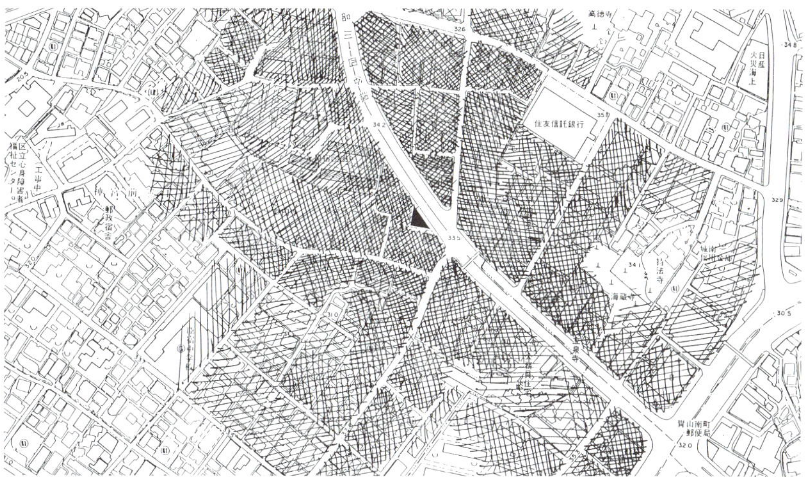

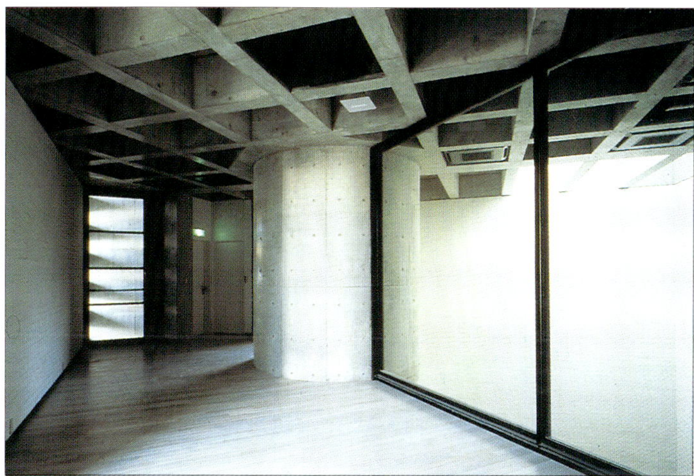

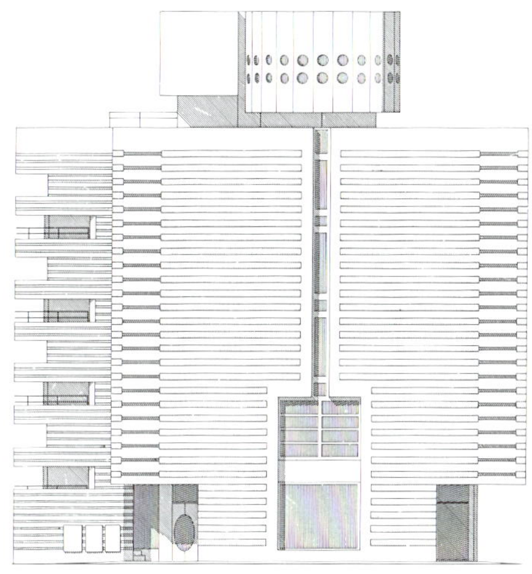

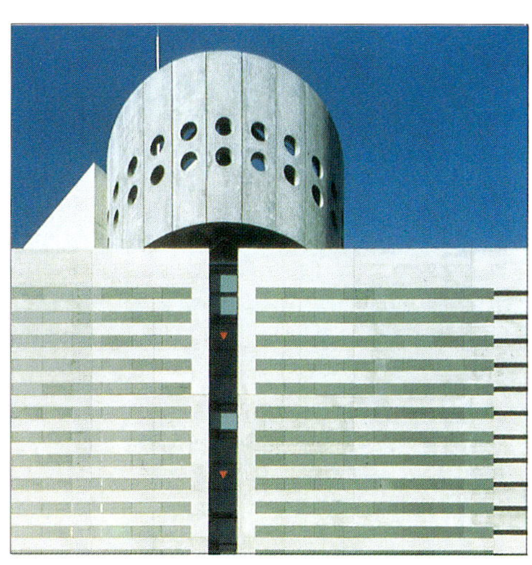

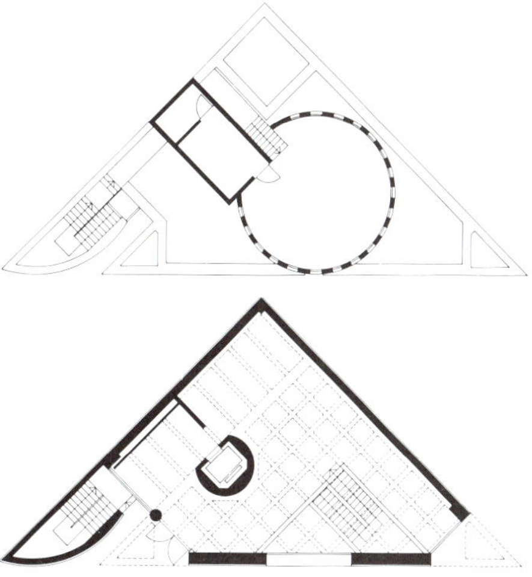

PREVIOUS PAGE: LEFT: Entrance facade; RIGHT: Sketch elevation and conceptual sketch
OPPOSITE: Axonometric
ABOVE: View from balcony and site plan
CENTRE: Interior view and front elevation
LEFT: Entrance facade detail and floor plans

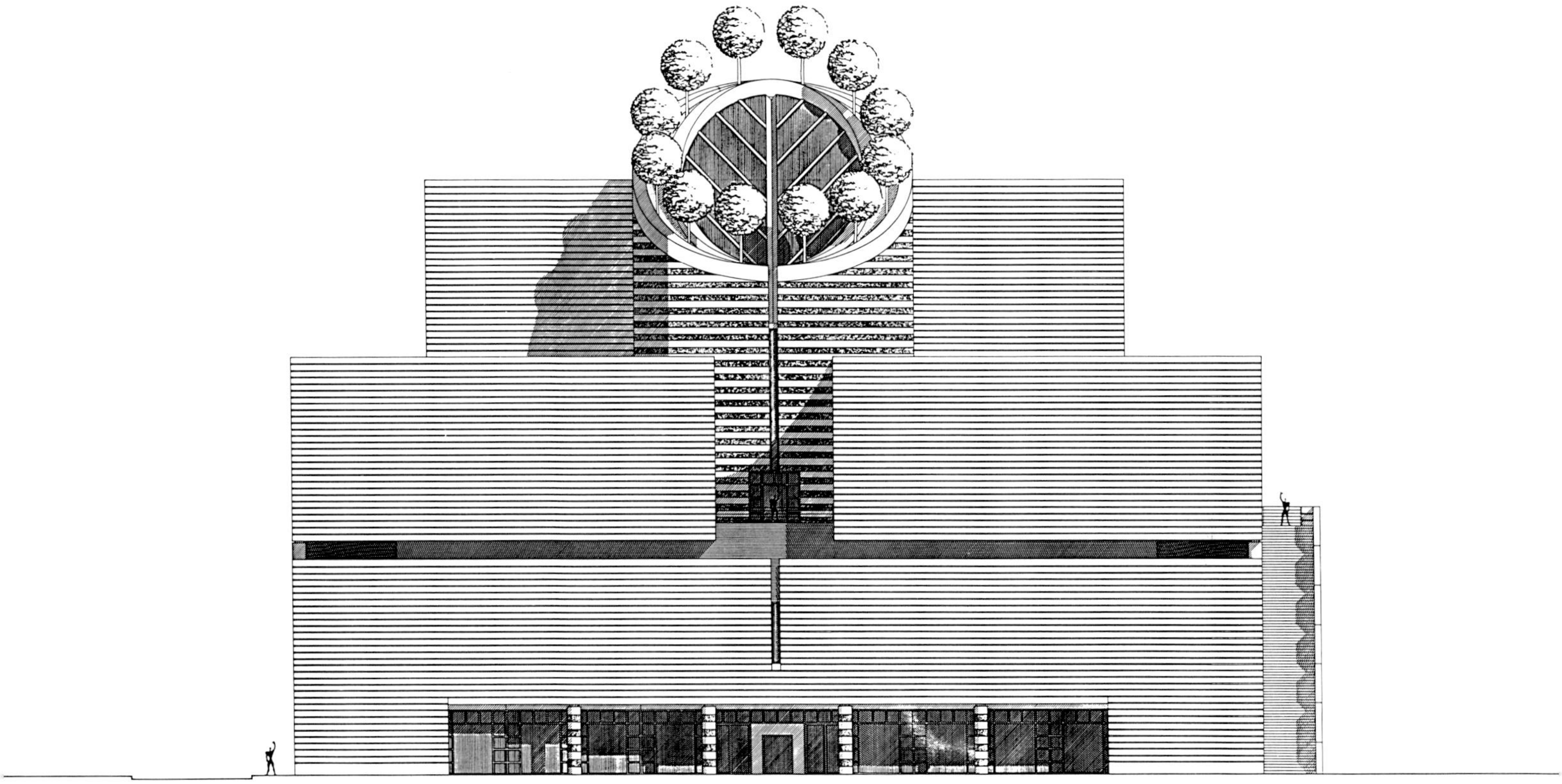

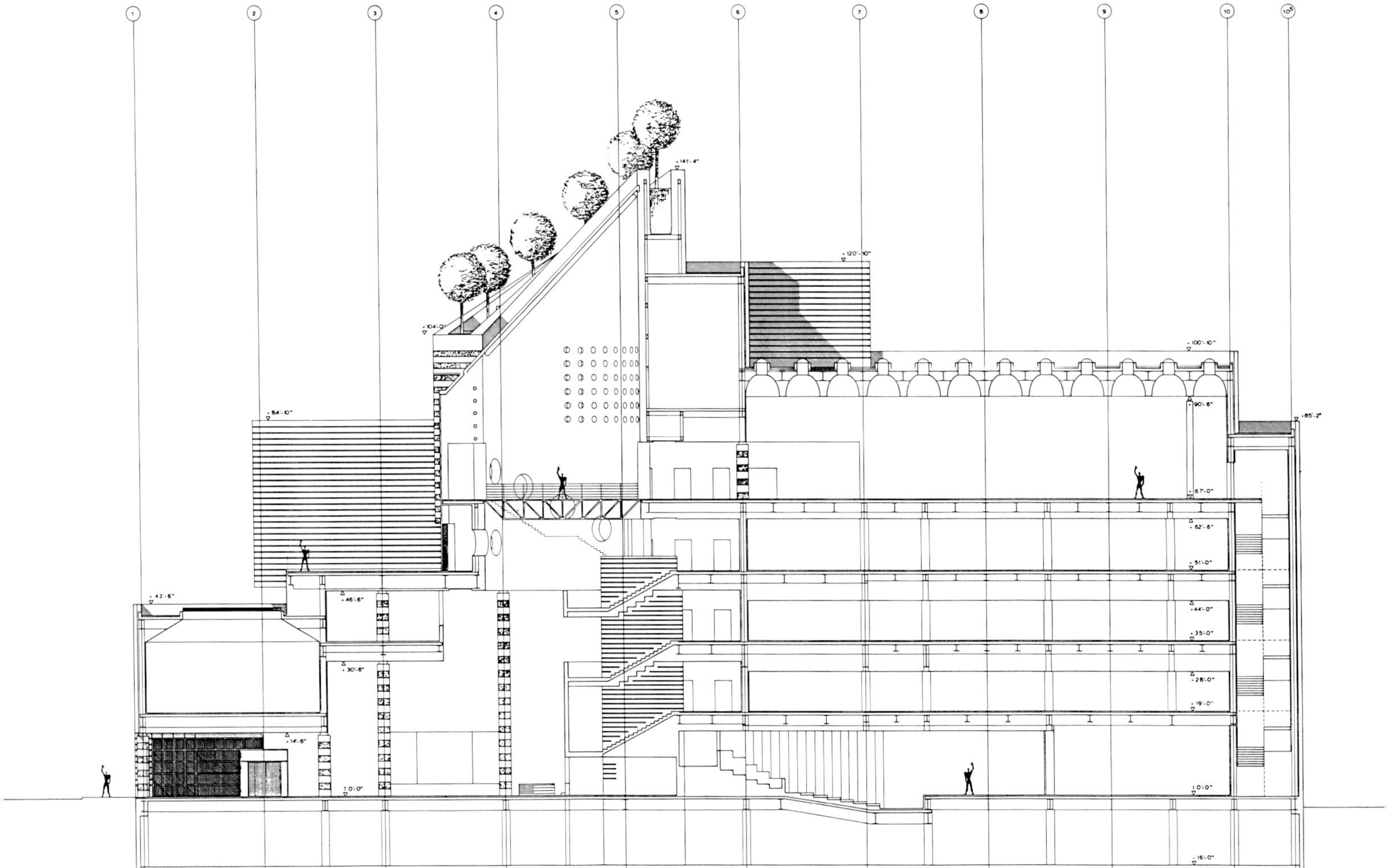

1 2 3 4 5 6 7 8 9 10 10b

+141'-4"
+120'-10"
+104'-0"
+100'-10"
+90'-6"
+85'-2"
+84'-10"
+67'-0"
+62'-6"
+51'-0"
+46'-6"
+44'-0"
+43'-6"
+35'-0"
+30'-6"
+28'-0"
+19'-0"
+14'-6"
±0'-0"
-16'-0"

Mario Botta's new building for the San Francisco Museum of Modern Art replaces the institution's present limited quarters in the War Memorial Veterans Building. A classic Modernist design, the new structure offers spacious, natural light-filled galleries, which will double the Museum's current exhibition space. Additional public spaces include an auditorium, classrooms, library, restaurant and bookstore.

The building features an impressive three-level stepped-back stone facade that is distinguished by a soaring central cylinder crowned by a ring of trees. While establishing a strong presence on Third Street, the facade also offers ample natural light to the galleries through the skylit roofs of the step-backs. To the rear, the building becomes a four-storey tower that houses the Museum's curatorial and administrative offices. In his signature style, Botta has called for the external surface of the central cylinder to be clad with contrasting bands of dark and light coloured stone, while the rest of the building's exterior consists of a single natural material that accentuates the unique quality of San Francisco's light. The building, which will be situated between two highrise office towers, will offer a striking and distinctive new architectural landmark for San Francisco.

Botta has created a building flooded with natural light and filled with open spaces. 'The atrium should serve as a piazza for people to come together and exchange ideas,' he explains. 'Within this space, the organisation and spatial relationships of all the areas that surround and define the atrium should be perceived.'

Visitors are drawn from the atrium up to the four floors of galleries above via a grand staircase. The first gallery floorwill house selections from the permanent collection. An intimate second-floor mezzanine will display photographs and works on paper. The top two floors will accommodate special temporary exhibitions.

In addition to the galleries, the new building will house numerous other public areas which open off the ground-floor atrium. A 300-seat auditorium will accommodate presentations on art history and contemporary art issues as well as films, symposia and seminars. An area dedicated to educational programming will include a large workshop/studio and a classroom with seating capacity for 100.

On a lower level, a photography and graphic arts study area will offer access to visiting scholars and artists to view the Museum's collection. Additionally, the Museum's library will be accessible to staff, the local art community and the general public.

In today's city, the museum plays a role analogous to that of the cathedral of yesterday. It is a place of common encounter and confrontation, a place we require in order to challenge the hopes and contradictions of our time. It is also a place where the values and aesthetics of the past are very much present and where the unique sensibilities of mankind are born witness throughout history. In fact, it might be possible to interpret the museum as a space dedicated to witnessing and searching for a new religiosity, which promotes and enriches those spiritual values that we so strongly need.

OPPPOSITE: Elevation and Longitudinal Section
BELOW: Cutaway Perspective

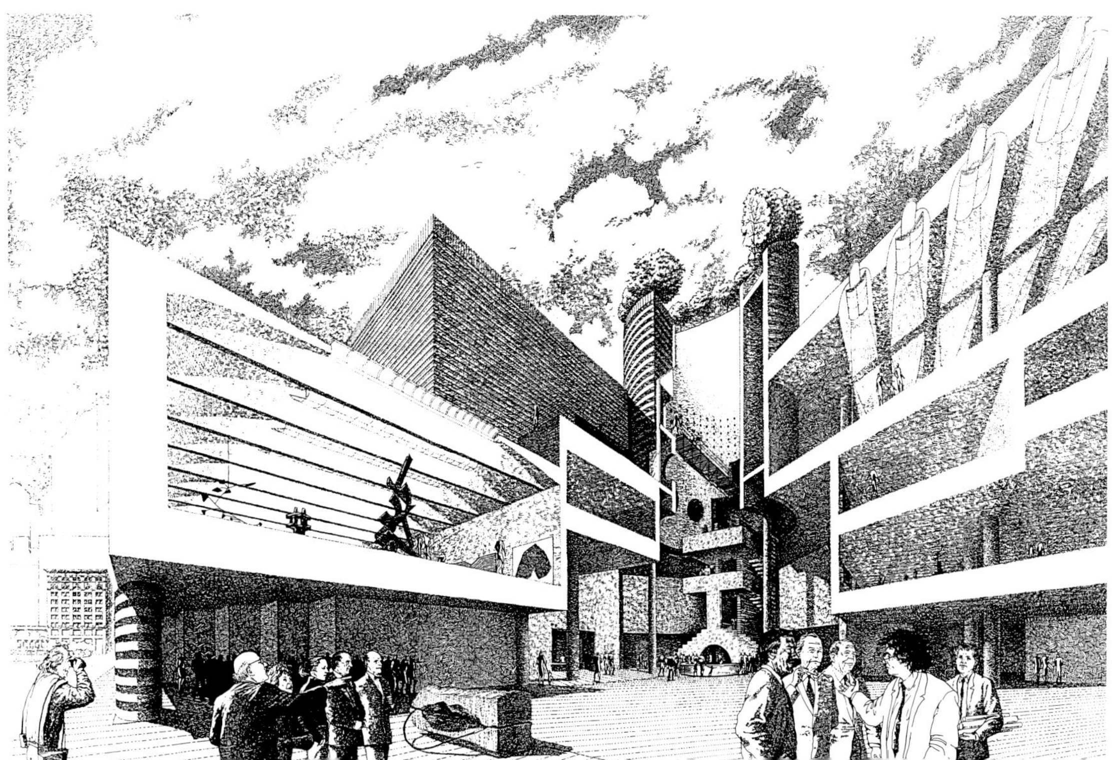

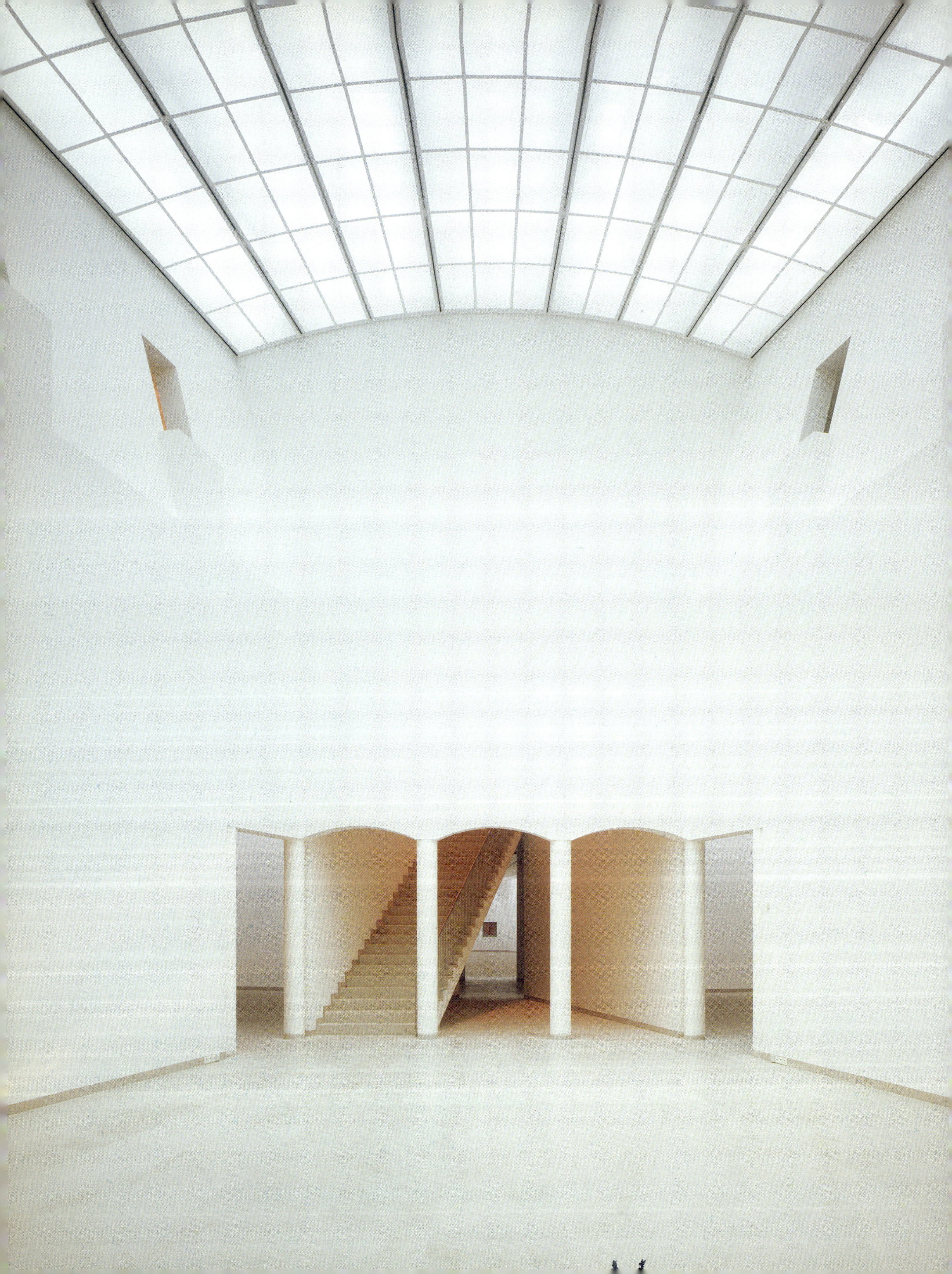

HANS HOLLEIN

FRANKFURT MUSEUM OF MODERN ART

The concept of the Museum of Modern Art in Frankfurt represents a development of my considerations regarding the construction of a museum, and is based on my concrete experiences with projects realised by us before. It is also based on my involvement in fine arts, both as a receiver and as a creator of art. The focus of attention is the artwork; its presentation and demonstration is just a compatible environment. This environment is in a dialectic relationship with the artwork, withdrawn but not without its own individuality and character. Considerations of space and light are of top priority; questions of optimum confrontation and the capability of experiencing art, problems of approach and access, of efficiency and functionality follow. Questions of architecture. Questions of art.

The draft is the result of two premises: firstly, considerations in terms of municipal planning, urbanity and urban character as well as the conditions of the building site and its specific layout; secondly, the programme, its functional consequences and the necessities of presentation of fine art objects to a wide public of different educational backgrounds.

The eastern end of the insular area formed by Berliner Straße and Braubachstraße is an important landmark in the approach to the historic core of the city – the old Stauferstadt district – characterised by a marked triangular shape. This was accepted as a structuring and form-giving element from which the specific shape of the building could be developed.

So, a compact triangular, chiefly symmetric building has been created. The apex of the triangle is conceived as a succinct solitaire, although integrated into the building proper. Visibility from long distances and noticeability of the design media are significant prerequisites.

However, in terms of accessibility and communication with the old town quarter, the Domstraße/Braubachstraße corner of the triangle is more important. In order that the building communicate optimally with the historical town centre – and with the activities concentrated there – it was consistent to strive to place the main entrance to the museum at that point.

This superimposition of an asymmetrical, diagonally oriented area of access on a symmetrical structure puts the building into complex interrelationships.

In the interior it seemed important to continue access by penetrating into and climbing up to various levels of event. A significant feature was to elevate the main action area of the entrance hall from a direct relationship to the street outside and also from the secondary functions like reception desk and cloakroom. (This area is designed to meet the requirements of security checks with minimum personnel, to relate to the cafeteria and to afford access to the collection and administration.) The entrance hall proper is therefore about 1.5 m above the entrance level, whereby the feeling of participating in an event is intensified and disturbances from the secondary functions are minimised. A 'by-pass' has been provided to avoid further disturbance, for instance in the case of events. From the central hall, the various departments and storeys of the museum are disclosed directly, in terms of both visual surveyability and physical accessibility. The lecture room, also accessible from the entrance area, is connected with the storeroom, a feature that is of particular advantage for a number of events.

In addition to the doorkeeper's cabin, administration and library areas are also accessible both from the entrance hall and directly from outside. From these rooms there is visual contact with the museum rooms themselves. The cafe is, on the one hand, close to the entrance and the museum area; on the other, it is an independent element which should animate the street in front, the fabric of which is reshaped by the new museum.

Besides the main entrance, there is an administration entrance, a large service bay in Domstraße and additional transport access in Berliner Straße, which is also assigned to the temporary exhibition area. The latter is conceived as a flexible instrument enabling the creation of different lighting situations with special walls and ceilings for easy assembly and with differentiated electronic safety devices. Headroom is almost without exception at least 4.5–5 m, a few special areas having much greater or smaller dimensions. Transport clearance is four metres practically everywhere; upper storeys are served by a goods lift. This also connects the basement, which contains storerooms, a picture depository, workshops and technical installations as well as the lecture room.

The collections are accessed from the large entrance hall. We avoided doing this only via lifts or high (psychologically inhibiting) vertical staircase shafts but endeavoured to achieve it by an experiential diagonal penetration of the building. Many round walks are possible; the desired outlooks are frequently broken down into zones serving communication. The roof window areas (and the layout of the loft area) have been planned so that the intentionally shaped roof structure – the result of necessary superstructures for air conditioning and light access – has an aesthetic effect and builds upon a clear moulding line on the main building mass. The silhouette has been articulated because of its significance in the cityscape.

The compact design of the exterior chiefly follows the site boundaries specified. Such a voluminous appearance has been chosen not only for economical reasons, but also under urban planning considerations. The building is articulated by small recesses and notches as well as by the selection of materials. The main building materials are – in compliance with the characteristic style of public buildings in Frankfurt – red sandstone and

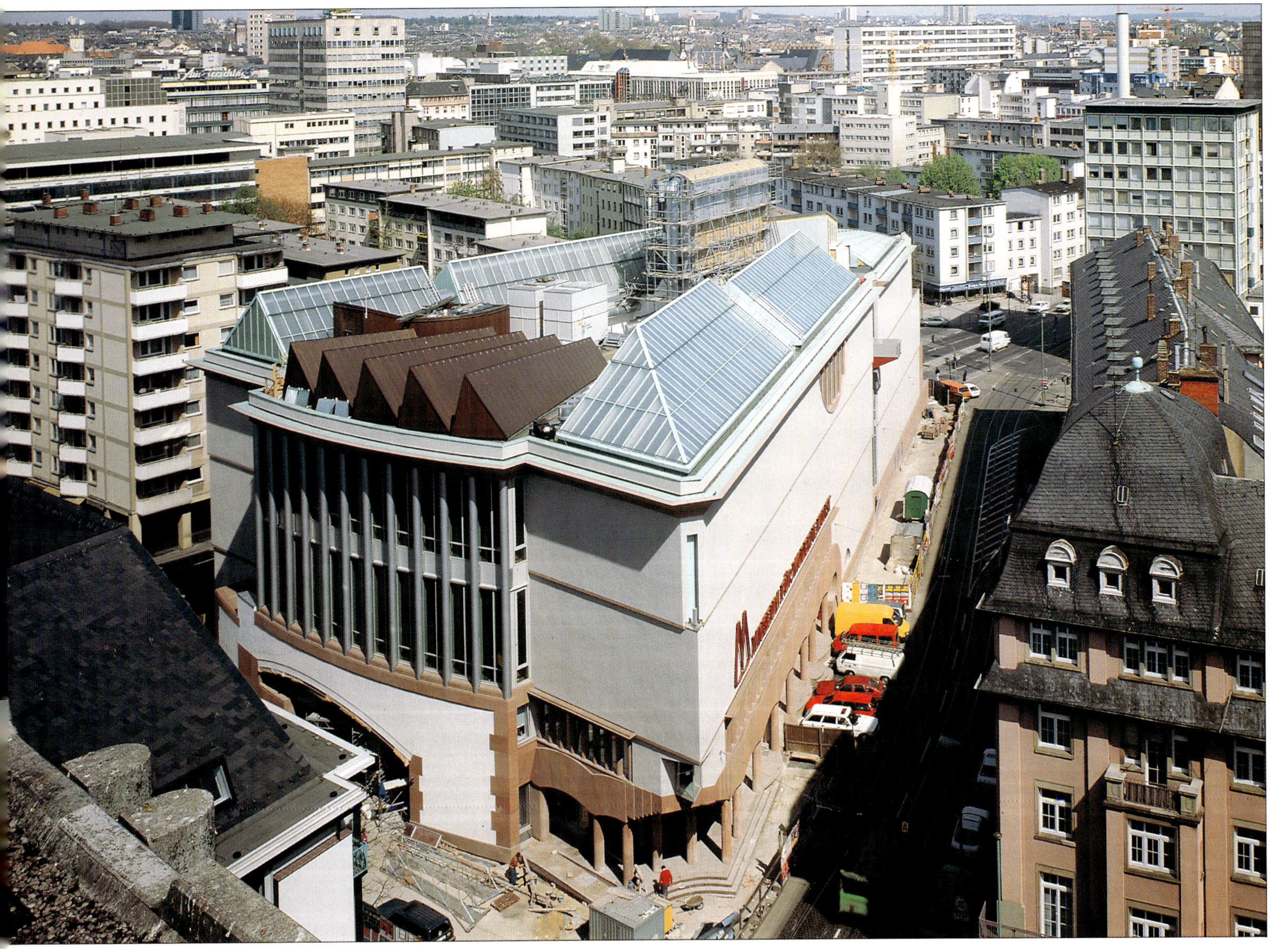

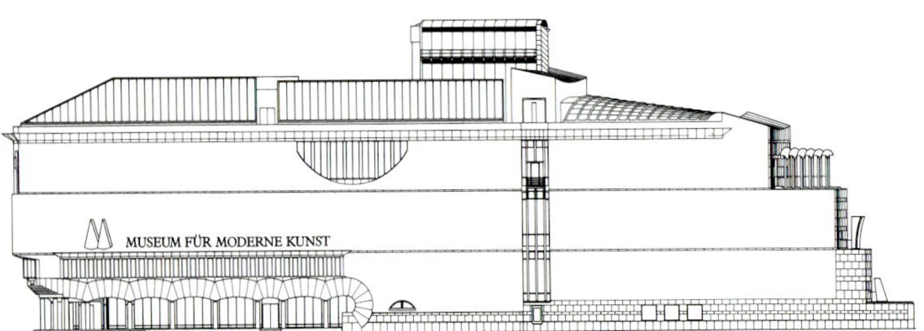

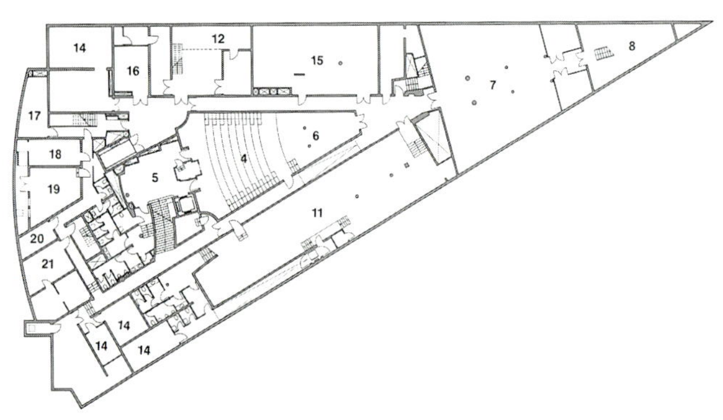

PREVIOUS PAGE: Interior view of main hall
ABOVE: Overall exterior view
BELOW: South elevation from Braubachstraße; Basement plan

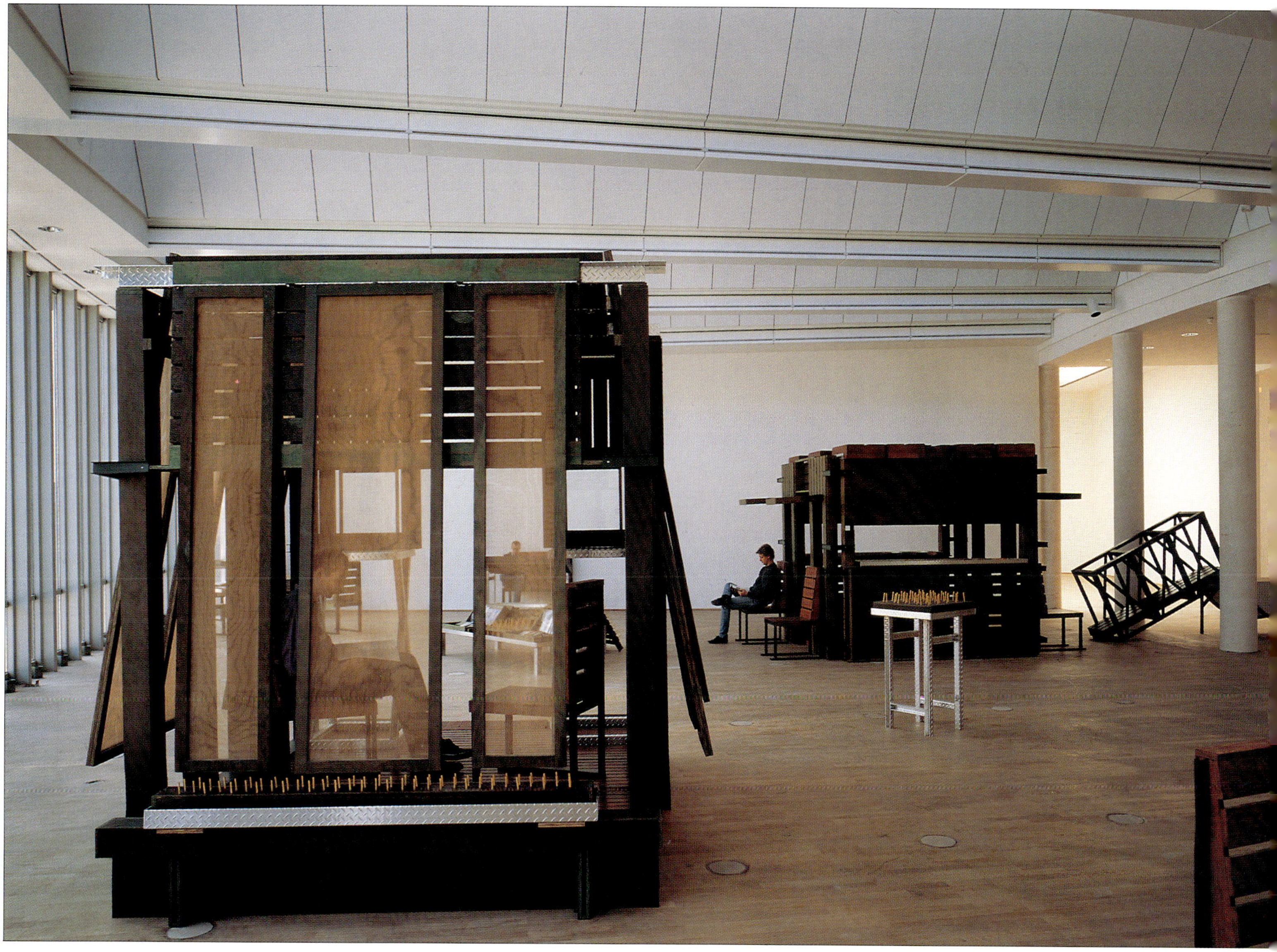

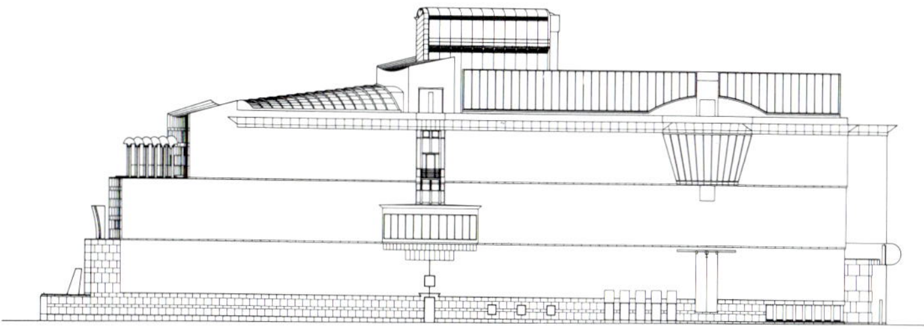

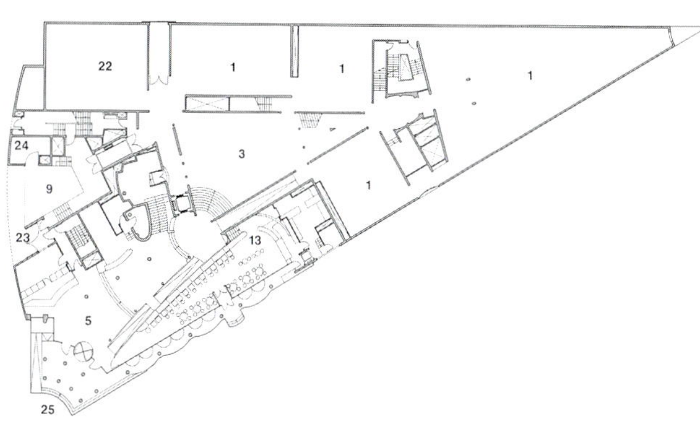

ABOVE: Reading Room *by Siah Armajani*
BELOW: North elevation from Berliner Straße; Ground-floor plan

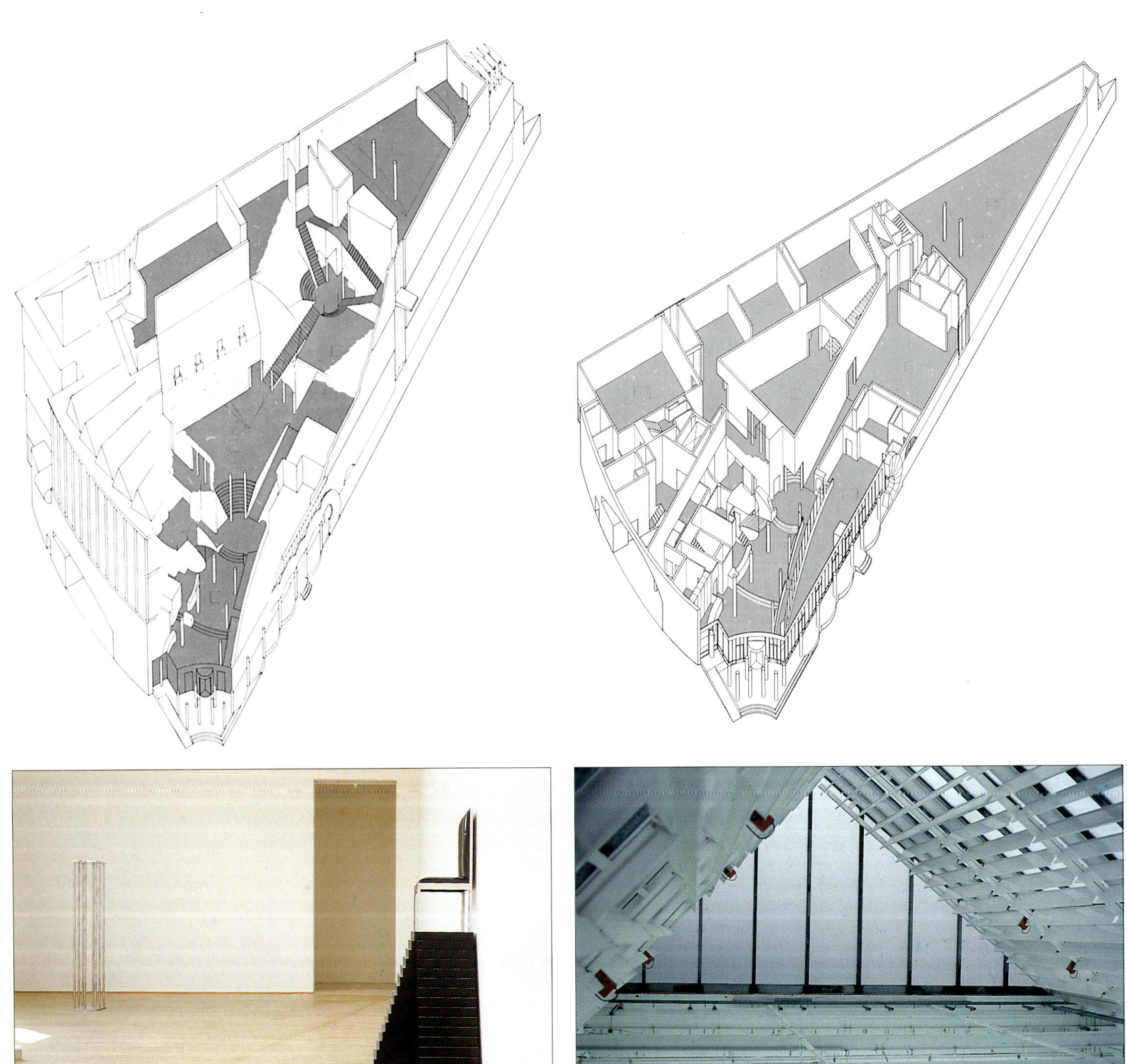

ABOVE: Isometric of exhibition spaces, system access and mezzanine level
BELOW: Gallery and ceiling void

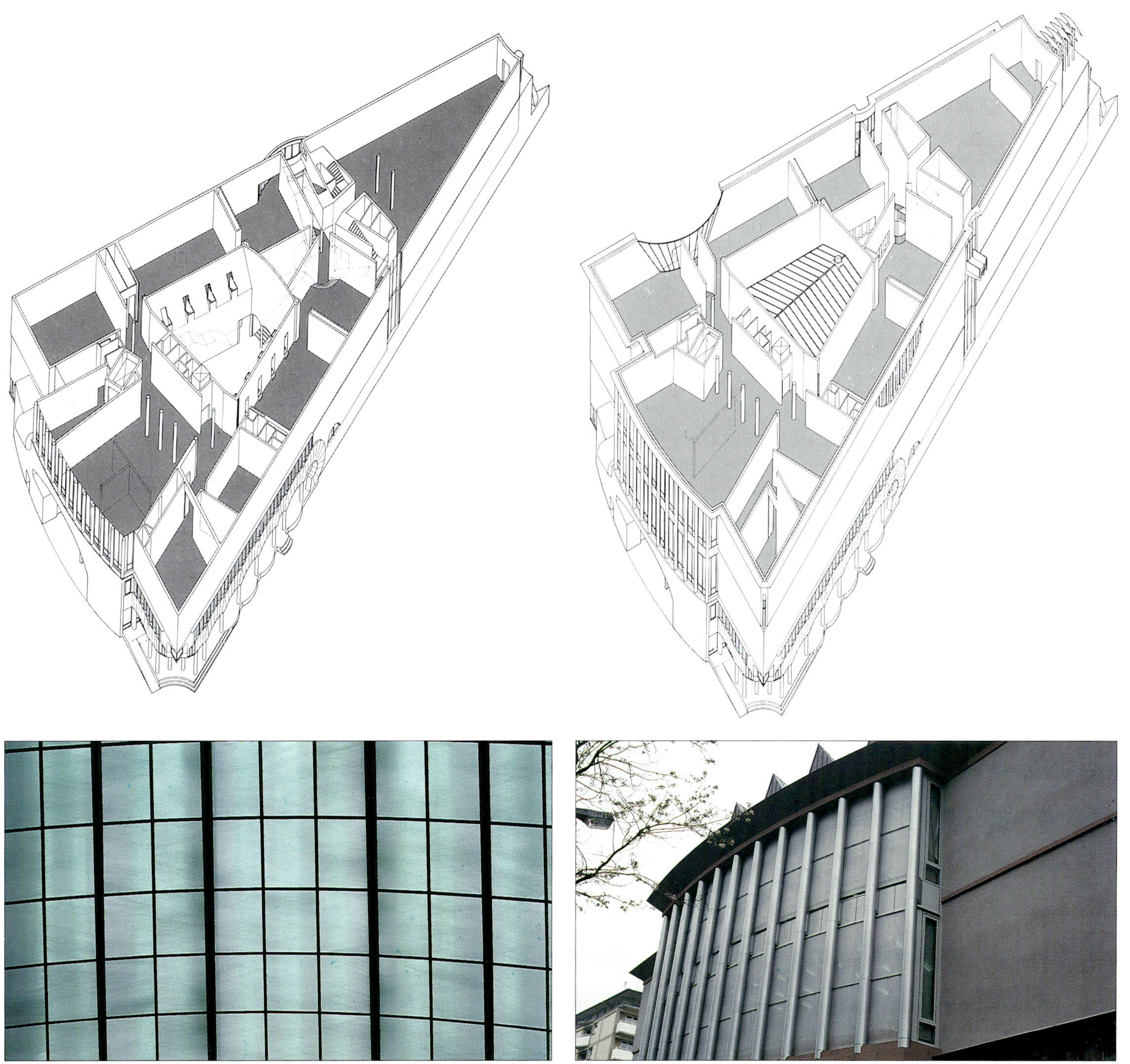

ABOVE: Isometric of exhibition spaces, level two and level three
BELOW: Ceiling and front facade details

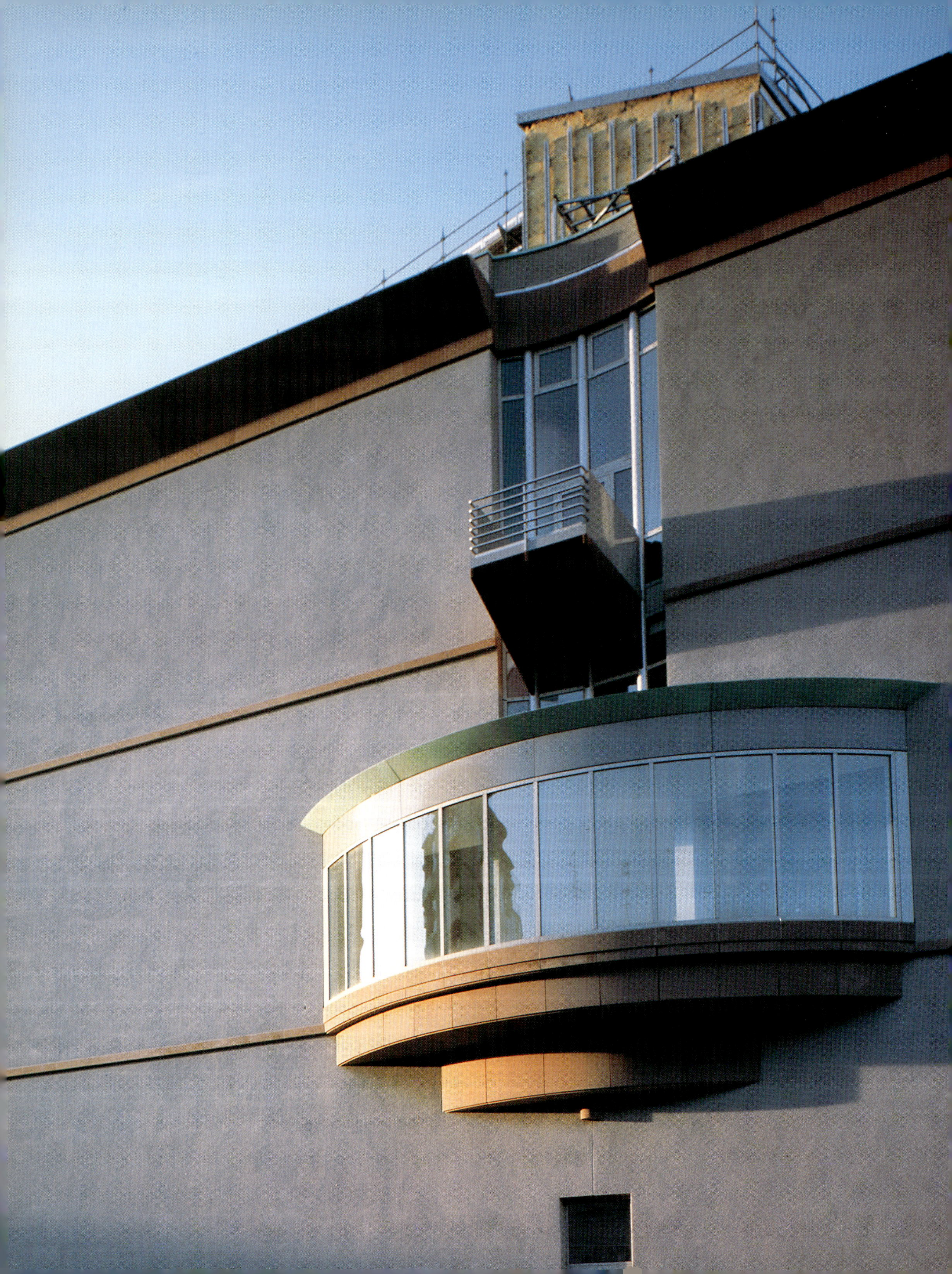

plaster for the walls, copper (and aluminium) for the roofs.

The stepped apex of the building is like a sculpture on an urban scale, both allowing for the urban planning aspect and assuming the function of an escape route. The motif of sculptural arcades existing in the neighbouring buildings of Braubachstraße was continued in the facade of the cafeteria area, thus placing the building in context.

The static system of the building is based on load-carrying walls and supports of conventional design, the surfaces of which are plastered inside and outside. In order to guarantee the desired variability and flexibility, the ceilings in the small rooms are without supports wherever possible. However, in principle, the building has been structured so as to avoid excessive span widths. The structuring of both ground plan and cross section permits an advantageous distribution and branching of the air-conditioning system.

The museum is conceived both as a daylight and as an artificial-light museum, special attention being paid to supporting illumination. In the rooflight areas, an illumination system has been provided which simulates the lighting effect of natural light. In the primary artificial-light areas, the spatial structural layout and the ceiling thicknesses are designed to provide various light effects, depending on the needs of the art work. New linear wall washers flood the walls continuously with light from floor to ceiling. In accordance with the programme, there are areas primarily illuminated by roof lights and others – above all in Domstraße – with side lights.

A building is also a work of art. But unlike many of the works exhibited in this museum, it is not the work of a single person but the result of great effort on the part of the architect, his staff, the user, the client and – not least of all – the builders involved in its realisation. All these people are to be thanked.

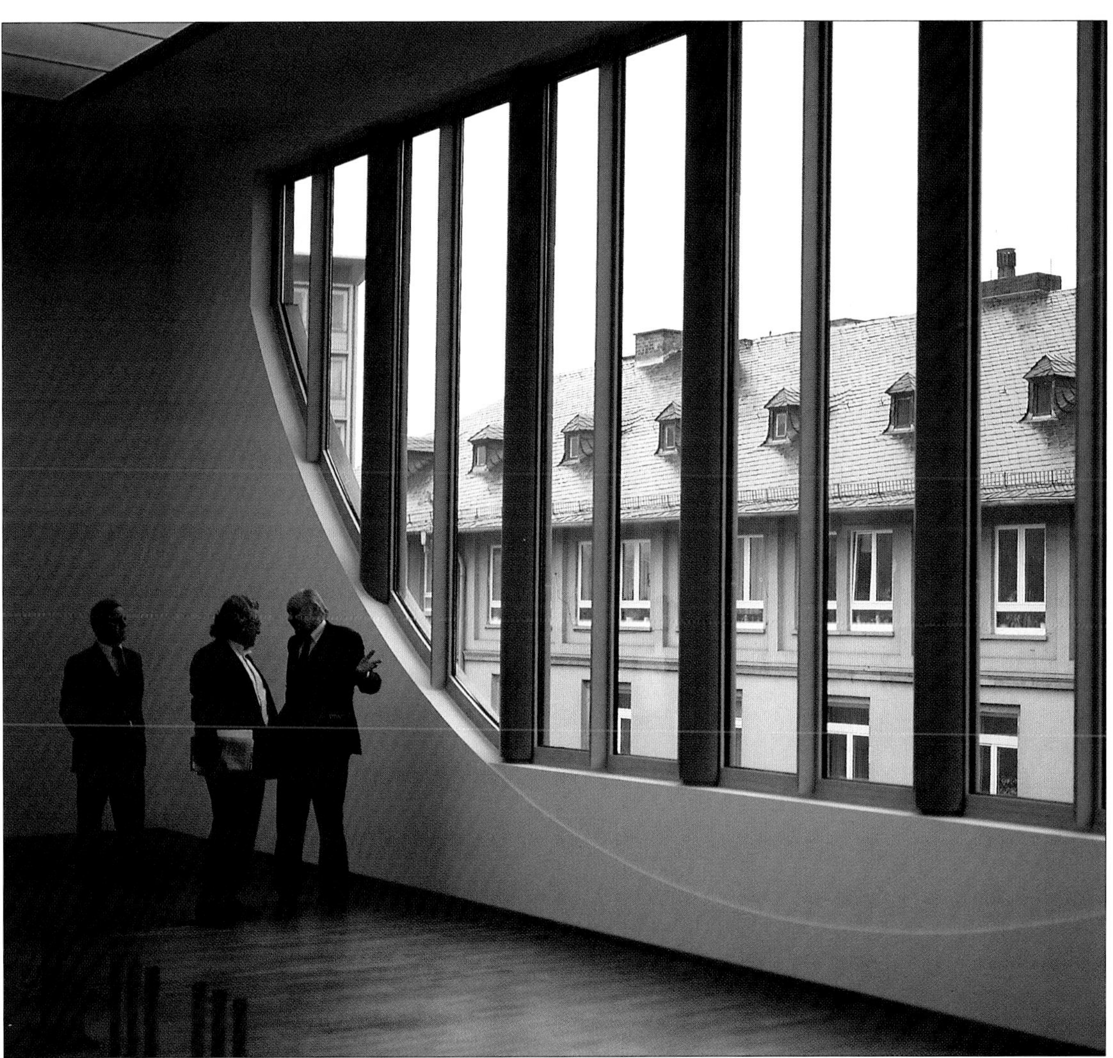

OPPOSITE: Exterior detail
ABOVE: Interior view showing Hans Hollein and Germano Celant

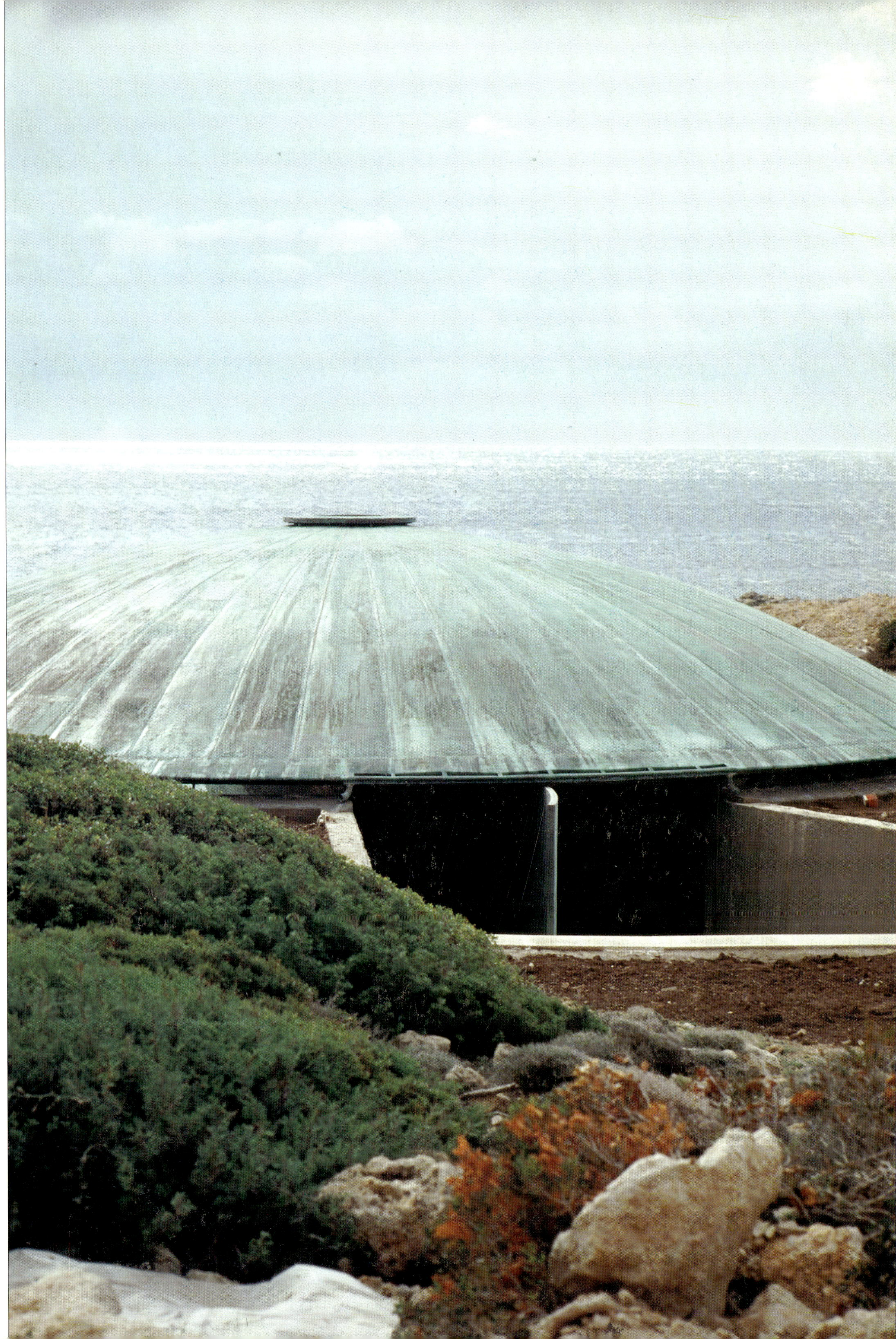

ANDREA BRUNO

MUSEUM OF ANTIQUITIES, MÀA PALEOCASTRUM, CYPRUS

When I was asked to draw a plan for a 'museum' to gather and present the visitors with the results of the archaeological diggings carried out by the Cyprus Department of Antiquities, at a site named Màa Paleocastrum on the Southern coast of the island near the well-known resort place of Paphos, I visited that area and examined the site and the diggings. On observing the aerial photos I felt a desire to see what this sharp pointed peninsula surrounded by two deep bays really looked like, when seen from ground level, while I also felt rather disturbed by the idea of building something on that area. I couldn't conceive of an acceptable architectural structure on that untouched natural landscape, where the marks left by the passage of men resulted in the traces, very light ones indeed, revealed by recent archaeological research.

My first pacing of this stream of land extending towards the ocean proved decisive enough to convince me that no museum, as a construction, could be built there.

I felt embarrassed at having to tell Professor Karageorgis of that decision because while walking through that space, the dimensions of which are those of a big modern aircraft carrier, I felt the past being present with such an intensity that I was struck by the very same emotions one feels when visiting some big museums built by men in foreign countries, where masterpieces are collected.

An intensely moving sky covers all that existed on this site which the archaeological radiography allows to be perceived with discretion. My project closed on these considerations. My job as an architect had already come to an end before starting and I felt perfectly satisfied with this thought.

While trying to give a convincing shape to such a consideration, I had thoughts coming from my past experience: that is my first coming into touch – through mere plans as well as accomplished projects – with a country where I have spent much of my professional life, from the late 50s to 1980. That country, Afghanistan, taught me how to view the widespread, precious and fragile testimonials of bygone civilisations that have been exposed with no interruption to decay and alterations, on a wider scale.

An inventory of the Afghan monuments I had made all over the country in those years suggested the idea of an immense open sky museum, where the big fragments left as a memory of past civilisations are to be found in the same position as they were created, being hundreds of kilometres distant from each other in space, deserts, mountains and hundreds of years of time. A museum itinerary in such a situation becomes a red thread defined by historical knowledge which binds together space and time and can be recognised on the ground with an absolute undebatable and moving exactness.

An object if taken to a museum loses at least some of its 'authenticity', as it becomes a referential element in different spaces and annulled situations. An object seen and kept in its original site connects the past with the present with no equivocation.

Well preserved and sheltered, it is the big unmovable objects, architectural constructions and carefully signalled urban dwellings that are the simplest and most correct accomplishment of a museum-like interest. When to a preservation effort an attentive and deepened historical knowledge is added, by means of archaeological researches that aim at giving a clearer presentation, the word museum allows the best possibility of defining and identifying the object taken into consideration.

Finally the red thread connecting space and time must be seen and comprehended by today's men.

The Màa museum extends its shape towards the sea from which the fleeing Achaeans came 2000 years ago. The landscape hasn't changed through the centuries. Simple lasting signs mark the museum ground, such as the defensive wall crossing behind, the huge corrupted and austere rocks defining a limit of frightening domination, the exhumed location plans of the dwellings and then the Mediterranean green bushy vegetation – an emerging shape from a rocky outline.

An acceptable suggestion: a covered space, where one can reflect and receive some suggestion from imagination; a pause before reaching the sea barrier at the end of the fortified wall of the watch tower.

All those signs cannot be read in their original shape without the precise cue of the archaeologists. The red thread goes back to the sea where the men came who built these memories from the past which are now offered up for the attention of a generation that has already gone to the moon. So it won't be a museum. But some other thing.

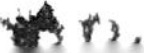

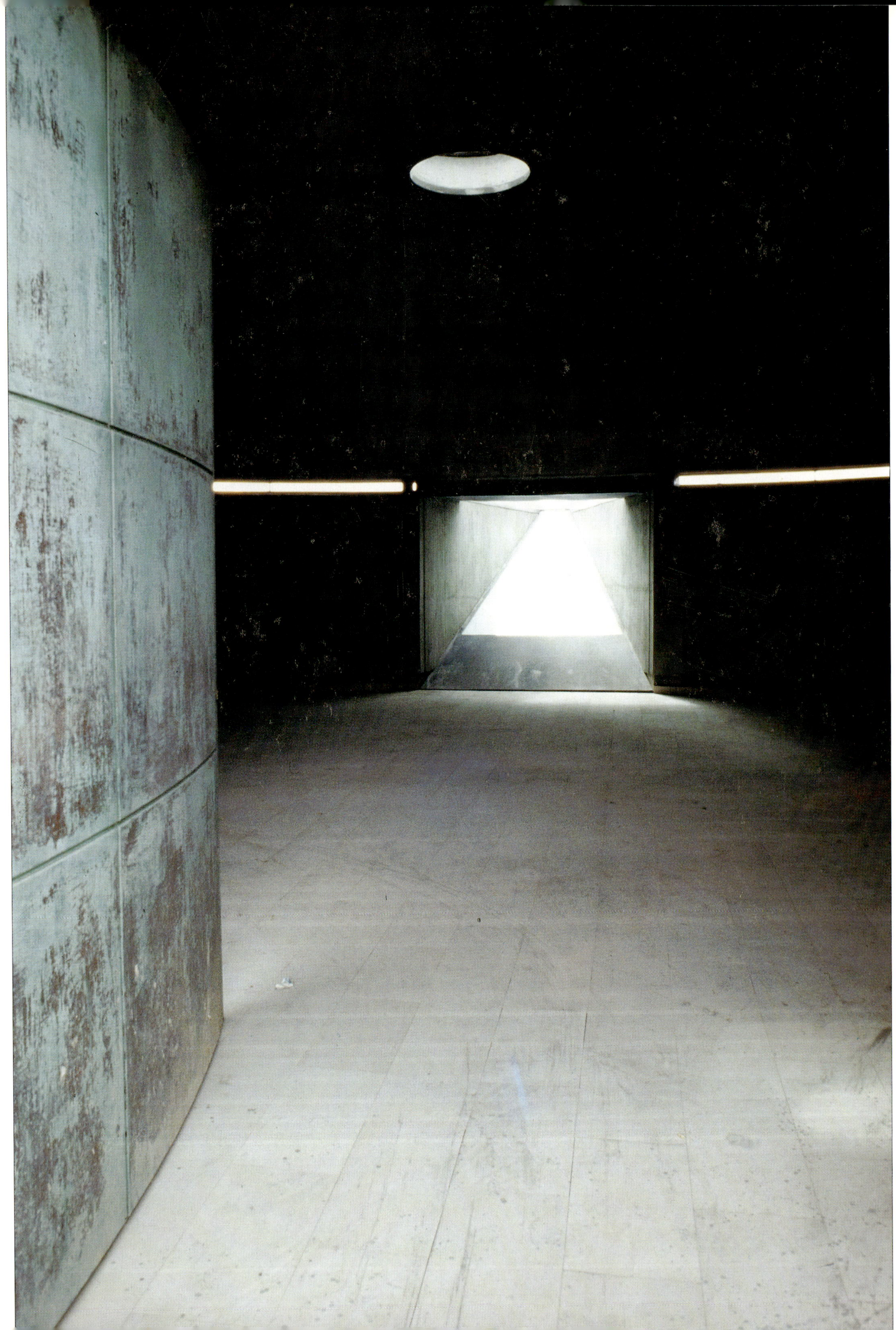

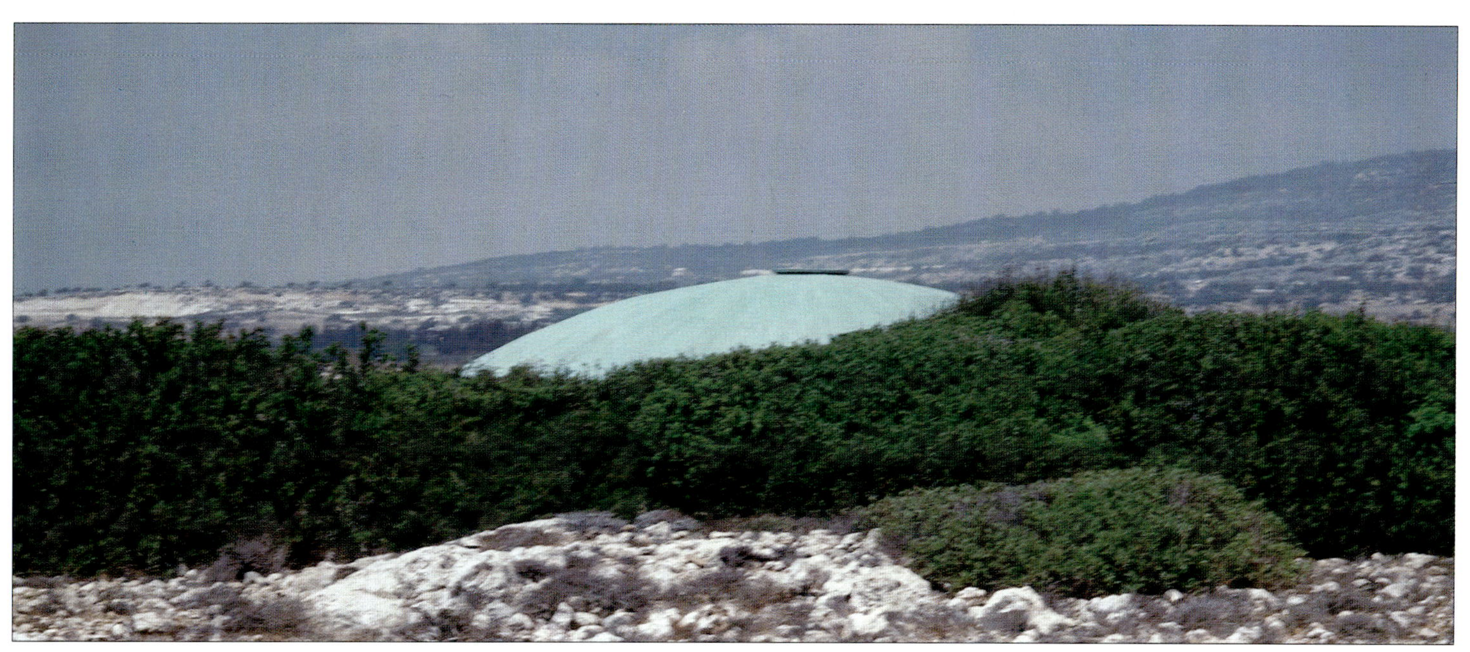

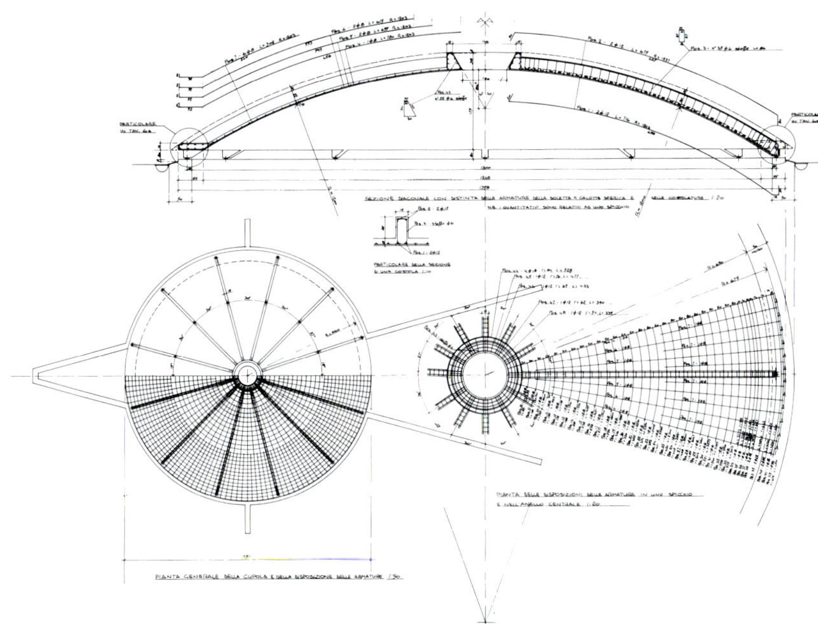

OPPOSITE: *Entrance*
ABOVE: *Landscape around site*
CENTRE: *Plan and construction details*
BELOW: *Museum set within its landscape*

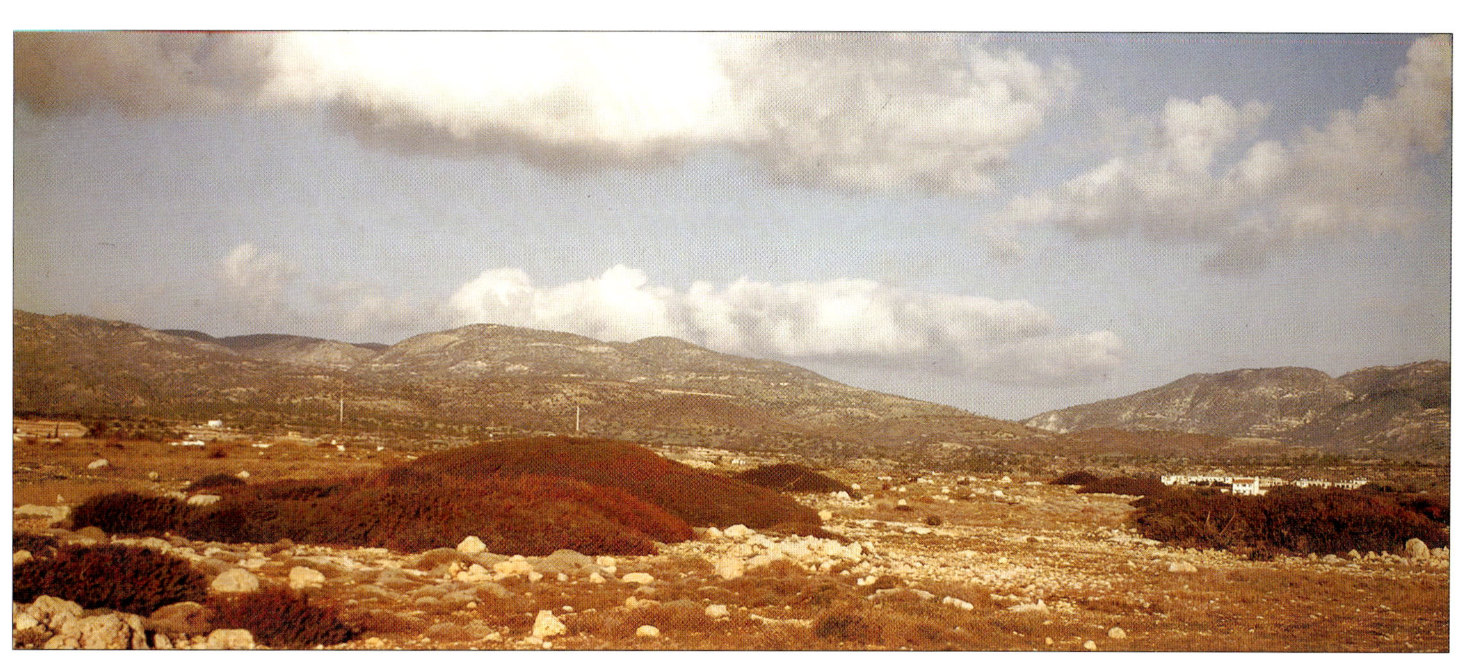

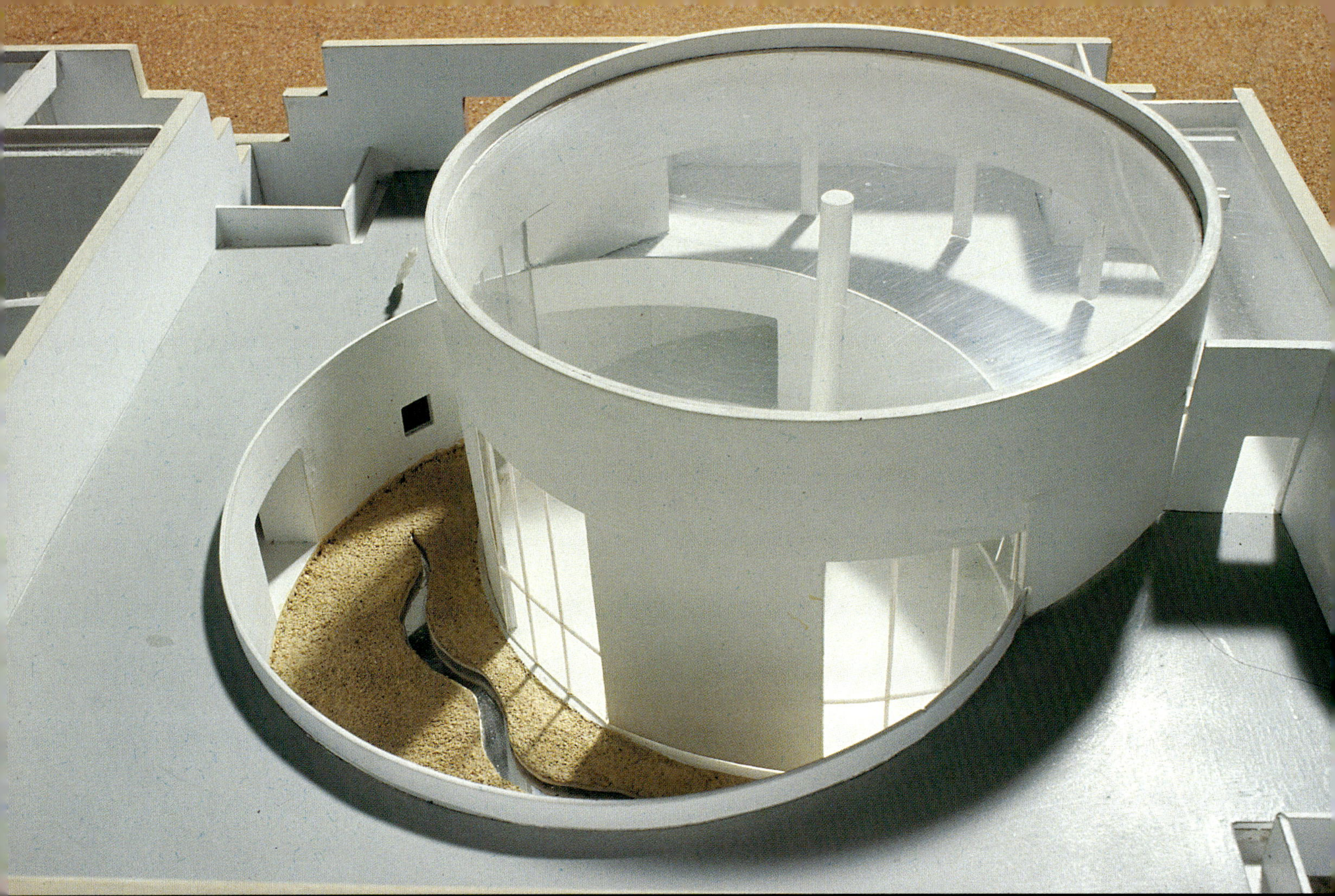

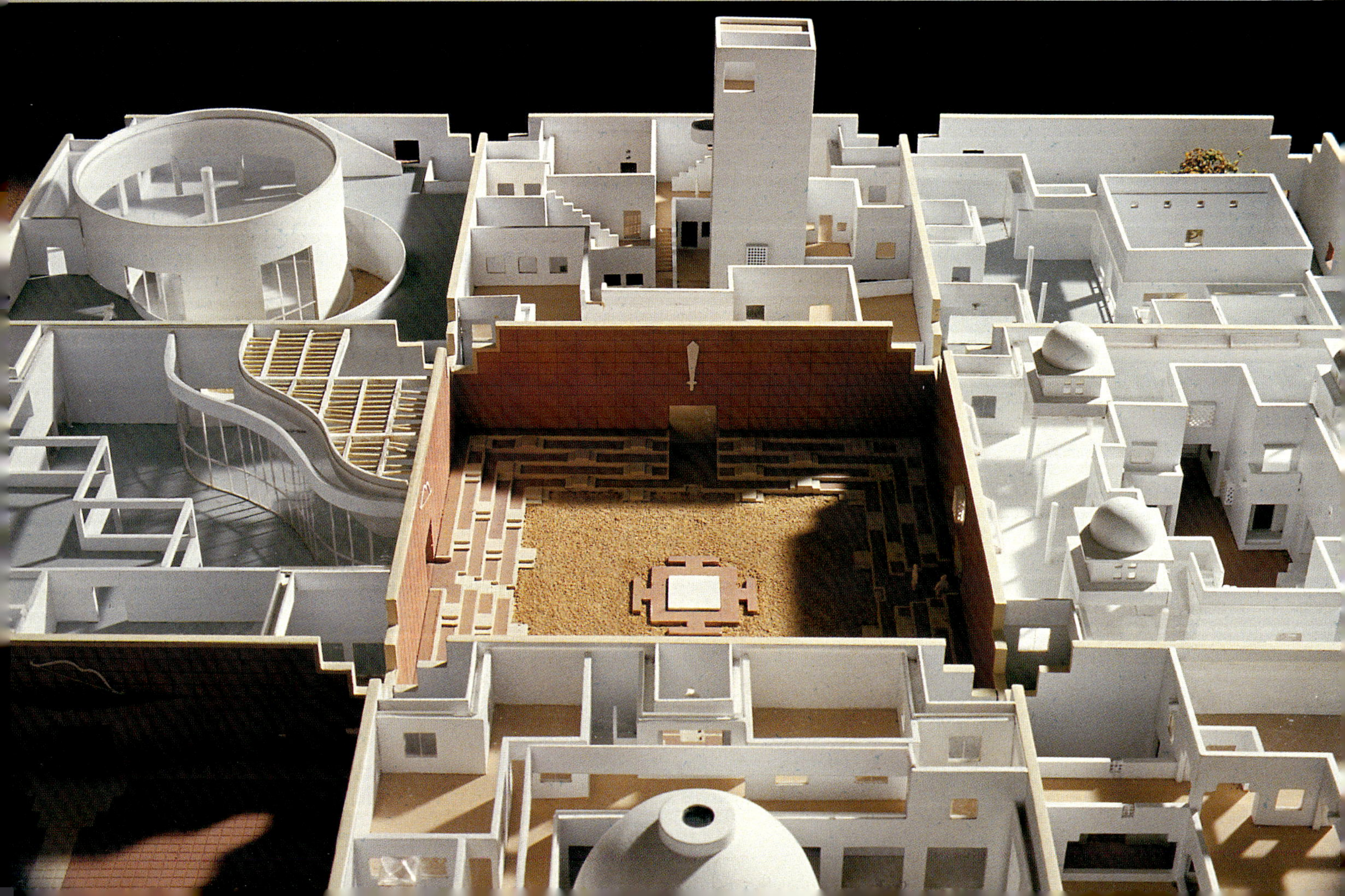

CHARLES CORREA
JAWAHAR KALA KENDRA, JAIPUR, INDIA

The Jawahar Kala Kendra is based on the Vastu-Purush Mandalas of the Vedic shastras, wherein architecture was conceived as a model of the Cosmos. The specific Mandala invoked is the Navgraha, which consists of nine squares. Each square is the house of a planet, including the two imaginary ones: Retu and Raku.

The building was designed for the Government of Rajasthan and is dedicated to the memory of India's first Prime Minister, Jawaharlal Nehru. It is located near the University in the city of Jaipur.

The original city plan for Jaipur, drawn up in the 17th century, was also based on the nine squares of the Navgraha – with one of the squares moved to the east side due to the presence of a hill. The Jawahar Kala Kendra directly imitates this original Navgraha – with one of the squares displaced so as to create a main entrance, and also recalls the gesture which generated the original plan of Jaipur.

It is designed to house a combination of facilities: collections of textiles, jewels, illustrated manuscripts and other crafts at which Rajasthan excels. It also includes a street of houses and studios for traditional craftsmen to carry out their work. In addition, there is a library and a small Performing Arts Centre consisting of a 600-seat auditorium and a small experimental theatre.

The building is a concrete frame construction with brick and stone infill. The external walls are clad in Rajasthan sandstone topped with a coping of beige Dholpur stone. These are the same materials used for the Jantar Mantar Observatory, as well as the Fathepur-Sikri and the Red Fort in Agra.

On the external facades, the presence of each of the planets is expressed by its symbol inlaid in white marble (embellished where necessary with black granite and mica slate), in a manner which recalls the calibrated surfaces of the Jantar Mantar instruments.

The construction started with just two planets (Mangal and Chandra) – all the available budget would allow. The following year further funds were released by the government which allowed three more planets to start construction. A year later the budget for the remaining planets was sanctioned. Thus three different contractors were working on the site simultaneously. In the final stages, they were joined by a fourth. This *adhoc* procedure of financing (often prevalent in India), usually mitigates against the successful completion of a project. In this case, because of the nature of design it did not matter. In each case, the first thing we would start were the four external walls which define the planets. Then, as further funds became available, we proceeded with the design and construction of the infill structure. Thus the use of the Mandala was conceptually relevant to the project, and had decisive constructional advantages as well.

In the centre of each of the 30-metre walls there is a doorway connecting adjacent planets. These form a continuous open-to-sky processional through the complex. The rhythm of these monumental walls, repeating every 30 metres, allow each planet to find its own expression – not only in form, but in terms of colour and ambience as well. This reflects the symbolic diversity of the Navgraha and the pluralism of India. These doorways open up powerful vistas across the Mandala.

In this Jawahar Kala Kendra, each of the nine square houses (*mahals*): *Mangal*, *Chandra*, *Budh*, *Ketu*, *Shani*, *Rahu*, *Guru*, *Shukra* and *Surya* has been named after a particular planet, and is designed to express their special qualities. To achieve this, the functional programme of the Kala Kendra has been 'disaggregated' into nine separate groupings, corresponding to the mythic qualities represented by each planet:

1 *Mangal Mahal*: The planet *Mangal* represents power. Its symbol is the square and its colour is red. In this *mahal* is the museum's administrative office. Along the walls there is an explanation of the *Navgraha*.

2 *Chandra Mahal*: *Chandra* represents the quality of the heart. It is crescent-shaped and its colour is milky white. It symbolises romantic and sensuous emotions and houses a restaurant and guest rooms for the visiting artists.

3 *Budh Mahal*: *Budh* symbolises education and instruction. Its colour is golden yellow and its symbol is the arrow. It contains five museums, four small ones in the lower level: jewellery, manuscripts, miniature paintings and musical instruments. The upper floor contains a large exhibition of terracottas, architecture and antiques depicting the lifestyles of Rajasthan.

4 *Ketu Mahal*: The symbol of *Ketu* is the serpent. Its colours are brown and black. In this *mahal* are displayed traditional Rajasthani costumes and textiles.

5 *Shani Mahal*: *Shani* represents knowledge. Its symbol is the bow and its colours are light and shadow, the browns and reds of the earth. In this *mahal* Rajasthani craftsmen demonstrate their work.

6 *Rahu Mahal*: *Rahu* represents the eclipse of the sun. Its colour is pearly grey (like the iridescent feathers around the pigeon's neck). Its symbol is the image of the moon devouring the sun. Here is located an exhibition of swords, daggers, helmets and suits of armour celebrating the legendary heroism of Rajasthan warriors.

7 *Guru Mahal*: This *mahal* serves as a library. *Guru* symbolises knowledge and meditation. Its colour is lemon yellow and its symbol is the circle.

8 *Shukra Mahal*: *Shukra* represents Art. It's symbol is the star and it's colour is white. Here is located a 125-seat Experimental Theatre for the Performing Arts.

9 *Surya Mahal*: *Surya* represents creative energy. Its colour is red. Since it is located in the centre of the mandala, it must personify both *shunya* and *bindu*. It takes the form of a traditional *kund*, where the visitor can see Rajasthani music, dance and drama, performed under the open sky.

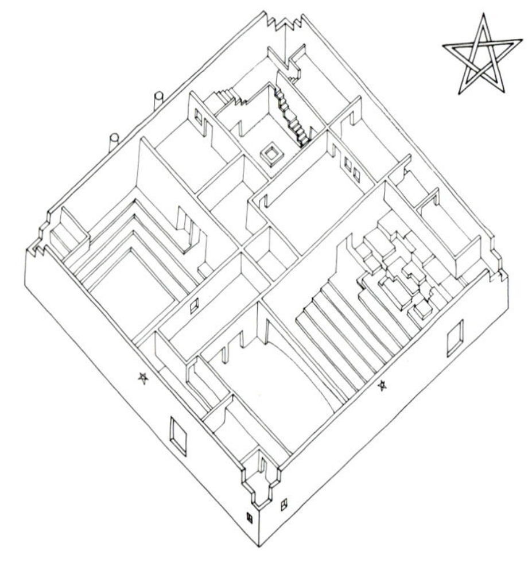

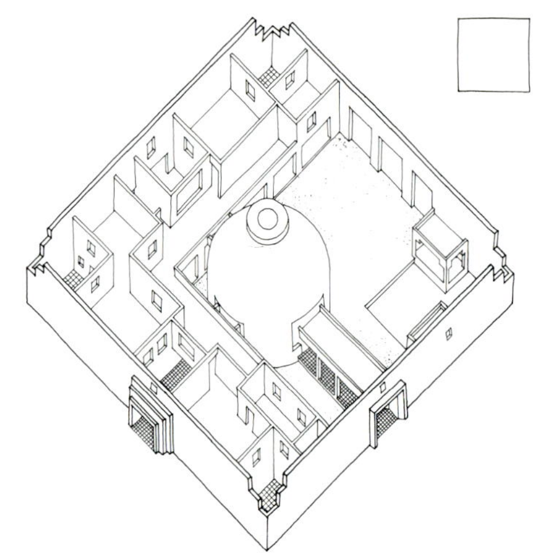

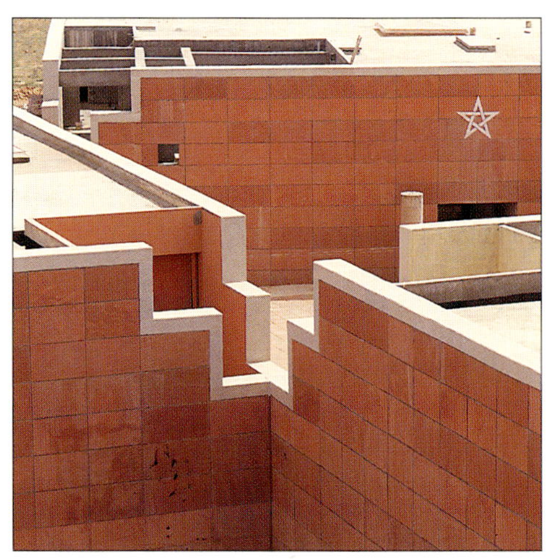

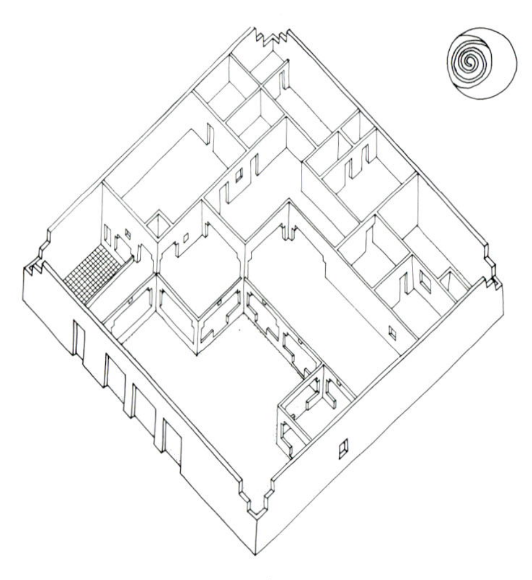

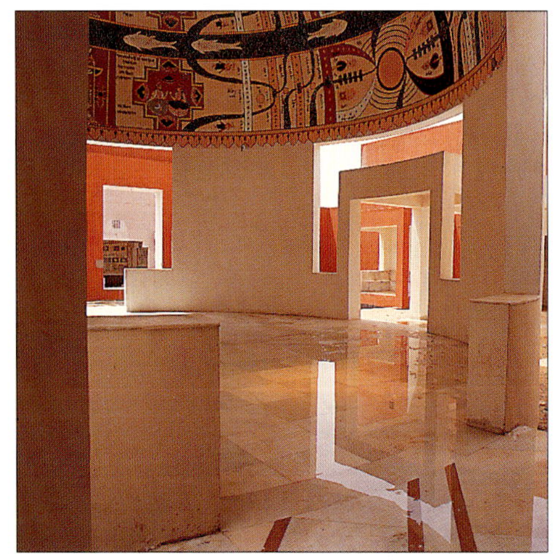

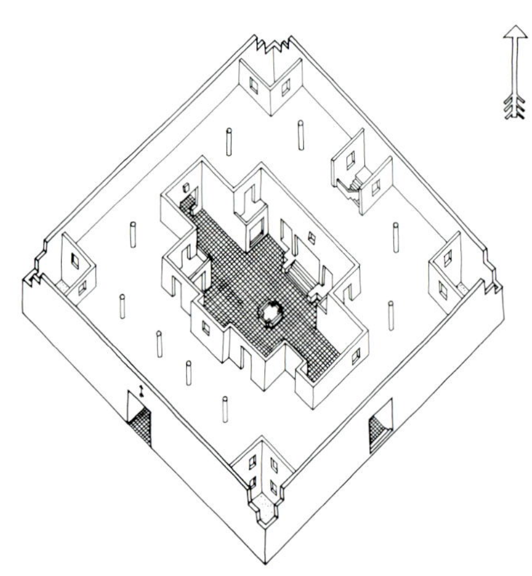

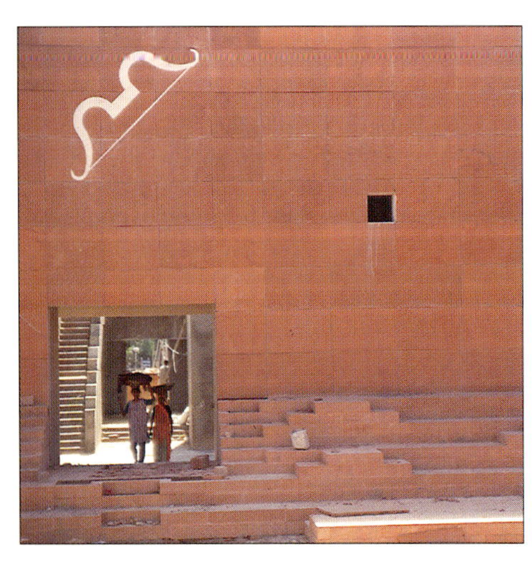

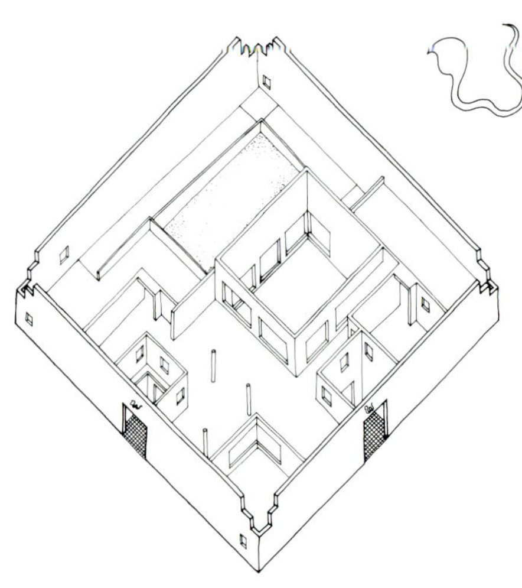

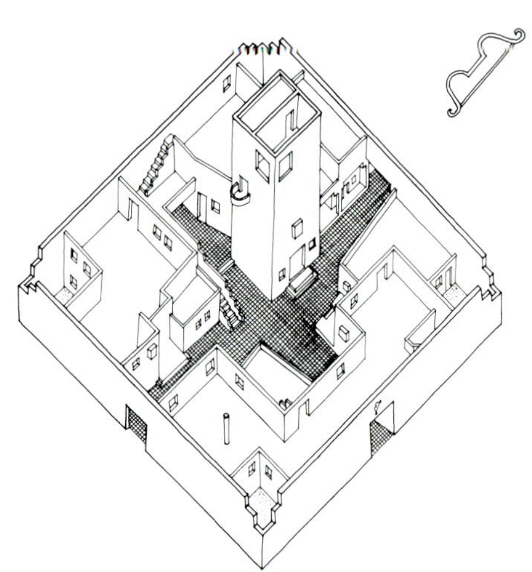

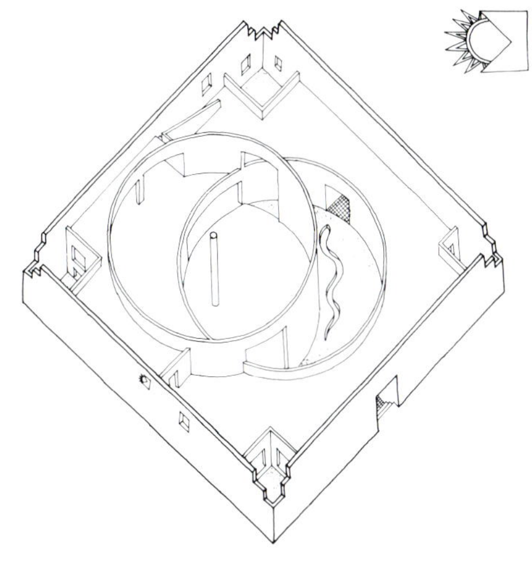
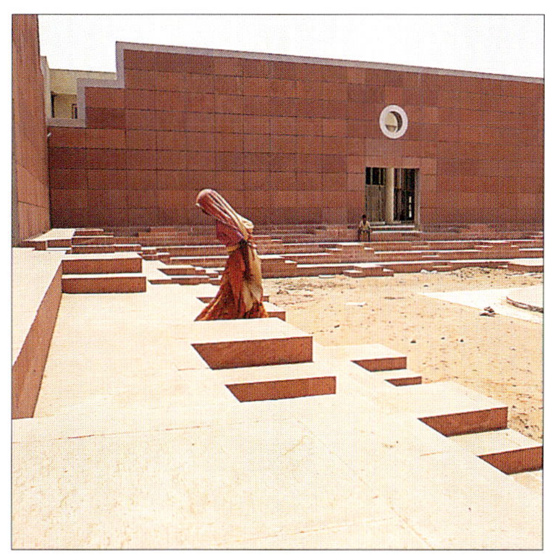
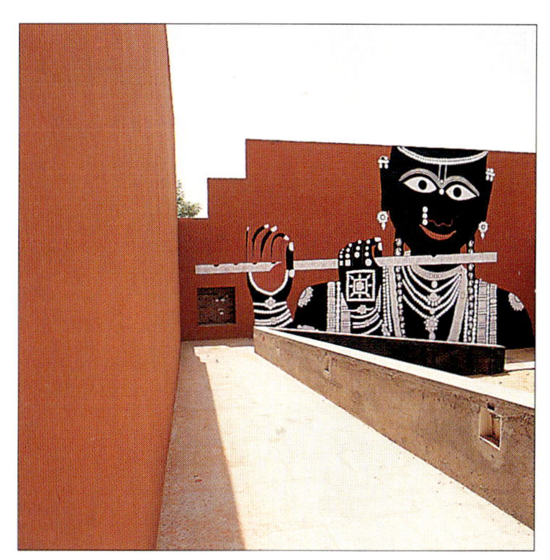
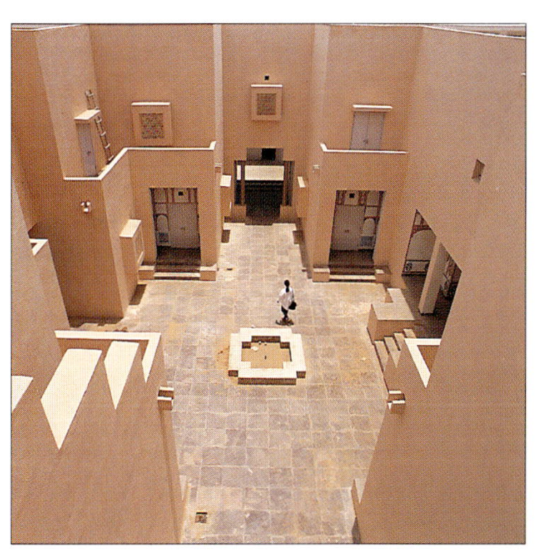
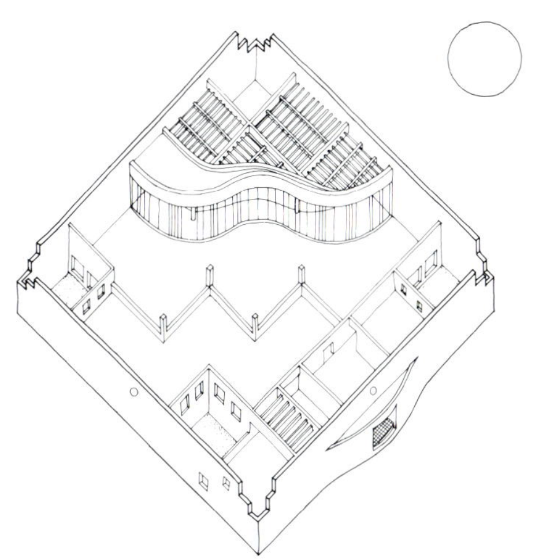
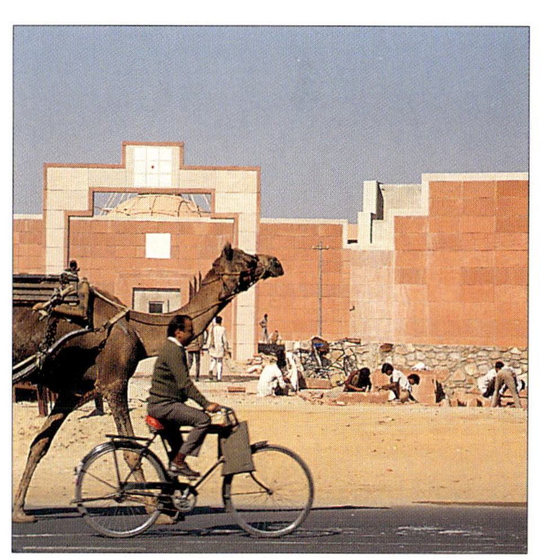
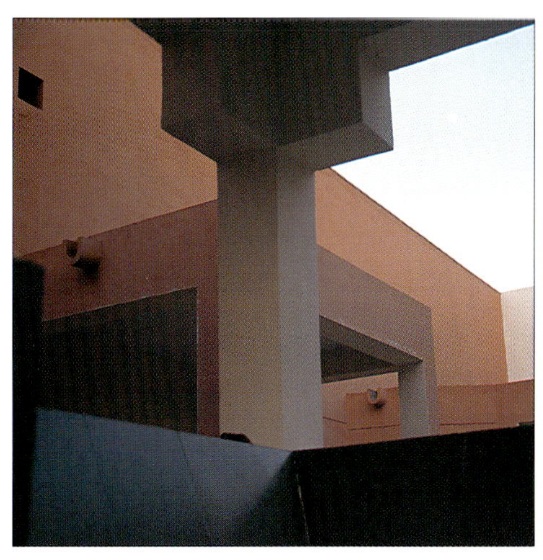
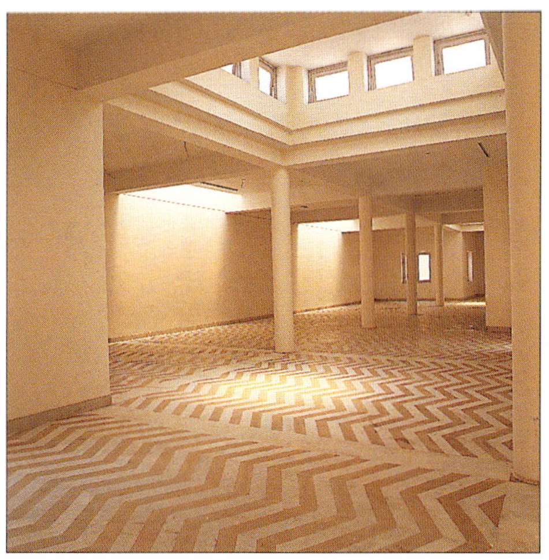
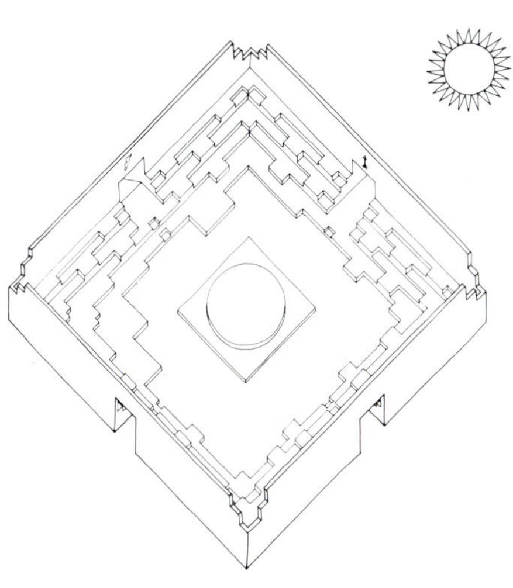

Mangal (Mars)
Red
Power
Administration

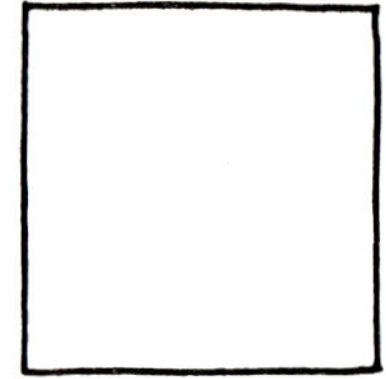

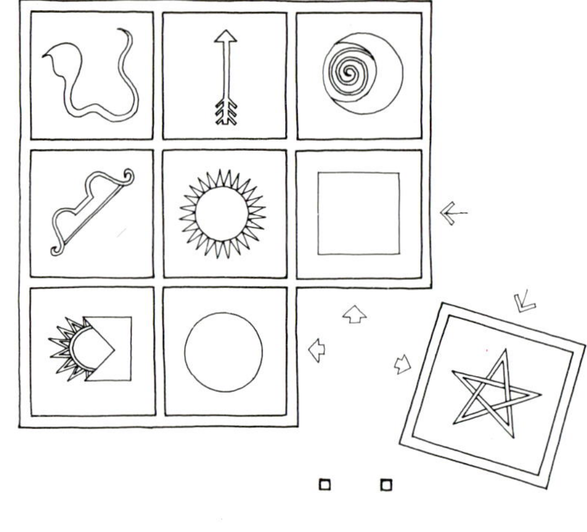

Chandra (Moon)
Milky White
Heart
Cafeteria

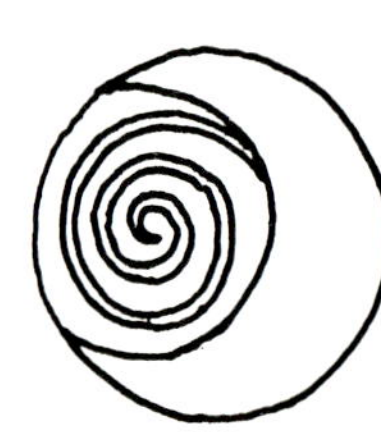

Budh (Mercury)
Golden Yellow
Education
Lok Kala Kendra

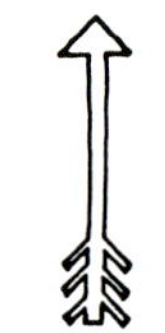

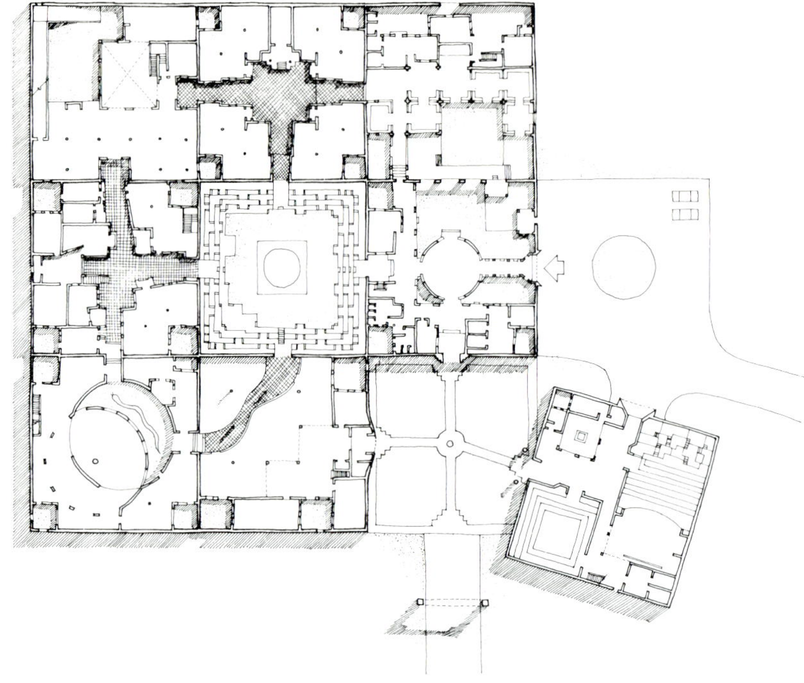

Ketu
Brown & Black
Anger
Museum I

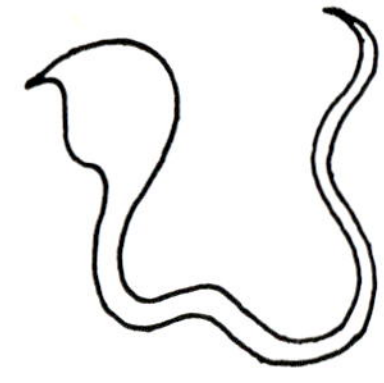

Shani (Saturn)
Earth Red (Light & Shadow)
Knowledge
Museum II

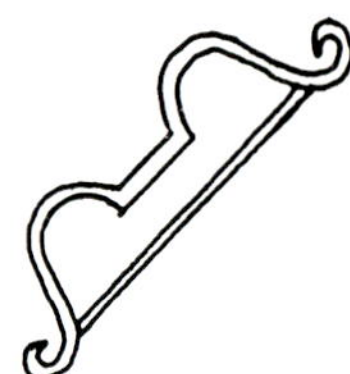

Rahu
Pigeon Throat Feathers
Devourer/Restorer
Documentation

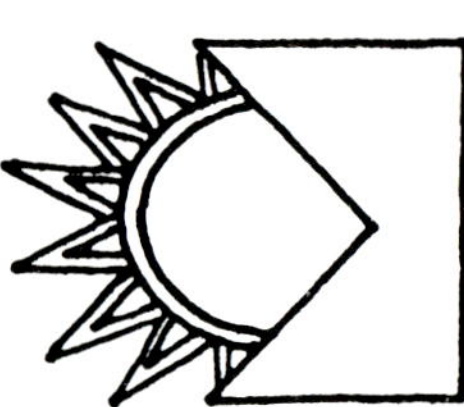

Guru (Jupiter)
Lemon Yellow
Knowledge (Meditation)
Library

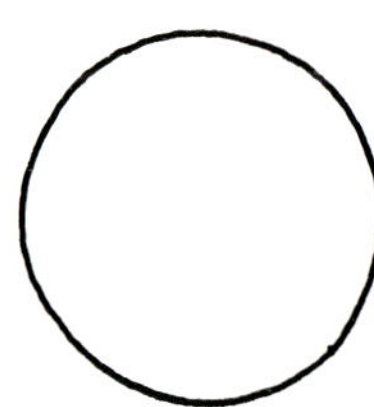

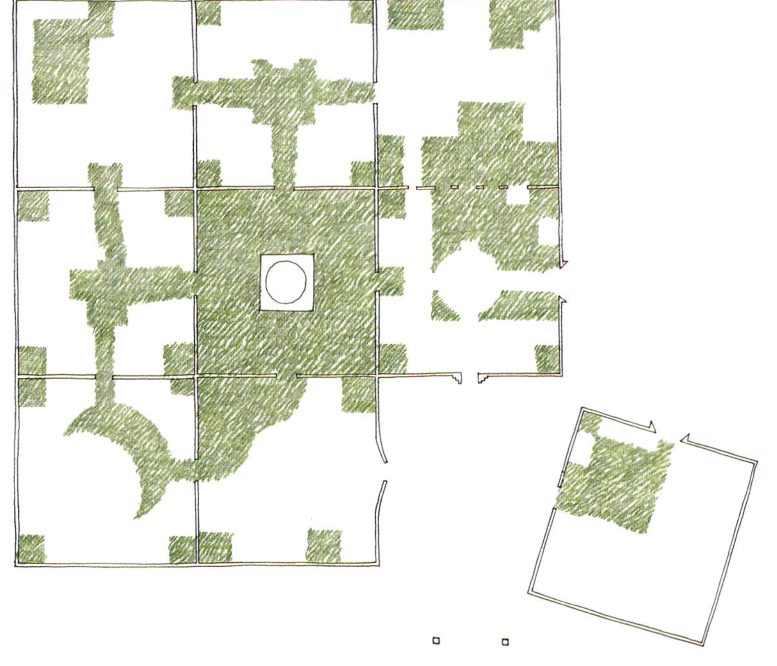

Shukra (Venus)
White
Art
Drama

Surya (Sun)
Red
Creative Energy
Kund